I Always Look Up the Word "Egregious"

Books by Maxwell Nurnberg

What's the Good Word?
Wonders in Words
Fun with Words
Word Play
Punctuation Pointers
Questions You Always Wanted to Ask About English
A Gathering of Poems (*Editor*)
I Always Look Up the Word "Egregious"

With Morris Rosenblum:
How to Build a Better Vocabulary
All About Words
What to Name Your Baby

With Harold A. Clarke:
Chalk Dust, a nationally produced Federal Theater Play

I Always Look Up the Word "Egregious"

Maxwell Nurnberg

PRENTICE HALL PRESS
New York   London   Toronto   Sydney   Tokyo

To Ellen and Eugene and Rose

Copyright © 1981 by Maxwell Numberg
All rights reserved, including the right of reproduction
in whole or in part in any form.

Published in 1987 by Prentice Hall Press
A Division of Simon & Schuster, Inc.
15 Columbus Circle
New York, NY 10023

Originally published by Prentice Hall, Inc.

PRENTICE HALL PRESS is a trademark of Simon & Schuster, Inc.

Library of Congress Cataloging-in-Publication Data

Numberg, Maxwell
   I always look up the word "egregious."

   Includes index.
   1. Vocabulary,   I. Title.
PE1449.N82   428.1   81-1460
ISBN 0-13-448720-6   AACR2
ISBN 0-13-448712-5 (pbk)

Manufactured in the United States of America

15   14   13   12   11

Acknowledgments

For most of the sentences cited as illustration of the use of a word in context, I am deeply indebted to *The New York Times* with its brilliant array of journalists, reviewers, critics, editorial staff, Op-Ed essayists, sports writers, and the often distinguished men and women who write letters to this prestigious newspaper.

When the New York newspaper strike was on, I moved to the *Times Literary Supplement* (of London) and, when that publication was suspended, I cast peripheral glances at *The New Yorker* and the *New York Review of Books*. Any excerpts that come from these sources are labeled *TLS, NY,* or *NYRB.* (All others except a few home-grown sentences are from *The New York Times.*)

Since I have used so much newspaper material—sometimes of a controversial nature—I wish to make the usual disclaimer: The views expressed in these excerpts do not necessarily reflect my views or those of my publisher or of any of the sources mentioned.

For material quoted from other sources I wish to make, with thanks, the following acknowledgments:

To Prentice-Hall and Dora Rosenblum for permission to use and adapt material from two publications, *How to Build a Better Vocabulary* and *All About Words*, on which I collaborated with the late Dr. Rosenblum.

To "Pleasures in Learning," a selection I contributed to a former New York University publication, for the epigraph that heads Chapter 1; copyright © 1964 by Maxwell Nurnberg.

To Harcourt Brace Jovanovich, Inc., for the excerpt from *The Golden Echo* by David Garnett and for two excerpts from George Orwell's essay *Politics and the English Language*, copyright © 1946 by George Orwell.

To Curtis Brown, Ltd., for permission to reprint a passage from Robert Graves's "Goodbye to All That," copyright © 1929 by Robert Graves.

To Oxford University Press for permission to reprint the anonymous clerihew "Spinoza" from *The New Oxford Book of Light Verse*, selected by Kingsley Amis (1978), no. 185.

To Random House, Inc., for permission to quote lines from Italo Calvino's *The Baron in the Trees*, © 1959.

To check on derivations and definitions I have consulted chiefly *Webster's Seventh New Collegiate Dictionary*; *Webster's New World Dictionary of the English Language*, Second College Edition; and the *American Heritage Dictionary of the English Language* with its unique Usage Panel and its appraisal of usage in dispute.

As a backup I used *Webster's Third New International Dictionary*, Unabridged (hereafter referred to as W3), and its supplement *6,000 Words*, and now and then, as will be seen, the *Oxford English Dictionary*, hereafter referred to as *OED*.

Finally, I wish to acknowledge my great indebtedness to Ruth M. Goldstein for her painstaking reading and typing of the manuscript as well as her occasional felicitous additions and wise subtractions.

Contents

Proem

This is a vocabulary book for those who don't need one—
unless you want to bring into sharper focus words that are now on the blurred fringes of your mind,
unless you want to have a safe landing place for words that are now precariously perched on the tip of your tongue, or
unless you want to meet some **difficult, unusual**, and **even rare words** to which you have not been properly introduced.
And if you didn't recognize that the rhetorical device used here of repeating the same words in successive clauses is known as **anaphora,***
or if you didn't recognize that the first sentence (in boldface) is by way of being an **antinomy,*** a built-in paradox,
then maybe this is just the book for you.

---

*These words are treated fully in the body of the book, as are other unfamiliar words you may come across. Consult the index.

1. Prolegomenon

A friend of mine was talking to a theatrical agent who was not particularly distinguished for the range or choice of his vocabulary. He was therefore a little startled to hear the word *eclectic* suddenly pop out.

"Joe! Where did you get hold of that elegant word?"

"*Eclectic*? Oh, I just happened to come across it in the dictionary."

"What do you mean you *just* happened to come across it in the dictionary?"

"Well, you see, I was looking up the word *egregious* and on my way to *egregious* my eye caught the word *eclectic* and I liked it."

"O.K., Joe. But how did you *happen* to be looking up the word *egregious*?"

"I always look up the word *egregious*!"

from "Pleasures in Learning," M. N., ©1964

Joe did two things right. He consulted a dictionary when he didn't know the meaning of a word. Moreover, he showed an interest in words in general when he made a short detour around the word *eclectic,* finding out what a rewarding, and sometimes exciting, experience thumbing a ride through a good dictionary can be. (All so-called desk dictionaries are good. The only bad dictionary is one that isn't used.)

Every pro, whether the game is baseball, tennis, or golf, will tell you that your game will be much improved if you follow through. Joe didn't follow through. He didn't file away *egregious* inside his mind; he only kept it on its surface, where it could easily be dislodged. In not taking the important step of following through, he behaved the way most people do, even you, perhaps.

If the definition of a word is connected to nothing but your desire to remember it, you haven't done enough. The process of forgetting begins the moment you close the dictionary, for memory is a sometime thing. In one way or another you have to forge a link. If you don't make some kind of association—genuine or artificial—to tie the word down, its meaning is sure to get lost in the multiplicity of words that crowd your mind.

To illustrate, let's see how to make the association that will help you remember a moderately difficult word: *jettison.* On the follow through, you come back with the information that *jettison* is related to the French word *jeter,* to throw, and to the word *jetsam,* what is thrown overboard. You have hooked into the meaning. To *jettison* is to throw overboard, to discard. An association has been made with something that you know. You have made a permanent *nexus.* (There's another example! If you associate the word *nexus,* which you may not know, with the word *connexion,* the British spelling of *connection,* which you do know, you have now annexed the word.)

But now let's get back to the business at hand. What would have happened if Joe had followed through or taken this step when he looked up his nemesis, *egregious,* and consulted *Merriam-Webster's Second International Dictionary,* Second Edition, Unabridged? After locating the word, he would have gone on to read what follows the pronunciation. He would have been told that *egregious* comes from the Latin *grex, gregis,* herd, flock. After the definitions he would have read: See *gregarious.* At *gregarious* he would have discovered the family to which *egregious* belongs: *aggregate* (prefix *ad,* becoming *ag,* added to), *congregate* (*con,* together), *egregious* (*e* for *ex,* standing out from the herd), and *segregate* (*se,* aside, set aside from the flock).

And so Joe would have come away with a fistful of words and would have returned to *egregious* for additional information. He would have learned that *egregious* once meant outstanding, distinguished, eminent, but these meanings are marked "archaic," no longer in use in that sense.* Today the word means something that is "outstandingly bad, flagrant" (as in an *egregious* blunder, an *egregious* fool).

At this point it is wise to sound a cautionary note. Don't try to use your inventive mind or your imagination to figure out the meaning of a word you don't know. The use of derivation is often very helpful in locking a word in, but it's dangerous to try to unlock the meaning unless you have the right key. Suppose we take the word *provenance.* If you know that it means "origin" or "source," *then* it's easy to explain with hindsight and confidence: "Oh, yes, *provenance* comes from the Latin root *ven,* come, + *pro,* forth, hence *provenance* means the place (French suffix *ance*) from which something comes: in other words, the origin, source, derivation."

Even if you know the derivation or provenance of a word, it may not be enough; the word *egregious,* Joe's addiction, is still only a word in the deep freeze of the dictionary. It has to be thawed out, activated. It has to be seen with other words in context. Here are two such sentences:

> The TV replay in slow motion shows that the officials were guilty of an *egregious* booboo.

> The American intelligence community was stunned: a 10 percent error was *egregious.*

That's what this book is about: to present words in

---

*In Italy, however, it is a common salutation used in letters: "Egregio Signore" (Distinguished Sir). The *Oxford English Dictionary* says the pejorative meaning in English came as early as the end of the sixteenth century, and cites Shakespeare's "egregious murderer." But as late as 1855, Thackeray still used it in its complimentary sense in *The Newcomes.*

current use, brought back alive in their native habitat, the wilderness* of written expression in which they roam.

My purpose is to provide sentences illustrating the unself-conscious use of words in actual experience, in real situations. To use a word significantly in a sentence when neither the need nor the situation exists is a difficult assignment. Try it yourself:

You know the fairly simple word *fatuous*. It means "foolish, silly." Now use it in a sentence. You will probably find that you suddenly become self-conscious. You have to *create* a situation in which the word *fatuous* belongs. Right here a mental censor steps in to save you from dredging up something from your subconscious and you finally settle for a sentence as neutral, bland, sanitized, bloodless, and non-committal as "His fatuous behavior made me dislike him intensely." †

How much better are these sentences taken from *The New York Times:*

> For ten years candidates have been going through the big food bazaars grinning *fatuously* and shaking hands with astounded females in the dubious belief that somehow this would assure the women's vote.

> Only the most *fatuous* of sports officials, pretending that the Olympics are non-political, will be prepared to boost Soviet prestige by going to Moscow for the Games.

> He also warned that it was quite *fatuous* to suppose that all is well with the world simply because Communist China and the Soviet Union are now at odds.

---

*Beautiful word, *wilderness*, not from Latin or Greek but from the mother tongue, Anglo-Saxon—*wild* + *dior*, animal (from which comes our word *deer*, a particular animal, though early on it meant all animals), + *ness*, state of being, place: *wilderness*, the wild animal place!

†This sentence actually appears as an illustration of the use of the word *fatuous* in a vocabulary book by an American linguistic expert. Not much more illuminating is a sentence in a book (published in 1979) on "confused words" by a British expert. To establish the difference between *sentimental* and *sentimentality*, he offers: "I can't stand his weak sentimentality."

Fatuous, as can be seen from this context, means more than merely silly, foolish. *Webster's Third* adds the qualification "especially marked by ill-founded hope or desire," and sometimes, I might add, a touch of smugness. The word comes alive in the newspaper sentences quoted. Why? Because the writer wanted to express *his* thought. He did not have to make up a fatuous sentence on demand.

I didn't go to the dictionary for the words presented and treated in this book. *I let the words come to me—in context.*

That's why for the past few years I've been hunting down words in *The New York Times.* Equipped with a red pencil, a pair of scissors, Scotch Tape, and index cards, I waited for words to come within range. There is a free-flowing immediacy about words used in a great newspaper. Ideas have to be banged out quickly, precisely, and, if possible, vividly. I have found my words in the news, editorials, Op-Ed essays, letters from readers, reviews of books, plays, films, art, ballet, music—and yes, even the sports pages.

Years ago the following words from the sports pages were tracked down: bellwether, cunctatious, debacle, flaccid, hiatus, impeccant, juggernaut, lagniappe, obsequies, paladin, pantheon, paragon, prestidigitation, puissant, pullulating, purlieus, ratiocination, and transpontine.

Sometimes in the sports pages the words may tend to be a little jaunty or flamboyant. And why not? Having to deal day after day with similar events and recurring situations, sports writers reach out for new ways to make their stories exciting. A winning homer is "a lethal blow"; but useless homers, punched out when the game is safely in the bag, put on ice, are "merely lagniappe."*

In his essay "Politics and the English Language," George Orwell takes Professor Hogben to task for playing "ducks and drakes with a battery [of English idioms] . . . and, while disapproving of the everyday phrase *put up with,* is

---

*Whenever a word is used that you may be unfamiliar with, you will probably find it treated somewhere else in this book. Just consult the index.

unwilling to look *egregious* up in the dictionary and see what it means."

Good old Joe! He's probably still looking it up!

READ THIS BEFORE YOU GO ON

Since this is in no sense a technical book, derivation is given only when it is helpful or provides insight. Sometimes the complete Latin or Greek words are given to add to your knowledge of these not so dead ancient languages.

Occasionally, for relaxation a fairly easy word is included—if it has resonance, provides interesting background, or has a historical dimension. From a pragmatic point of view, this book can be looked upon as a short dictionary of long words, in which you will learn more about particular words than you can expect to find in a regular dictionary.

2. Warming Up

In the room the people come and go, talking of words like *imbroglio.* Usually they are *somber* and *worried,* which they find more worthwhile than being *serious* and *nervous.* Sometimes they are *glad,* even though they much prefer *jolly.* They know that a *miss* is as good as a *mile,* and they can never be *quizzical,* unless, of course, they draw a blank. To clear up any confusion, they are Scrabble players—men and women who know the value of words far better than their meaning.

NY Times (December 3, 1979. Clyde Haberman)

acronym

As Moscow developed its own vast arsenal, credibility came to rely on the doctrine of Mutual Assured Destruction (MAD, the aptest *acronym* ever).

acronym—a word formed from the initial letters of a sequence of words. Today the formation of acronyms has become a sort

7

of game, to come up with initials that produce a word indicating the meaning or purpose of the original sequence of words. The acronym MAD above is one example. A more constructive acronym is AID, Agency for International Development. (From Gr. *acro-* topmost, highest + -onym, name;* that is the topmost or first letter.)

Also: *acrobat; acropolis* (*polis,* city); *acrophobia* (*phobos,* fear). Words with the combining form *-onym* will be found under *eponym* in Chapter 4.

We aren't the only ones to play around with acronyms. Fiat, the popular Italian car, has three counts in its favor: It is an entire Latin sentence: *Fiat,* "Let it be done (or made)"; it is an English word meaning a decree: *fiat,* an order coming from high places that must be carried out; and it is made up of the initial letters of Fabbrica Italiana Automobili Turino.

adumbrate

> And when the catastrophe so richly *adumbrated* finally occurs, he can only murmur, "Why, why, why?"

adumbrate—literally, "to cast a shadow" (from L. *ad,* to + *umbra,* shadow). *Adumbrate* means to foreshadow, suggest, and predict, as well as to outline, to sketch lightly.

Other words with the same root are: *penumbra,* the area in an eclipse where an intervening body cuts off the light partly (*pen,* from *paena,* almost, which also appears in *peninsula,* "almost island," and in *penultimate*); *somber,* dark, gloomy; *sombrero*; and *umbrage,* generally found with the verb *take* or *give,* where the word means annoyance, displeasure, resentment.

ailurophile

> *Ailurophiles* just can't get their fill of feline antics, as the continuing popularity of B. Kliban's cat cartoons demonstrates.

---

*The hyphen after *acro-* and the one before *-onym* not only indicate that these are combining forms but also indicate at which point they are usually attached.

ailurophile—lover of cats (from Gr. *ailuro-* cat + -*phile,* love).
Philo- and -*phile* are combining forms* found in hundreds of
English words. The opposite of -*phile* is -*phobe,* fear, sometimes hatred. *Xenophobes* fear and hate foreigners (*xenos,*
stranger).

anagram

> Sanche de Gramont, having fulfilled his residency for
> citizenship, changed his name to Ted Morgan (the
> *anagram* of de Gramont which he chose from a list
> that included, among other names: O. D. Garment,
> Tom Danger, Rod Magnet, and R. D. Megaton).

anagram—A rearrangement of the letters to form another
word, preferably a word that is apt or humorous: *astronomers*
to *moonstarers; funeral* to *real fun.* (From Gr. *ana,* backward
+ *gramma,* letter.)

   Perhaps the longest anagram, and the most ingenious,
transforms "Washington crossing the Delaware" to "He saw his
ragged Continentals row."

   Many seventeenth- and eighteenth-century French
authors used anagrams of their actual names as pseudonyms,
and one of them is today known by no other. François Marie
Arouet l.j. (l.j. = *le jeune,* junior) changed his last name by
rearranging the letters, so that we read in Carlyle about "Mon-
sieur Arouet Junior, who by an ingenious anagram—arouet + l
+ j (with *u* equivalent to *v* and *j* to *i*)—writes himself Voltaire
ever since."

anathema

> For such leaders as the Ayatollah Khomeini, the
> political doctrines of foreign lands are *anathema.*
> Capitalism and communism have both been condemned
> as the "creed of Satan."

---

*Greek combining forms that come at the beginning of a word usually end in *o*;
at the end of a word, in *e* or *y*.

anathema—a formal curse; a strong denunciation, used mostly for a person or thing detested.

ancillary

The agreement between the two heavyweights calls for 30 percent shares of gate and *ancillary* rights to receipts for challenger and champion.

ancillary—supplementary, additional (from L. *ancilla,* maid servant).

androgynous

Much significance is attached to the fact that his mother, his wife, and other women who have been important to him are all tall, gaunt and *androgynous,* with a preference for mannishly tailored clothes.

androgynous—having both male and female elements, in flowers and humans (from Gr. *andro-,* male + *gyne,* female).

Androgynous has won out over *hermaphroditic* (Hermes + Aphrodite) and the seldom seen *monoecious* (*monos,* one + *oikos,* house—both stamen and pistil in one plant).

There is a tendency in the United States to give androgynous names to children. A woman I know told me that if she gave birth to a girl, she would name her Samantha so that she could call her Sam or Sammy! Of course, there are so-called androgynous names: Merle, Jean, Shirley, Shelley, Lee, Mickey come to mind. With *hypocoristic,* or pet, names the field has become overgrown: Billie, Freddie, Jackie, Frankie, Marti, etc.

Also: philanderer; polyandrous (*poly,* many). Also gynecology; misogynist (miso-, hate).

android

The 90-pound robots, or *androids,* as their developers prefer to call them, move on three rubber-tired feet, talk, sing . . . whistle and rotate their domes.

android—an automaton made to resemble a human being (*-oid*, resembling).

anomalous

> For more than a decade the Federal Government has been in the *anomalous* position of discouraging cigarette smoking while encouraging the growth of tobacco for cigarettes.

anomalous—not conforming to the normal; hence irregular, inconsistent, and—almost—contradictory, paradoxical (from Gr. *a(n)*, not + *homalos*, even, which comes from *homos*, same, not to be confused with L. *homo*, man). It can therefore be seen that *homosexual* means one who has a sexual preference for one of the same sex and therefore can be applied as well to women as a synonym for *Lesbian*, which term comes from the homosexuality attributed to the poet Sappho, who lived on the island of Lesbos in the Aegean Sea.
> Also: *homogenized; homonym; homogeneous.*

apocalyptic

> As the alternative to the *apocalypse*, humanity must learn to live in peace and at last emerge from the prehistoric era.

apocalyptic—prophetic, revelatory, often in terms of the final destiny or doom of the world, used frequently since the proliferation of atomic weapons in these troubled times.

apocryphal

> The plays adapted were Alfred Jarry's "Ubu Roi" and the Elizabethan "Arden of Faversham," *apocryphally* ascribed to Shakespeare, one of the greatest of the lesser-known Elizabethan plays.

apocryphal—not authentic, not true, spurious, not documented (from Gr. *kryptien,* to hide, becoming English *crypt*). Speakers like to begin an anecdote with: "Of course, this story is probably apocryphal, but. . . ." *Crypto-* plugged into a word denotes someone or something hidden or secret, like crypto-Communist, crypto-Nazi, anyone accused of working secretly for an objective he is unwilling to declare.

apogee

> Donizetti's earlier opera "Il Furioso" after all has enough mad scenes to furnish several operas, and it may well be that it took all of these to reach the *apogee* in "Lucia."

apogee—the highest or farthest point (from Gr. *apo,* away from + *ge,* earth). Usually it is used for an orbiting object around the earth: *apogee,* its farthest point, and *perigee,* its closest.

> These tides are even higher if the moon is in *perigee,* the closest point to the earth in its elliptical orbit.

(From Gr. *apo,* away from = L. *ab, abs;* Gr. *peri,* around = L. *circum.*)

Also: *geology; geopolitical; geometry* (which originally meant a measuring of the earth).

Words similar in meaning are *nadir* and *zenith,* both from Arabic.

apostasy

> Although the two men (former CIA agents) have different backgrounds and styles, there is the same pattern of early orthodoxy followed by disillusionment and then *apostasy.*

apostasy—abandonment of a cause one has believed in; defection; desertion (from Gr. *apo,* away + *stasis,* a standing).

arcane

> The rules of evidence and procedures in a trial are *arcane* to most laymen—including reporters and editors.

arcane—mysterious, hidden, recondite, understood by only a few, as contrasted with something clear, lucid, and direct. Some official in Washington, reading some bureaucratic instructions for the public, coined a useful word when he said, "We'll have to laymanize it."

In Latin, *arcana,* plural of *arcanum,* means secret things.

autism, autistic

Autism, a behavioral disorder appearing in early childhood and characterized by language difficulties and extreme withdrawal, affects an estimated 100,000 people in the United States.

autistic—may also include a disregard of external reality.

autodidact

He and I have in common the fact that we are *autodidacts* and suffer the loss and gain of not having gone to universities.

autodidact—one who is self-taught (from Gr. *auto-*, self + *didaktos,* taught).
Also: *didactic,* teaching a moral; *didactics,* pedagogy.

bellwether

On the trading floor of the New York Exchange, brokers like to keep their eyes on several *bellwether* issues in order to judge the tone of the general market.

bellwether—a word beloved of writers for the sports and financial pages. The bell rings in this word because it is tied around the neck of the *wether,* or male sheep, that leads the flock. The others, being sheep, follow.

The word is gradually developing an additional meaning (probably influenced by the word *weathervane*) to indicate which way the wind is blowing, a kind of barometer, something from which a prediction can be made, as seen in the following headline:

A BELLWETHER COUNTY IN WYOMING
IS LEANING HEAVILY TOWARD THE PRESIDENT
(This meaning has not yet reached the dictionaries.)

bionic

> Tommy John, the 35-year-old lefty with the recon-
> structed *"bionic* arm," allowed only three hits and had
> the opposition beating the ball into the ground with
> monotonous regularity.

bionic—refers to the practical science of designing instruments
modeled after living organisms.
    Also: Gr. *bios,* life, is in too many words to mention
here. One of them, *symbiosis,* much used, will appear later.

burgeon

> Because the American theater is *burgeoning* with new
> creative female talent, the program, helped by a grant
> from the Ford Foundation, is potentially a significant
> one.

burgeon—once spelled *bourgeon* like its French original,
meaning "to bud," is used as a weaker form of *proliferate,*
meaning to grow rapidly, to flourish, to expand quickly.

cacophony

> Protests at graduation are a dim murmur compared
> with the anti-Government *cacophony* of the Vietnam
> War and Watergate years.

cacophony—ugly noise, clamor, din, unpleasant sound (from
Gr. *kakos,* bad, evil + *phone,* voice, sound). The combining
forms *phono-* and *-phone* have given us many words too obvious to mention; however, the other combining form *kako-*
gives us *cacography,* bad writing, incorrect spelling, and *cacoethes,* an itch to do something, usually writing: *cacoethes
scribendi.*

catalyst

> Some people felt that it was Wilson, the speedy switch-
> hitter, who served as the *catalyst* of the offensive
> attack that led the Royals to the first league pennant in
> their 12-year history. However, Brett was the man who
> was feared the most by opposing managers and pitchers.

catalyst—mentioned here only because it is beginning to take
on the meaning of "something that triggers an action or
reaction."
    Also: Gr. *kata,* down, yields such words as *catastro-
phe, cataclysm* (washing down, tremendous flood, disaster).

Catch-22*

> In one *Catch-22* situation, reporters could not drive
> into the sprawling grounds of the Salaam Hotel, where
> the press center was set up, without an official car pass,
> which had to be picked up at the hotel press center.

Catch-22—the above is a classic Catch-22 situation. Too
often, any hitch, any obstacle is labeled Catch-22.
    Even Greek mythology comes close to having a Catch-
22 situation. Tithonus, a handsome Trojan prince, is beloved
of the goddess of dawn, Eos (Aurora), who offers to grant him
anything he asks for. He chooses immortality, but neglects to
ask for eternal youth. Like any other, he grows older and
weaker and finally prays for death.
    Tennyson takes it from there. Tithonus speaks:

> "The woods decay, the words decay and fall,
> The vapors weep their burden to the ground,
> Man comes and tills the field and lies beneath,
> And after many a summer dies the swan.
> Me only cruel immortality
> Consumes. I wither slowly in thy arms."

---

*Joseph Heller's original title was *Catch-18,* but a book by Leon Uris titled
Mila 18 caused a snag. Finally, Heller's editor came up with the catchier
Catch-22.

In the myth, Eos, unable to grant his wish for death, transforms Tithonus into what he has almost shriveled to—a grasshopper.

catharsis

On the West German mainland, newspapers report the reaction to "Holocaust"—realization, anguish, *catharsis.*

catharsis—the purification or cleansing of the emotions. Originally applied by Aristotle to the purging of pity and terror through the viewing of a tragedy.

cenotaph

"Beloved Prime Minister Chou, you lie sleeping in the snow, but *we will never forget you*," said the note attached to the *cenotaph.*

cenotaph—a tombstone honoring someone whose body lies somewhere else (from Gr. *kenos*, empty + *taphos*, tomb).
Also: *epitaph* (*epi*, upon).

charisma, charismatic

When Ramsey Clark . . . returned last week from a visit to Iran, he said that 99 percent of its people support Ayatollah Ruhollah Khomeini, the *charismatic* Moslem leader who hopes to return from exile.

charisma—this word is entered only for the record. Not so long ago the word *charismatic* was known only in its religious sense, describing an evangelical, somewhat controversial movement within the Christian faith. Harold Macmillan, former Prime Minister of England, when interviewed by William Buckley on "Firing Line," said, "I had no charisma. There was no such word then." *Charisma* is seen and heard daily now, to describe a leader who captures the popular imagination, has personal magnetism, people appeal, even charm. Indeed, *charisma* breaks down anagrammatically into *is a charm.*

circadian

> Before the advent of jet planes, travel by ship was slow
> and time lags were easily adjustable, but with the
> speed of modern jet planes, the *circadian* rhythm is
> definitely disturbed.

circadian—a recently coined word; therefore its origin perhaps
gets nearer to the meaning than words that have traveled
through the centuries. *Circa* is Latin for "about" (only *c.* is used
with a date: c. 1500), and *di* is part of the word *dies*, "day," with
an, the adjective suffix. It means the round-the-clock rhythm of
daily life.

The word *circadian* was frequently used in the recent
25-day experiment in which a volunteer was sealed off from
outside contact, with no timepiece, no sun to give her a calculated guess at the time of day. One of the conclusions arrived
at was that a biological day lasts 25 hours as compared with a
24-hour solar day.

cliché

The number of clichés heard or read each day is legion (there's
one). They are generally fixed idiomatic phrases, some of
which may have originally been valid, fresh, and colorful but
through constant use have become about as personal as a
rubber stamp or a mimeographed love letter. Examples which
you can fill in easily are:

> take the bull by _____ _____
> swept it under _____ _____
> runs a tight _____
> breathe a sigh of _____
> life takes its _____
> perish the _____
> without fear of _____
> proud _____ of
> doomed to _____
> beyond the shadow of a _____
> like a bolt from the _____
> leave no stone _____

Nevertheless, you can see that many of the expressions given here are at times clearly unavoidable. Wishing to avoid "like a bolt from the blue," a journalist trying to describe a situation that suddenly became a near riot came up with "like a bolt of lightning from a clear sky." Maybe it's better to go along with rather than around such clichés.

The clichés most frowned upon are those that are pompous like "doomed to disappointment," "perish the thought," "proud possessor," "point with pride." They should be avoided like the plague (there's another).

If you do use a cliché—and it's almost impossible to get along without them in informal conversation or writing—it's important to get it right. If you don't, this may happen:

> *Malclichés overheard over the years*
> 1. He has it down to a pat.
> 2. When the burglar struck her, she fell down with a thug.
> 3. They're as alike as three peas in a porridge.
> 4. He behaved like a bull in a china closet.
> 5. It's an error to be human.
> 6. The fog was so thick it was like a knife.
> 7. My husband's so busy, he's working like a Trojan horse.
> 8. I never take airplanes. I like to be on terra cotta.
> 9. She sticks to him like a leash.
> 10. She burnt the candle with both hands.

And—that's the (11.) whole thing in a bombshell.

clone

> Dame Agatha herself had no other comparable stage success ("The Mousetrap" is nearing its 30th year) and those who have tried to *clone* her novels into dramatic shape have proved scarcely luckier.

clone—a figurative use of *clone*, which in science means to reproduce an exact duplicate, asexually, by fission. The word was a sensation for a while when a controversy arose over reports of human cloning, which Dr. Steptoe described as science fiction.

coefficient

Like Erich Fromm, he believes that neurosis is a *coefficient* of freedom.

coefficient—a difficult word to define even in mathematics or physics, but as used here figuratively it means "a contributing factor toward a result, a joint agent."

cognition, cognitive

Marshack . . . has been building a case for some years that the surviving works of Cro-Magnon peoples contain evidence of a *cognitive* ability that exceeds anything suggested by conventional archeologists.

cognition—a much used word meaning the mental process by which knowledge is acquired or, more simply, the learning process (from L. *cognoscere,* to get to know; p.p. *cognitus*).

concatenation

This explanation the authors see as a *concatenation* of events on a national scale that was bound to affect adversely an urban locale made vulnerable by rotten political and economic leadership.

concatenation—a linking together or being linked together in a series. Derivation is very helpful: L. *catena,* chain + preposition *con,* together. *Catenary* describes the curve made by a chain or cord suspended between two points: "In a winter freeze, ice formed on the *catenary* curves of the wires from pole to pole."

condign

He was then reminded of the *condign* punishment that, according to regulations, awaited those who supplied false information to the occupation forces.

condign—richly deserved; usually followed, as here, by the word *punishment* (from L. *con,* with + *dignus,* worthy).

Also: *dignity; indignation,* a nobler word than *anger,* since it suggests that the resentment is probably justified.

congeries

The Bronx is a stretch of earth seared by a *congeries* of urban problems, including arson, heavy unemployment, and general neglect.

congeries—a heap, a collection of or a mass of objects, forces, or individuals; an aggregation; accumulation not necessarily linked together as in *concatenation.*

contravene

The Revolutionary Council a few days ago said that women's service in the army *contravened* the spirit of Islam.

contravene—conflict with, contradict, go against the law (from L. *contra,* against + *venire,* to come).
Also: *circumvent* (*circum,* around + *venire,* to come): to get around and so defeat, especially by strategy; to get the better of or prevent from happening by means of craft or ingenuity.

contumacious

Without for a moment agreeing that the conduct of any one of the petitioners was in fact *contumacious,* the petition states that their acts and statements were the result of their being harassed, beaten, and held in very high bail.

contumacious—obstinately resisting authority, insubordinate, "swollen" with one's own importance (from L. *tumere,* swell).
From the root *tum* also come: *tumor; tumid* (often used to characterize a swollen or pretentious style, as is the word *turgid*); *tumescence,* swelling; and *tumult.* Also related is the word *contumely,* insolence (swollen with pride). In his famous soliloquy, Hamlet asks:

"For who would bear the whips and scorns of time,
    The oppressor's wrong, the proud man's contumely?"

countervailing

If containment requires greater *countervailing* local
and American strength, why not admit so much and
get on with it?

countervailing—acting against with equal force (from L. via
French: L. *contra*, against + *valere*, to be strong).
    Also: *convalesce; valiant; equivalent; valor; avail;* and
valetudinarian (infirm, sickly, thinking constantly of one's
health).

deleterious

Even as I write [just before the opening of the 1980
Olympics] Moscow is being purged of "*deleterious*
elements": activist dissidents or just non-conformists,
"refuseniks," or just people who applied to emigrate and
still wait for answer, unemployed people, alcoholics.

deleterious—injurious to health, harmful; destructive (from Gr.
deleterios, injurious (to health); damaging, destructive).

demography, demographic

The reasons for this phenomenon are essentially
demographic, and include age, ethnic origin, income,
and class factors that are fundamentally related.

demography—a science dealing with distribution, density, vital
statistics of population (from Gr. *demos*, people + *graphein*, to
write).
    The root *demos* gives us the words: *democracy;
demagogue; endemic* (peculiar to a people, hence, native,
indigenous); *epidemic* ("upon the people," therefore, widespread); *pandemic* (*pan,* all).
    Graph, which is used as an English word, appears in
too many words to enumerate. It is one of those dependable

roots that do not change in spelling, except when the word comes to us from the Italian, as *graffiti* (singular, *graffito*), writings or scribblings, especially on walls or posters.

Demotic, of the people, describes a simplified system of writing in ancient Egypt, as distinguished from the *hieratic.* Sometimes *demotic* is used to mean *vernacular.*

diaphanous

Miss Green was resplendent in a *diaphanous* outfit that offered a goodly glimpse of what lay underneath.

diaphanous—transparent, describing a see-through blouse, etc. (from Gr. *dia,* through + *phanein,* to show).

Also: *cellophane; phantasmagoria; epiphany.* The last two words are, of course, treated elsewhere in this book.

dichotomy

This pervasive outlook, which is based on an absolute *dichotomy* between East and West, lurks under much of what is written about Turkey.

dichotomy—two divisions, two opposing schools of thought, a bifurcation (from Gr. adverb *dicha,* combining form *dich(o)*, in two, apart + Gr. combining form *-tomy,* to cut.

Also: *appendectomy; tonsillectomy,* etc.

disparate

One of the most alarming facts of today's world— perhaps ultimately more menacing than nuclear over-kill—is the gross *disparity* of material wealth between the rich minority and the poor majority of the peoples of earth.

disparate—essentially not alike; unequal; distinctly different. At the heart of this word is the L. root *par,* equal. *Dis* is one of the negative L. prefixes along with *in, contra,* and *mal.* Corresponding Gr. prefixes are *a(n), anti, dys, caco.*

divagation

> Remembering his 10-year-old contract with his pub-
> lisher, he has dusted off his old notes and book
> reviews, and has strung them together, retaining all
> "the redundancies, asides, *divagations.*"

divagation—a wandering from the subject, digression (from L.
vagari, to wander, to roam). The *vagus* nerve is so called
because it wanders so far along the human body.

Also: *vague; extravagant; vagabond; vagary; vagrant.*

dragoman

> Our *dragoman* took us everywhere and saw to it that
> we bought everything. (*TLS*)

dragoman—in the Near East, an interpreter and often a guide
who almost always steers you toward the "best" shops.

ebullient

> The serious problems afflicting Prime Minister Tru-
> deau's Government seem to have neither affected his
> *ebullient* personality nor lessened his popularity.

ebullient—bubbling over, overflowing with enthusiasm (from
L. *e,* out + *bullire,* to boil, to bubble over).

An interesting spelling/pronunciation aspect: *bouillon*
and *bullion* may be pronounced the same but they have totally
different meanings: *bouillon* (Fr. *bouillir,* to boil), clear broth;
bullion, gold and silver in ingots before being coined.

eclectic

> Mr. Gruber has become the best known of a group of
> young Viennese composers who have attempted to
> pull music back from excessive cerebration and return
> to an *eclectic,* overtly communicative musical idiom.

eclectic—selecting what is best from various sources (music in
this case). (From Gr. *ec,* out + *legein,* to choose.)

effluvia, effluvium

The press room is so dank and ridden with scraps of press-release *effluvium* that it seems better suited to cultivating mushrooms than news stories.

effluvium—a generally disagreeable outflow (from L. *ex* to *ef*, out + *fluere*, to flow). Plural, *effluvia*.
  Also: *fluent; effluence; influence; influenza.*

eleemosynary

Coming at the end of an impoverished musical season, this sprightly little show is an act of beneficence. For the deprived theatergoer, it seems positively *eleemosynary.*

eleemosynary—for charity, given as charity, alms (which is a reduction of *eleemosynary* to a four-letter word).

encomium, encomiastic

It is deadly to read such an enthusiastic, uncritical appraisal, because it overwhelms the reader with *encomiastic* prose.

encomium—high or extravagant praise (from Gr. *en,* in + *komos,* revel). Synonyms: *panegyric, eulogy.*
  In Milton's famous masque, Comus tries to persuade Innocence to join the revels with the honeyed lines:

"What need a vermeil-tinctur'd lip for that,
Love-darting eyes, or tresses like the morn?"

ephemeral

Thus George Brett is not just one of the boys of summer attempting an *ephemeral* feat. If he succeeds in the incredible—batting over .400 for a full season—he will also stock the memories of a new generation and recall to life prodigies long past.

exponential; geometric; logarithmic

> The signs of the impending dangers of *exponential* growth in consumption in a world of finite resources are frequently clear only to the experts.

> Other factors come into play, and they assure that the rise in crime will not be arithmetic but *geometric.*

> Because the decibel scale is *logarithmic,* the difference between 85 and 90 represents a doubling in loudness.

exponential, geometric, logarithmic—these three words describe different ways in which a quantity may increase or, for that matter, decrease. If a quantity increases by constant increments (e.g., 3, 6, 9, 12, ...) it is said to increase *arithmetically* or *linearly.* If it increases by a constant multiplier (e.g. 3, 9, 27, 81, ...), it is said to increase *geometrically* or *exponentially,* which is obviously much faster than *arithmetically.* A *logarithmic* increase is much slower than either of these (as when the decibel scale goes only from 85 to 90 even though the loudness doubles); it is the inverse of exponential increase.

extrapolate

> There are dangers in *extrapolating* from a single tooth to a reconstruction of a skull or a life style.

extrapolate—to draw conclusions or make predictions on the basis of facts available at the time. Election returns are an example of how on the basis of 5% of the votes a network can predict the results. The networks, however, call it a projection.

    To interpolate is to insert material—thrown in—to alter what has been said or written.

febrile

> The *febrile* combination of Islamic fundamentalism, anti-Americanism and terror tactics now sweeping Iran last week spread to other Moslem nations.

febrile—feverish; here it seems to be the kind of fever that spreads quickly to others.

feckless

> The C.I.A. is not filled with amateurish bunglers. They are not *feckless,* clumsy, innocent, pedestrian, sentimental, easily deceived, impetuous, spendthrift, or dim.

feckless—look upon this much seen word as a shortening of *effectless,* i.e., *ineffectual, ineffective,* and you can't miss.

fecund, fecundity

> Do we live in a society which, as Dorothy Parker said, so often confuses the first rate with the *fecund* rate?

> He has stunned us with his pre-emptive strike, and a relationship that could have remained *fecund* until February may be jejune in January.

fecund—productive, fertile, fruitful
Both excerpts (the second is by William Safire) illustrate clever puns; however, I'm afraid that Dorothy Parker confused *fecund* (related to *fetus*) with *feculent* (related to *feces*), but, of course, the pun wouldn't work with *feculent.*

feisty

> A *feisty* old derelict made what the patrolmen thought was a threatening gesture.

feisty—much overused. Means lively, spirited, frisky, exuberant, full of nervous energy; also aggressive, belligerent.
Actually, the word is Anglo-Saxon in origin, from a word that means "breaking wind." It is often used appropriately enough to describe some older person who is still "full of beans."

feral

> In both homicides the assailants came from the thousands of Brazil's slum youngsters whose brief life

stories read like those of the *feral* youths accused of attacking the elderly in decaying parts of New York.

feral—wild, savage, untamed (from L. *fera*, wild beast).

flagellation

Several instances of punishment by *flagellation* have been reported from the provinces, ordered by religious courts set up by ayatollahs or mullahs outside the framework of civil law.

flagellation—a whipping or flogging, especially as a religious discipline or for sexual stimulation.

The word *flail* is, of course, related, a kind of shorthand version, though its use is restricted to flailing of arms or threshing.

forensic

William Fitzpatrick, the assistant district attorney who prosecuted the case, said hypnosis was gaining acceptance as a *forensic* tool.

forensic—suitable for a law court, employed in legal proceedings, especially as used today: forensic medicine; forensic scientists, referred by the police as "the lab boys."

It also has to do with formal argument, debate: "having forensic skill." In the ancient Roman world the name *forum* was applied to the marketplace and civic center of a city. Since public business was transacted and orators declaimed there, the word *forum* itself means not only a public meeting place but also a program involving discussions of a problem.

fractious

Strategists for the rival Presidential candidates reached a series of early-morning agreements on the allocation of support, averting the possibility of a *fractious* floor fight.

fractious—breaking the rules, refractory, unruly, tending to cause trouble, unmanageable (from L. *fractus,* p.p. of *frangere,* to break).

Also: *fracture; fragile; frangible* (breakable).

There is a plant called *saxifrage,* which grows in crevices and therefore breaks the rocks in which it is imbedded. *Irrefragable,* however, comes from a different root. Although it means indestructible, it comes from L. *refragari,* to resist, oppose.

fulminating

Only when he was destitute and close to 46 did Rolfe exploit his fabulous talent for invective, *fulminating* in one book after another against those who had thwarted his ambition.

fulminating—shouting denunciations, thundering against (from L. *fulmen, fulminis,* thunderbolt, lightning).

Fulminating powder is an explosive material used in detonations.

gelid

Here stands Wellington—his raucous laugh, his shrewd grasp of political and diplomatic, as well as tactical, realities, his *gelid* calmness in the heat of battle.

gelid—cold, icy (from L. *gelidus,* icy cold; *gelare,* to freeze).

In Puccini's *La Bohème,* the beautiful and poignant aria that Rodolfo sings to Mimi at their first meeting, and that foreshadows the tragic ending, begins with the words: "Che gelida manina" (How cold your little hand!).

Also: *gelatine; congeal; jelly; gelato,* Italian for ice cream.

gnomes

Nothing excites the *gnomes* of Zurich and their colleagues in the world money markets more than political uncertainty.

gnomes—dwarflike creatures in folklore who were the reputed guardians of treasure. The term was first used and probably coined by Paracelsus.

graffito

> The title of Miss Signoret's autobiography, *Nostalgia Ain't What It Used to Be,* was inspired by a *graffito* the actress had once noticed in New York.

graffito—the not much used singular of the much used plural *graffiti*. My favorite graffito was the work of two scribblers of apparently different philosophical outlooks.

The first one had written on the ledge above the steps leading down to the subway station: THE END. A second scribe, not an existentialist and evidently not as tall, added a Y to the first word and URE to the second word, conveying a Faulkneresque message of affirmation for the future of mankind: THE$_Y$ END$_{URE}$

hagiographic

> Still, his short unhappy life makes for moving reading even in the biographer's *hagiographic* account.

hagiographic—worshipful (from Gr. *hagios,* holy, saintly, sacred + *graphein*, to write).

A *hagiography* is a biography of saints, or any idealizing biography. *Hagiology* is literature dealing with the lives of saints, or history of sacred writings.

hegemony

> Mr. Brezhnev expressed concern about a passage in the joint Chinese-American communique opposing *"hegemony,"* which is a Chinese codeword for Soviet expansionism and has been used in Chinese-Soviet polemics.

hegemony—domination of one state over another (from Gr. *hegemon,* leader).

hierarchy

> Despite the left-hander's absence from the mound most of last season, he has impressed the Yankee *hierarchy* with his throwing this spring.

hierarchy—a governing church body, though it is as often used in a secular sense to designate any governing body that is classified according to rank. It means those higher up, the top echelon of any organization. (From Gr. *hieros,* sacred, holy.)
   Also: *hieratic,* consecrated to religious uses.

holograph

> Not long ago, in the library of Madrid, 700 pages of the notebooks of Da Vinci with drawings and descriptions of the drawings in his own handwriting were discovered—a historic *holographic* find.

holograph—a document wholly in the handwriting of the author (from Gr. *holos,* whole + *graphein,* to write).

holography, hologram

> *Holography* is three-dimensional photography without the use of a lens. Through the use of coherent beams of light, it provides a means of recording a whole image—not just the flat surface of ordinary photography. Dr. Gabor gave the new type of photography the name of *hologram,* after the Greek words *holos,* meaning whole, and *gramma,* meaning letter or message.

holography, hologram—the perfection of this process through the use of laser beams has produced three-dimensional photographs and x-rays (still in its early stages).
   Also: *holocaust,* literally complete destruction by fire (*kaustus,* burnt). Incidentally, *encaustic* (*en,* in, into) was the purple ink used by Roman emperors to burn their signatures into their decrees. Cut the word *encaustic* down to the first three letters and you get our word *ink.*

hubris

> His downfall is the consequence of political heavy-handedness, economic mismanagement, cultural dislocation, and what can only be termed the *hubris* of the Shah.

hubris—put the words *arrogance* and *overweening pride* together and you have a definition of *hubris,* which is a strong and useful word (from Gr. *hubris,* insolence, outrage).

hyperbole

> President Carter was indulging in Nixonian *hyperbole* when he called the invasion of Afghanistan the greatest threat to world peace since World War II.

hyperbole—exaggeration for effect, especially in poetry and humor. Mark Twain once remarked that German words were so long they had perspective.

> "Ten thousand saw I at a glance
> Tossing their heads in sprightly dance."
> > Wordsworth, "I Wandered Lonely as a Cloud"

hyper—always means over, above, more than normal. Latin twin is *super* (just as *hypo* has its twin in *sub*). *Hyperkinesis* (also *hyperkinesia*) means pathologically excessive motion (*hyper* + *kinesis,* movement, from *kinein,* to move).

iambics and trochees

> After the surprise victory of his team, the coach's enthusiasm was not actually expressed in *iambics* and *trochees,* but what he said had its own exuberant rhythms.

iambics and *trochees*—*iambic, iamb* is the normal rhythmic line in English verse just as the *alexandrine* is the normal rhythmic line of French tragedy. Listen to commercials on television: "It isn't just for breakfast any more" is a perfect *iambic* pentameter (five feet, ten syllables, with the accent on the second syllable in almost every foot).

In his plays Shakespeare employs the iambic pentameter, for the most part unrhymed (called blank verse). In his sonnets, of course, the framework is a rhyming scheme (ababcdcdefefgg), but the lines are still iambic pentameter.

An example of iambic pentameter can be seen in the famous lines of Marlowe's play which Dr. Faustus speaks on first beholding the apparition of Helen of Troy:

> "Was this the face that launch'd a thousand ships
> And burnt the topless towers of Ilium?"

Familiar poems employing the *trochaic* rhythm are a mere handful, the most famous being Poe's "The Raven," Tennyson's "Locksley Hall," and Leigh Hunt's delightful:

> "Jenny kissed me when we met,
> Jumping from the chair she sat in;
> Time, you thief, who love to get
> Sweets into your list, put that in:
> Say I'm weary, say I'm sad,
> Say that health and wealth have missed me,
> Say I'm growing old, but add,
> Jenny kissed me."

Because the first syllable in a foot is accented in a trochee, the beat seems to be longer:

> "In the Spring a livelier iris changes on
>   the burnish'd dove;
> In the Spring a young man's fancy lightly
>   turns to thoughts of love."
>   Tennyson, "Locksley Hall"

immanent

For most people, ultimate reality is not transcendent but *immanent*—"God" is understood as "nature" or a force or forces within this world.

immanent—inherent, remaining or existing within (from L. *manere,* to remain + *im,* within).

immolation

> His self-destruction was an exemplary one, and can even be understood as a self-sacrifice, a *self-immolation* for the benefit of others.

immolation—a sacrifice (from L. *mola,* a millstone). *Molars,* the name of the grinding teeth, is derived from the same word. The Latin word *mola* came to mean the thing ground, a kind of grain or meal. In accordance with prescribed ritual, Roman priests sprinkled this finely ground grain, with a portion of salt added, over a sacrificed animal's head. By another transfer of meaning, the word *immolatio,* literally "the act of spreading the ground grain," was applied to the sacrifice itself.

impecunious

> A major general with a comfortable fortune, now he could marry the girl whom he had courted while a young subaltern and whose family had scorned him as too *impecunious* for their daughter.

impecunious—without money, poor (from L. *im,* not + *pecunia,* money, from *pecus,* cattle, sheep, which meant wealth in many ancient communities).

impinges

> Apologists for his Catholicism have pointed out that he repudiates the Church in *A Portrait* [*of the Artist as a Young Man* by James Joyce] only to the degree that it *impinges* upon his hero, and not absolutely. (NYRB)

impinges—encroaches, touches. Note that *apologists* almost always means defenders.

implode, implosion

> In order to play with the concept of black holes— *implosions* of matter in space—he has intensified his sideline work in physics.

implode—to burst inward (from L. *in* + [*ex*] *plode*, from *plaudere*, to applaud). *Explode* originally meant to drive off (*ex*) the stage by clapping of hands and hooting. *Implosion* is sometimes used in connection with "the black holes."

imprimatur

> The main outcome of Vanderbilt University's sponsorship of the Davis Cup matches is the addition of the *imprimatur* of a prestigious educational institution in the South to a non-academic activity involving the world's most prejudiced nation in Africa.

imprimatur (chief accent on *mat*, which may be pronounced *maht* or *mate*)—approval, sanction (from L. *imprimere*, to print; impress). The Latin one-word sentence *Imprimatur* means, "Let it be printed."

impugn

> He believes the actor to have been a largely asexual figure who was deeply wounded by a press that *impugned* his manhood.

impugn—attack with words, call into question, make insinuations against (from L. *pugnare*, to fight).
　　Also: *pugnacious, repugnant,* and *inexpugnable* (that cannot be defeated by force, impregnable, unconquerable).

incantatory

> Sadat's message, which became almost *incantatory* with each repetition, was: Let's fight no more wars; let's solve the very real differences between Arabs and Jews at a table, not on a battlefield.

incantatory—chanted like a ritual, cantorial (from L. *cantare,* to sing). *Incantation:* the chanting of verbal charms in the hope of achieving some magical result. A pointed exchange about incantation appears in Shakespeare's *King Henry IV, Part I:*

Glendower: I can call spirits from the vasty deep.

Hotspur: Why, so can I, or so can any man;
But will they come when you do call for
them?

Also: *recant (re,* back), "to sing a different tune."

incunabula

The two editions of the *Nuremberg Chronicle,* both
printed in 1493, are very exceptional *incunabula.*

incunabula—early printed books, especially before 1500 (from
L. *incunabula* [neuter plural], swaddling clothes, cradle).

ineluctable

To some, Paris is the home of the good life in full
philosophic awareness of the horror of history and the
ineluctability of death.

ineluctable—inescapable, inevitable. From L. *in,* not + *ex,* out
+ *luctare,* to struggle + *able,* which beautifully adds up to
"something that cannot be fought or struggled against."
Also: *reluctant,* "fighting back."

inexorable

Political realization of these identities is an idea whose
time is drawing *inexorably* near.

inexorable—relentless, that cannot be halted. From another
lovely combination: L. *in,* not + *ex,* out of + *orare,* to talk +
able, adding up to "something you're not able to talk your way
out of."

internecine

Internecine fighting that threatened to destroy Leb-
anon's uneasy balance of power broke out today

among the heavily armed militias of both rightist and leftist factions.

internecine—pernicious, death-dealing, deadly, or harmful struggle within a group or a nation; civil war (from L. *inter,* between + *necare,* to kill). A related Greek word, *nekros,* dead body, gives us the words *necromancy,* black magic; *necropolis,* cemetery (especially one in an ancient city).

interpolate (see extrapolate)

intransigence, intransigent

Her situation appears to reflect Soviet *intransigence* in face of pledges at Helsinki nearly two years ago to promote the freer flow of persons and information.

intransigent—in negotiations that are deadlocked it's always the other country or the other party which is *intransigent,* unwilling to yield any point, unwilling to come halfway. Again the derivation is interesting: L. *in,* not + *trans,* across + *agere,* to drive: "unwilling to cross the line."

irony

It's *ironic* that the fur that protects the seals from the cold weather subjects them to the greed of men.

irony—if you asked someone to define *irony,* he'd probably stammer: "Oh, you know," or give you an example of irony. It's hard to define. Try this: the opposite of what might be expected or intended, as in Mark Antony's use of "honorable men" to characterize the murderers of Julius Caesar.

irredentism

The resolution certainly gave no support to the idea of increasing the previous number of sovereign states in the Middle East or of giving Israel a new neighbor rampant with *irredentism* and aflame with a denial of Israel's legitimacy.

irredentism—an unflagging desire or intention to regain territory lost by war or partition; comes to us through Italian *irredenta* (from L. *ir,* for *in,* not + *redemptus,* redeemed).

jejune

> The biographer's own comments are almost always *jejune* or banal.

jejune—empty, barren, dull, flat, inane, vapid—and therefore, by extension, immature, juvenile, puerile. The *jejunum* (Latin) is part of the small intestine between the duodenum and the ileum and is so called from a belief that it is empty after death. You can remember the meaning of *jejune* by associating it with the French word *dejeuner,* literally "to break one's hunger" or, as we say, "to break fast." Also compare our slang expression "from hunger" for something empty, inane.

lapidary

> The baritone handles the merger of words and tones with *lapidary* precision.

lapidary—of an elegance associated with inscriptions on stone (from L. *lapis, lapidis,* stone).
> Also: *lapis lazuli,* an azure-blue semi-precious stone; *dilapidated,* fallen apart stone by stone.

libation

> Pouring himself some sparkling Burgundy, he interrupts his *libation* with a sudden start.

libation—the ritual of pouring the first portion of wine on the ground to honor the gods (from L. *libare,* to pour out). When a teacher explained the *libation* in Homer's "Odyssey" as a first offering to the gods, one bright pupil asked, "Could you call it 'one for the road'?"
> An advertisement announcing a celebration to honor Beverly Sills ends with the injunction: Now on with the ball! *Libiamo.*

limpid

> This book is written in a *limpid,* hard-hitting prose with a bare minimum of footnotes.

limpid—transparent, crystal clear, usually used, as here, to describe a writer's style, or to describe a girl's eyes (limpid pools).

linear, nonlinear

> This is one of those *linear* biographies that open with the birth of the subject and end with his death.

> His script, unlike the chronological style of the auto-biography, is *nonlinear;* incidents are shifted back and forth in their associative patterns, portraying the heroine during various stages of her long life.

linear—a term much used for narratives that have a beginning, a middle, and an end, in that order. *Nonlinear* is used for works that are not so constructed, especially when even the flashbacks (just as they are recalled in life) are not in chronological order.
William Faulkner's novel *The Sound and the Fury* is a supreme example of nonlinear narration. (The late Jean-Paul Sartre, in reviewing it, asked: "Why has Faulkner broken up the time of his story and disarranged the fragments? . . . Faulkner did not first think in terms of an orderly narrative and then shuffle the parts like a pack of cards; he could not have told the story in any other way.") In contemporary cinema, the non-linear screenplay is much in vogue, and filmgoers are becoming inured to flash-forwards as well as flashbacks, in such foreign films as Resnais' *La Guerre est Finie* and Losey's *The Go-Between.*

litigious

> It had to happen in this *litigious* nation. A San Francisco woman has been sued in Small Claims Court here by a San José man for breaking a date.

litigious—in the clipping the operative word is *sued. Litigious,* given to legal action (from L. *litigare,* to dispute, quarrel, sue), may also mean quarrelsome.

logarithmic (See exponential)

logo

> This emblem of the Pittsburgh Steelers, by the way, is the *logo* of the steel industry.

logo—short for *logotype*: distinctive emblem identifying a company, team, institution, etc. *Logo* is gradually replacing the word *colophon,* which has the same meaning and is sometimes still used when referring to emblems used by publishers.

macaronic

> What she studied there was Russian, which she was able to imitate brilliantly in *macaronic* gibberish, and Sanskrit, which she has wholly forgotten.

macaronic—referring to verse or prose in which a mixture of languages is used for humorous effect. Here are two stanzas of *macaronic* verse (Latin-English mixture):

Puer ex Jersey	(A boy from Jersey
Iens ad school.	Going to school.
Vidit in meadow	Saw in a meadow
Infestum mule.	A hostile mule.
Ille approaches.	(It approaches.
O magnus sorrow!	O great sorrow!
Puer it skyward	Boy goes skyward.
Funus ad morrow.	Funeral tomorrow.)

The word *macaronic* probably comes from the Italian *maccaroni,* macaroni (plural, *maccheroni*), which was originally a mixture of grain, eggs, and cheese.

Jonathan Swift liked this sort of thing (*macaronics*), especially where authentic Latin words, meaninglessly strung together, formed a good English sentence. In correspondence with Dr. Sheridan, he asked: "*Is his honor sic? Prae letus fells pulse.*" (Latin: *is*, this; *his*, these; *sic*, thus; *prae*, before; *letus*, a form(?) of *letum*, death, from which our word *lethal*, into which the *h* has crept, probably through association with Lethe, the underworld river of forgetfulness or oblivion; *felis*, cat; *pulse*, a form of *pulsus*, beat.)

Italo Calvino, one of Italy's most famous contemporary novelists, inserts this verse into *The Baron in the Trees,** a mixture of three languages (the Spanish, I am told, defective):

> *Il y a un pré where the grass grows toda de oro*
> *Take me away, take me away, che io ci moro.*
>
> *(There is a meadow . . . every hour*
> *Take . . . for here I die.)*

Macaroni is obsolete for a fashionable fop, an English dandy, a member of a class of traveled young Englishmen of the late eighteenth and early nineteenth century who affected foreign manners and fashions. That may help to explain what is meant in the first stanza of "Yankee Doodle." It was first sung by the British to taunt the American troops, who later adopted the song as their own; it was first printed in America in 1795.

> "Yankee Doodle came to town
>   Upon a little pony
> He stuck a feather in his hat
>   And called it macaroni."

maladroit

> The President has wisely chosen to address himself to this as the first policy of his Administration, even if caught up in the miscalculations of his sometimes *maladroit* staff.

maladroit—clumsy, bungling (from L. *mal*, bad, wrong + Fr. *à*, to + *droit*, right).

Translated by Archibald Colquhoun. Translation copyright © 1959 by Wm. Collins Sons & Co. Ltd. Reprinted by permission of Random House, Inc.

megalopolis

Headline: A *MEGALOPOLIS* GROWS IN ITALY
MILAN-TURIN

megalopolis—an urban region in which several large cities are close enough to be considered a single urban complex. The word *conurbation* (from L. *con*, with + *urbs*, city) is used in much the same way. *Megalopolis* breaks down to Greek *megalo-*, large + *polis*, city: as in Annapolis; Sevastopol (city of Sebastian).

In the United States the metropolitan areas in a giant urban sprawl are BosWash, ChiPitts, SanSan, JaMi.

Also: *megalomaniac.*

melding

As is often the case with Mr. Stoppard, the play is a *melding* of past efforts.

melding—amalgam, blend. The word *meld* is itself a blend of *melt* and *weld.* In pinochle, *meld* refers to cards laid on the table in partial fulfillment of the bid made.

meliorist

"I call myself a *meliorist*—a man who believes that by human actions wisely directed the world can be made a better place."

meliorist—the excerpt speaks for itself. All that is necessary to add is that just as we have good, better, best, so Latin has *bonus, meliorus, optimus.*

metaphor, simile

The play *Gin Game* is a *metaphor,* as so many of our plays about the aged and the ill are these days.

The field of human cancer research is haunted by viruses. *Like tiny malignant ghosts* [a simile] they appear and then vanish; leave their footprints, but defy pursuit.

metaphor, simile—the familiar metaphor "the autumn of one's life" (also see **cliché**) had new meaning poured into it by Shakespeare in Sonnet 73:

> "That time of year thou may'st in me behold
> When yellow leaves, or none, or few, do hang
> Upon those boughs that shake against the cold,
> Bare ruined choirs, where late the sweet birds sang."

By extending the metaphor, he tells us in that beautiful fourth line that his early life was an active, happy one. "Bare ruined choirs," yes, but once "the sweet birds sang."

Metaphors and similes are poetic lies—lies which reveal truth more vividly than do most literal statements. With a metaphor, we boldly say that something *is* something else; with a simile we say that something is *like* something else. Metaphors and similes are also referred to as *imagery,* because it is natural for them to present pictures.

midden

Upon this medieval *midden,* popes and contractors erected a new town, Avignon, and a new order.

midden—a refuse heap, especially of a primitive habitation, one found by archeologists. A *kitchen midden* is a refuse heap or mound of the Mesolithic or later periods, containing shells, artifacts, and often animal bones.

misogyny

His theory is that Strindberg's *misogyny,* the contempt for women that shows in so much of his work, is a chauvinism undermined by something deeper.

misogyny—hatred of women (from Gr. *miso,* from *misein,* to hate).

Also: *misanthrope,* hater of mankind; *misoneism,* hatred of change or innovation (Gr. *neos,* new).

mutagen

> The W.H.O. says: "Those who oppose the use of DDT suggest that it may present a hazard as a carcinogen and *mutagen.*"

mutagen—any agent increasing the possibility of mutation, a variation in inheritable characteristics. Here are two important combining forms: L. *mutare,* to change + Gr. *-gen,* born.
Also: *mutation; immutable; mutant; oxygen; hydrogen; psychogenic; carcinogenic.*

mystique

> Mexico is one of the leading nations of Latin America and her revolutionary *mystique* is still strong.

mystique—a difficult word to define, carrying its own mystery with it. It doesn't appear in *Webster's Second,* and *Webster's Third* takes forty-one words to define one meaning of it. The word *mystique* implies a complex of mysterious beliefs or skills gathered around an idea, a feeling, or a person that can magically form a whole—an occult cult, so to speak.

mythic

> Gabriel García Márquez's new book, like his masterpiece, *One Hundred Years of Solitude,* once again is set in a *mythic* Colombian village.

mythic—a much used word, sometimes meaning *mythological,* but more often used to mean *imaginary,* as in this excerpt. It is often difficult to ascertain the meaning as in: "There is a mythic faith in the idea that such a strategy would accomplish the goal."

nebulous

> The main obstacles to reading his historical work are his *nebulous* terminology and, to give him the benefit of the doubt, his habit of not saying what he means.

nebulous—vague, unclear (from L. *nebula,* mist, cloud).
Also: *nebulize,* to reduce a liquid to a fine spray or mist; *obnubilate,* becloud.

nubile

The director begins the play with the aging wizard, Prospero, and his *nubile* daughter, Miranda.

nubile—marriageable, but more often used in the sense of voluptuous, a meaning not given in some dictionaries (from L. *nubere,* to marry).
Also: *connubial; nuptials.*

obduracy

After supporting Mr. Schmidt's *obduracy* for months, the German employers' federation has just called for more economic stimulus.

obduracy—stubbornness, stubborn persistence (from L. *durus,* hard, lasting, tough).
Also: *endure; duress; indurated,* hardened to.

obloquy

Pollution's first memorable part in the theater was in Ibsen's classic 1882 play, *An Enemy of the People,* about a doctor who drew *obloquy* from his community for publicizing a tainted reservoir.

obloquy—verbal abuse, vituperation (from L. *ob,* against + *loquere,* to speak).
Also: *colloquy* (*col,* together); *loquacious.*

onomatopoeic (or onomatopoetic)

One can keep time to his word-music, to the rolling cascade of language, as in "catfish stew, corn fritters, potato pone, fresh cold buttermilk," or the *onomatopoeic* "Roll. Roll. The subway rolls. Take it to the city. Take it to the city."

onomatopoeic—from noun *onomatopoeia,* the sound of the words suggesting their meaning. Words like *crash, roar, tinkle* are the more obvious examples. Its use in poetry is more subtle: Shakespeare's "Like sweet bells jangled out of tune and harsh," in *Hamlet,* or Swinburne's "lisp of leaves and ripple of rain." Swinburne's line also illustrates *alliteration,* a repetition of the same consonant sound.

opprobrium

> The word peasant has nearly everywhere been a term of *opprobrium.*

opprobrium—as here used, means reproach or contempt, but it usually is a very strong term, meaning disgrace, ignominy, shameful conduct.

oxymoron

> This is the best new *oxymoron* since "guest host."

oxymoron—a figure of speech in which opposite or contrary ideas or terms are combined (from Gr. *oxys,* acute, sharp + *moros,* foolish), beautifully illustrated in these lines from Tennyson's "Idylls of the King":

> "His honour rooted in dishonour stood
> And faith unfaithful kept him falsely true."

> Other words: *sophomoric* (from Gr. *sophos,* wise + *moros,* foolish).

paean

> Consider the perfection of Voyager 1, from which scientists learned more in one week near Saturn than in all previous history. Everything worked. It was a demonstration of excellence, a *paean* to American ingenuity and skill.

paean—a song of praise (to Apollo).

paladin

> Texas has been a defensive *paladin,* chary about throwing passes and relying on a solid ground attack for the 10 victories it pieced together during the year.

paladin—related to the word *palace.* It is the name specifically given to the twelve famous warriors of Charlemagne's court but is often applied to the Knights of the Round Table as well. Today the word is used for a noble defender of the right, or a renowned champion.

palindrome

> Such reversals and retractions, which give the appearance of moving backward and forward at once, may be embodied perhaps in a *palindrome*: TO LAST, CARTER RETRACTS A LOT.

palindrome—a word or a sentence reading the same backward and forward (from Gr. *palin,* back, again + *drome,* running).

The excerpt above is from a letter to *The N.Y. Times* written by Edward Scher after the U.S. vote against Israel in the U.N. which was afterward retracted and explained as a failure in communication between the government and the U.N. representative—a clever example of a sentence that reads the same backward and forward and made timely sense.

A palindrome is a more sophisticated form of the anagram. A famous palindrome, reputedly the first, is Adam's introduction of himself to his new-found mate: "Madam, I'm Adam," an introduction which the first lady acknowledged with the perfect palindrome, "Eve." Napoleon, in a philosophic mood, is reported to have said, "Able was I ere I saw Elba." However, the assumption that Adam and Eve and Napoleon spoke English casts a shadow of doubt on the authenticity of their statements. But there's no such doubt cast on "A man, a plan, a canal, Panama."

panache

> He gives a grand performance, with the *panache* and glamour of a Barrymore or Gielgud.

panache—the French word for plume or bunch of feathers. Anyone who has read Edmond Rostand's *Cyrano de Bergerac* knows that *panache* refers to the white plume on Cyrano's hat. However, the word today carries its symbolism—the sweep and flourish that Cyrano could make with it in the face of death. And so today *panache* has come to mean a gallant or heroic gesture, a splendid swagger, flamboyance, brio, dash, verve. In a long explanation of the word to the French Academy, Rostand said in part: "A little frivolous perhaps; a little melodramatic certainly, the *panache* is no more than a charming gesture. But this charming gesture is so difficult to make in the face of death and supposes so much strength that it is a charming gesture I would wish for us all."

panoply

> The music is all Weill and the lyrics are by a grand *panoply* of wordsmiths, among them Bertolt Brecht, Marc Blitzstein, Ira Gershwin, Ogden Nash, Maxwell Anderson.

panoply—an impressive array, a magnificent display. From the Greek combining form *pan-*, all + *hopla*, weapons, arms (from which we get *hoplite*, a heavily armed foot soldier of ancient Greece).

paradigm

> It [the Republican Party] may be the party of Lincoln, but no one imagines it, any more than the Democratic Party, to be a *paradigm* of financial nobility.

paradigm—a word whose practice used to bedevil pupils who numbly recited, "I am, you are, he is, we are," etc., or "amo, amas, amat," etc., without knowing that they were presenting a paradigm of the verb *to be* or of the Latin verb *amare*, to love. Used otherwise, *paradigm* means a model, a pattern, an example. John Leonard's apt pun "Brother, can you paradigm?" tells you how the word is pronounced.

Don't confuse *paradigm* with *paragon*, which means a model of *perfection*.

parameters

> The mayor said that the increase in salary for firemen and policemen was well within the *parameters* of wage increases suggested.

parameters—this much used—some say abused—word comes from a difficult concept in mathematics and as a vogue word means limits, boundaries, probably influenced by the word *perimeter.*

peccadillo

> The famous Senate courtesy did not conceal the determination to make every past *peccadillo* into a manifestation of gross misbehavior.

peccadillo—a small sin, a venial sin. Through Spanish from Latin *peccare,* to sin.

Also: *peccant; impeccant; impeccable* (flawless, faultless).

There's an English expression "to cry peccavi," which means to admit one's guilt, to confess an error or wrongdoing (L. *peccavi,* I have sinned).

A famous historical pun: Sir Charles Napier, after capturing the district in India called Scinde (now spelled Sind), whose largest city, Karachi, became the capital of newly created Pakistan), sent to Lord Ellenborough a dispatch notable for both brevity and truth: the one word "*Peccavi*" ("I have Scinde," sinned). Maybe the pun was the work of someone other than Napier, say historians, but no matter, if it serves to fix the word in your mind.

penurious

> For all the efforts of its recent rulers to wrench the country into the 20th century, Afghanistan remains a *penurious* family of fiercely squabbling tribes and cliques that unite only against the threat of foreign domination.

penurious—Penury in modern usage is generally restricted to the meaning of "extreme poverty," but its adjective, *penurious,* "impoverished," may also be used to mean stingy, parsimonious, or niggardly.

peremptory, peremptorily

"If his career should *peremptorily* come to a close because of this injury, etc., etc., etc., etc." (Howard Cosell)

peremptorily—absolutely, completely. (From L. *emptus* (p.p.), bought, paid for, as in the expression *Caveat emptor,* "Let the buyer beware."

perigee (See apogee)

peripatetic

The son of an electrician, Mr. Hirsch spent a *peripatetic* childhood in the West Bronx, where his family changed addresses some 13 times before he entered the second grade.

peripatetic—walking around, itinerant (from Gr. *peri* [twin of L. *circum*], around).
   The Peripatetic School was founded by Aristotle, so named because Aristotle used to walk about as he taught his disciples. The covered walk of the Lyceum was called Peripatos.

peripheral

For biologists, then, the anti-evolution issue is not *peripheral* and should be given critical attention.

peripheral—marginal, around the border, side (as in peripheral vision). From Gr. *peri,* around + *pherein,* to carry, bear.

piscine

At a later stage, its embryonic gill slits would recall a *piscine* forebear, a later step in evolution.

piscine—of or resembling fish (from L. *piscis*).
Also: *piscatorial. Piscine* is the French word for swimming pool.

placebo

The proponents of Laetrile either believe in the efficacy of apricot pits or in the value of unacknowledged *placebos.*

placebo—a harmless pill used in control tests, having no effect either good or bad except psychologically (from L. *placebo:* "I shall please").
Also: *complacent,* pleased with (*com*) oneself; *placate.*

plethora

Obviously, the present *plethora* of mini-parties will have to be reduced to facilitate orderly debate in the new Cortes (parliament).

plethora—excess, overabundance (from Gr. *plethein,* to be full).

polemic(s)

Having appeared with him many times on opposing ends of lecture platforms, I was in no way taken aback by the usual *polemics,* name calling and hysterics which are his trademarks.

polemic—either describes or is a controversial argument that is fiery, highly charged (from Gr. *polemos,* war). *Polemics* is also used in this sense.

polymath

He has become a *polymath* capable of enchanting a dinner table with authoritative pronouncements on miracle plays, on medieval pottery, on Stradivarius

> violins, on the Buddhism of Ceylon, and on the war-
> ships of the future—handling each as though he had
> made a special study of it. (*TLS*)

polymath—a person of great and diversified learning, sometimes called a Renaissance man (from Gr. *poly*, many +
mathein, to learn).
  Also: *polyglot*, many tongues, that is, speaking many
languages; *polymorphous*, having many shapes; and many,
many more.

postulate

> In the last century such an invisible ether was *postu-
> lated* as the medium through which light waves are
> propagated and through which the earth flies in its
> orbit.

postulate—as a verb, to assume to be true, only as the ground-
work for a chain of reasoning. As a noun, an assumption that
something is true. Very much like *hypothesis* and *hypothesize*,
which apply to a well-founded conjecture which still has to be
proved or tested.
  Also: *postulant*, a candidate, especially one for admission to a religious order.

prescient, prescience

> When Edison died, President Hoover was urged to
> order all electricity throughout the U.S. turned off on
> the day of the funeral, as a one-minute observance.
> Cooler heads had the *prescience* to warn that a power
> outage in New York and elsewhere was no way to me-
> morialize genius.

prescience—foresight, foreknowledge (from L. *pre*, before +
scire, to know). Pronounced *shent* and *shens*.
  The root *sci* is found in too many words to catalog, but
here is one: *nescient*, not knowing, ignorant of.

primordial

The whole attraction about diamonds is how they can best reflect light and appeal to some *primordial* instinct to be dazzled.

primordial—primitive, first in time (from L. *primus*, first + *ordire*, to begin).
    Also: *primeval*; *primogeniture*, the firstborn, with all the perquisites *he* is entitled to, traditionally.

pristine

How much of our still unspoiled national forests should be preserved in *pristine* wilderness?

pristine—unspoiled, in original or prime condition.

progenitor

The author sees the terrorists as the evolutionary *progenitors* of the guerrillas, who, in turn, give rise to the full-fledged revolutionaries.

progenitor—a forefather, precursor, forerunner (from L. *pro*, forth + *genitum*, p.p. *gignere*, to beget).
    Also: *progeny*, descendants; *congenital*, born with (*con*).

proliferate

In the 60's and 70's regional theaters *proliferated* from New Haven to Los Angeles; by 1979, there were more than 60 in 51 cities.

proliferate—multiply rapidly, increase, spread at a rapid rate. *Proliferate* is an interesting word. It comes from the Latin word *proles*, offspring, plus the root *fer*, to bear, and so has the idea of spreading, multiplying, expanding.
    Words containing the same basic root are *prolific* (abundant, profuse), and *proletariat*. Because *proles* is the

Latin word for offspring and because the poor were *prolific* and served the state not with their property but with their offspring, they were given the name *prolitarii,* from which come our words *proletarian* and *proletariat.*

provenance, provenience

> The art market should be less important than the *provenance* of the objects that are being sold. Why an object or an artifact was produced when it was—its cultural context—could provide a better story than the big bucks version.

provenance—the place from which something comes; an object's past possessors (art); in other words, the source, origin, derivation.

quark

> Since music is a tricky and unstable amalgam of science and mystery, of mathematics and the black arts, he was on solid ground in naming his new chamber work "Quarks." For, you see, *quarks* are not only subatomic particles hypothesized by nuclear physicists, but mysterious items referred to by Joyce in *Finnegans Wake.*

quark—in physics, any of three hypothetical subatomic particles having electric charges of magnitude one-third or two-thirds that of the electron, proposed as the fundamental units of matter. From a line in James Joyce's *Finnegans Wake,* that treasury of coined words: "Three quarks for Mr. Marks."

quasar

> Einstein demonstrated that nothing could travel faster than the speed of light, and yet observations of mysterious distant objects known as *quasars* create the illusion that this absolute constant is being exceeded.

quasar—distant starlike objects that emit immense quantities of light and powerful radio waves (from L. *quasi,* like + *stellar,* like a star).

quiddity

> If there is anything that Mr. Angell regards as unsavory in the upheavals baseball has visited upon itself in the last decade, it is the disrespect it has shown for its *quiddity,* what with the introduction of designated hitters, yammering ABC telecasters and World Series games played in freezing weather.

quiddity—essential quality of a thing; its whatness. From L. *quid,* what, as in *quid pro quo,* what in exchange for what.

quintessence, quintessential

> The *quintessential* difficulty in achieving a balance acceptable to both sides is, I feel, the tradition of mutual distrust existing within each superpower, especially in their military establishments.

quintessence—literally the fifth or highest essence, because the Greeks recognized only four elements (earth, air, fire, and water). The word therefore means the purest, finest form or expression of anything.

> When Hamlet speaks of man, he says, "And yet to me what is this quintessence of dust?"

quotidian

> His novel is haunted by the high level of *quotidian* American violence and the vulnerability of American lives.

quotidian—as adjective, daily; as noun, daily round of things (from L. *quot,* as many as + *dies,* day).

> Also: *diurnal,* and via French, *journal.*

raffish

> They shun the commonplace and embrace the extraordinary with the same sort of *raffish* glee that once

made the Brooklyn Dodgers of sainted memory the darlings of the multitude.

raffish—a difficult word to define, because though the dictionaries give "disreputable, rakish, tawdry, low," its use now is frequently sneakily admiring. Although the tendency is for words to pejorate, this one has ameliorated. It suggests a certain kind of swagger, yes, but not so unfavorable as its origin (*riffraff*) would indicate. It's a word to watch. Associate it with *riffraff* in its bad sense but realize that it has developed upward mobility.

ratiocination

Poe's masterpieces of detection, like "The Purloined Letter" and "The Gold Bug," depend for their intellectual excitement on *ratiocination*.

ratiocination—the process of reasoning methodically and logically (from L. *ratio*, reason).

Also: *rational; rationalize,* to find plausible or untrue reasons or explanations for one's questionable behavior or conduct. If someone says, "Now you're rationalizing," he's implying that you are trying to find good reasons for actions that appear to be not good.

recherché

Although submarine warfare may seem a bit *recherché*, the reporter points out that NATO strategists believe it would be the crucial element in any conflict between the two alliances, especially if nuclear weapons were not used.

recherché—overrefined, too studied, forced; also uncommon, rare, intensely sought after (from Fr. p.p. of *rechercher*, to search for). Accent is on the *ché*.

The word *research*, which is related, has had numerous definitions: copying from one source is plagiarism; copying from many is research. One wag described research as writing out in longhand what has already appeared in print. Long ago,

Charles Lamb (1775–1834), answering a charge of plagiarism leveled at him, remarked: "I have milked twenty cows to get the milk, but the butter I churned is all mine."

recidivism

> One of the criticisms noted in his analysis of the existing penal system was that *recidivism* (the return to jail of former inmates) ranged from 60 to 80% in the juvenile institutions.

recidivism—falling back to former criminal habits; relapse (from L. *re,* back + *cadere,* to fall).
Also: *accident; decadent; deciduous* (trees).

recondite

> This manual gives ample homely advice to appease the student who does not care about the most *recondite* theories of bridge play.

recondite—not easily understood by the general reader, abstruse, profound (from L. *re,* back + *conditus,* p.p. of *condere,* to hide).
Also: *abscond,* run away and hide from the law.

recrudescence

> There was much German mail in response, and a good lot of it furious, in part because I asked whether a *recrudescence* of Nazism was possible again in the future.

recrudescence—starting all over again, a revival (from L. *re,* again + *crudus,* raw). In French cuisine *crudités* are those crisp raw vegetables—celery, carrots, cauliflower, scallions, mushrooms—found on the table ready to be dipped into a sauce.

recuse

> The Attorney General's ownership of National Bank of Georgia stock caused him to *recuse* himself from the

Lance case. ("Recused" usually comes out "rescued" which shows there can be truth in typographical error.)

recuse—disqualify (in the legal sense). *Recusant:* any dissenter or nonconformist.

redolent

Terrified civilians are fleeing north to Beirut, where the air is *redolent* of orange blossoms.

redolent—sweet-smelling, fragrant; figuratively used as "suggestive of" or "evocative of" (from L. *oleo,* smell of).
   Oleum, olive oil, oil. *Pecunia non olet,* "Money doesn't smell."

replicate

A few years ago, two groups of scientists, neither initially hostile to their fellow scientist, tried to *replicate* his key experiment.

replicate—generally to duplicate an experiment under controlled conditions.
   Also from *plicare,* to fold: *complicate; implicate; explicate; supplicate.*

reprobate

Edward is portrayed as a combination of peace-making statesman and incurable *reprobate.* Running about Europe with Mrs. Keppel, he carouses with his somewhat vulgar entourage.

reprobate—an unprincipled scoundrel; someone worthy of reproof (from L. *reprobatus,* p.p. of *reprobare,* to disapprove, reprove).

revanchism, revanchist

The logical next move would be direct but secret contacts with Jordan to explore both the serious territorial issues that stand between them, and the even more serious issue of avoiding the creation of a *re-vanchist* P.L.O. state that unites them.

revanchism—a foreign policy motivated by a desire to regain territory lost earlier to an enemy (from Fr. *revanche,* revenge). Similar to *irredentism* (which see) but stressing the idea of revenge.

rococo (See baroque)

romantic (See baroque)

schwa or shwa

Because English is such a strongly accented language, a word of more than two syllables is usually awash with *shwas.*

schwa—the name given to the symbol ə. In Hebrew the word *sh'wa* is the name of the diacritical marks placed *under* letters to indicate the slightest possible vowel sound—a short, mild emission of sound. In English words that are more than two syllables long, *shwas* often predominate. For example, *medicinal* is pronounced mədicənəl; *anathema* is pronounced ənathəmə. You can associate the word *shwa* with the German *schwach,* weak.

scion

He comes on strong in his first book as the *scion* of H. L. Mencken, adopting his master's cheerful icono-clasms and resurrecting such old Menckenisms as "flubdub," "flapdoodle," and "tosh."

scion—offspring, descendant, child of. Not related to L. root *sci,* to know. Germanic in origin, it can also mean a twig containing buds from a woody plant used for grafting, coming close to the colloquial "a chip off the old block."

sedulous

> So much of the book consists of pages of praises received and *sedulously* reproduced, that it resembles a scrapbook more than an autobiography.

sedulous—diligent, assiduous, persistent, industrious.

Robert Louis Stevenson attributed the development of his literary style to his assiduous study and his imitation of writers he admired, to his having "played the sedulous ape to Hazlitt, to Lamb, to Wordsworth, to Sir Thomas Browne, to Defoe, to Hawthorne, to Montaigne, to Baudelaire, and to *Obermann*."

Don't be fooled by the *sed*. It does *not* mean *sit* as in *supersede, sedative* (invites your nerves to sit down), *sedate, insidious* (sitting in ambush ready to pounce, hence sly, treacherous, wily), *residence,* and *assiduous* (sitting close to).

Sedulous breaks down to L. *se*, without + *dolo*, guile, trickery, hence sincere, and all the adjectives following *sedulous* above.

self-fulfilling prophecy

> There is the peril of setting up the *"self-fulfilling prophecy,"* where the very act of prediction sets in motion the forces that result in the dreaded event.

Just a beautiful explanation of a much used phrase.

seminal

> Nothing was done about Nietzsche in the college, though Professor Stern rightly places him in the company of Marx and Freud as one of the *seminal* and most influential thinkers of his century.

seminal—like seeds in being the source of development; germinal (from *semen, seminis* L. for seed). Writers who are considered by some to be seminal are James Joyce, Franz Kafka, Walt Whitman, Marcel Proust, Samuel Beckett, and Ernest Hemingway, among others.

Also: *disseminate,* to scatter seeds; *insemination; seminar; seminary*, where the seeds of knowledge are sown.

shibboleth

What the world needs today are not the *shibboleths* of democracy but its dynamic practice.

shibboleth—a test word, password, slogan, catchword. The word comes to us from the Old Testament. After the Gileadites under their leader Jephthah had defeated the Ephraimites on the banks of the River Jordan, Jephthah wanted to make sure that none of the enemy escaped. He took advantage of the difference in the speech habits of the Ephraimites by putting each of them to the test. He asked them to pronounce *shibboleth,* a Hebrew word meaning stream, knowing that Ephraimites would pronounce it *sibboleth.*

Shibboleth has come to have the meanings given above. In Southey's "The Battle of Blenheim," the grandfather, when asked about the war, what started it, what good it accomplished, can answer only with the shibboleth "But 'twas a famous victory."

simile (See metaphor)

solipsism, solipsistic

(a) No one wants to revive a *solipsism* that says a tree doesn't exist unless a person is looking at it.

(b) In other words, I cannot be a *solipsist* like some of these writers who really feel that no one exists except themselves. I know that the world . . . exists.

solipsism—the theory that nothing exists but what the self experiences (a); *solipsistic*—egocentric (b).

These words are much used and the more they are used the more they come close in meaning to *egocentric.* From L. *solus,* only + *ipse,* oneself. Here derivation says it all.

It was Mme. de Pompadour who said, after the Battle of Rossbach in 1757, *"Après nous le déluge"* (After us the deluge), which might be considered a neat solipsism.

splenetic

He *splenetically* attacks a biographer, when his real target is the biographer's subject.

The setting of "The Impossible H. L. Mencken," appropriately enough, is a bar. The trouble with the show, however, is that the evening remains just that—a barside chat with a *splenetic* gentleman.

splenetic—irritable, bad-tempered. The cliché is "to vent one's spleen." The spleen, an organ near the stomach, was thought to be the seat of such emotions as malice, spite, and bad temper.

When Hamlet joins Laertes, who has jumped into Ophelia's open grave, and Laertes tries to throttle him, Hamlet says:

"I prithee take thy fingers from my throat,
For though I am not splenetive and rash,
Yet have I in me something dangerous."

sporadic

These and other Iranian towns that lie in country dominated by Kurdish-speaking Sunnite Moslem tribe members have been the scene of *sporadic* violent uprisings against the central Government.

sporadic—scattered, occasional (from Gr. *sporadikos,* scattered).

Also: *spore; diaspora,* dispersion throughout (*dia*) the world.

suborn

The new generation of railroad desperadoes of the 1950's and 60's again *suborned* Government officials, this time to destroy the passenger trains the 19th-century bruisers had gouged to create.

suborn—to bribe for criminal purposes, especially for perjury. From L. *sub*, under(hand) + *ornare*, to decorate, to furnish. Its derivation comes close to our colloquial expression "to decorate the palm."

Also: *adorn; ornament; ornate*, which has come to mean overdecorated.

subsumed

The main theme, all the complications *subsumed* in the word *plot*, has not in the past been Miss James's strength. (*TLS*)

subsumed—included within a larger group, class, or order (from L. *sub*, under + *sumere*, to take).

Also: *assume; consume; resume; presume.*

supererogatory

In the face of the critical and biographical literature on Wilde, the present author's attempt is *supererogatory*.

supererogatory—superfluous in a pejorative sense, over and above what is asked for (from L. *super*, above + *rogatus*, asked, p.p. of *rogare*, to ask).

Also many *ask* words: *abrogate; arrogate; derogatory; prerogative; prorogue*, to adjourn a legislative body.

On May 25, 1950, the following exchange took place in the Senate:

MR. TAFT: What does the Senator mean by supererogation?

MR. CONNALLY: The Senator can look in the dictionary for that. I do not have time to educate the Senator from Ohio.

surfeit

Innumerable complaints have been made about a *surfeit* of costume dramas and British accents on public television. But the television schedule is capable of encompassing a startling variety of material.

surfeit—excess; overabundance; nimiety; sometimes too much of even a good thing. The prefix *sur* is the French version of the L. *super*: above, over.

Shakespeare's *Twelfth Night* opens with the famous lines:

> "If music be the food of love, play on!
> Give me excess of it, that, surfeiting,
> The appetite may sicken, and so die.
> That strain again! It had a dying fall."

surreptitious

In the course of the operation, in which most meetings between undercover agents and public officials were *surreptitiously* videotaped and recorded, the agents paid out hundreds of thousands of dollars in cash.

surreptitious—done in a secret or stealthy manner; clandestine (which usually implies illicit). From L. *sur* for *sub,* under(handed) + *rapere*, to seize.

surrogate

If television, which, after all, is now more than 30 years old, can still be likened to a baby, its *surrogate* parents, the viewers, may one of these days decide to face the fact that the creature in the cradle is not simply a slow learner but is in fact seriously retarded.

surrogate—as used today almost always means a substitute, a deputy (from *sur* (*sub*) *rogatus,* asked for, or chosen in place of another). In England in the past, the scion of nobility had a surrogate, a boy educated with him who was punished for the other's misdeeds; he was also known as the whipping boy.

sycophant

When members of Ali's entourage comment, at least publicly, there is never a discouraging word. They could give Norman Vincent Peale lessons in positive thinking. Yes, they are *sycophants* who tell Ali or tell others what he wants to hear.

sycophant—a fawning self-seeker; a servile flatterer; a yes man.

How does a word like *sycophant,* which breaks up into Gr. *sycon,* fig, and *phanein,* show or reveal, come to mean a fawning self-seeker? In ancient Athens informers were called *sycophantes.* Many explanations, ancient and modern, have been given for the use of the word in this sense. Here is what Plutarch says on the subject in his *Life of Solon:*

> One cannot, therefore, wholly disbelieve those who say that the exportation of figs also was anciently forbidden, and that the one who *showed* up, or pointed out, such exporters was called a "sycophant" or *fig-shower.*

symbiosis, symbiotic

> Italy is undergoing a unique experiment, an uneasy *symbiosis* between the strongest Marxist movement in the West and the Roman Catholic party that has furnished all heads of government for the last 32 years.

symbiosis—the biological term for an often mutually beneficial relationship between two organisms (from Gr. *sym,* together + *bios,* life). Much used for such a relationship between countries, between parties as above, between groups generally in the phrase *symbiotic relationship.*

symbol

> Since Easter *symbolizes* the opening of a new season of life, as well as the Christian Resurrection, not much more could have been asked of the weather.

symbol—a word hard to define, but saying that it represents something else by association, especially a concrete object for an abstract idea, comes close.

Right now the albatross around the neck of Coleridge's ancient mariner is a frequently used symbol for burdens, incubuses, etc., that people or governments have to bear. Many modern critics and readers see symbols in every kind of literature—plays, novels, poems, even films—and though critics can often go off the deep end, such analyses are frequently persuasive and certainly ingenious. But many of us may come to the same conclusion reached by Jonathan Swift (1667–1745) when he wrote:

> "As learned commentators view
> In Homer more than Homer knew."

syndrome

> We may be faced with the Flying Dutchman *syndrome* and that may in the end lead to the Shah's staying here, even though it didn't seem that way when we started on this. In legend, the Flying Dutchman is a phantom ship condemned to sail forever because of a blasphemy uttered by the captain.

syndrome—comes to us from medicine, where it describes a number of symptoms occurring together and characterizing a specific disease. From Gr. *syn*, together + *dromos*, a running; in other words, symptoms running together to form a recognizable condition. However, it is used loosely, and certainly overused, to designate any cycle, any combination, anything— almost like a metaphor. To mention only a few, we have the battered wife s., the sardine s., the sandcastle s., hit or flop s., the holier than thou s., the Vietnam s., the Norman Rockwell s., second best s., etc., etc.

Also: *dromedary*, a camel known for its running ability.

tendentious

> The United States Embassy told the Soviet Foreign Ministry that the reporting was *tendentious* and very unhelpful at a time of unrest in Iran, and also in terms of our bilateral United States-Soviet relations.

tendentious—biased; written or said to promote a cause; advancing a definite point of view. From L. *tendere*, to stretch ("the truth"). Sometimes a euphemism for falsity or outright lying.

trauma, tramatic

> Jimmy Carter has been playing hell with what might be called the "source" system, and Washington journalists have been *traumatized* psychologically.

trauma—another medical word. From Gr. *trauma,* wound, it is used for any painful, shaking emotional experience that can leave a psychological scar. In psychiatry, a trauma creating substantial damage to the psychological development of the individual generally leads to a neurosis. Plural *traumas* or *traumata.*

trenchant

> In Ghana, where travel by land is at best adventurous and at worst hazardous, the most appropriate metaphor for life is a road. So it is fitting that the most *trenchant* comments about life are the names painted lovingly on the bulging passenger trucks that ply the byways.

trenchant—forceful, penetrating, cogent, incisive. From the Middle English word for *cutting,* from Old French p.p. of *trenchier,* to cut.
    Also: *retrench,* to cut down, curtail, reduce.

trochee (See iambic)

truculent

> With the Russians taking a *truculent* stand in public as well as complaining privately about the atmosphere of Soviet-American relations, the Administration plans to sidestep a confrontation at the forthcoming meeting in Belgrade.

truculent—pugnacious, bellicose. In recent years, usage accepts the meanings surly, defiant. From L. *truculentus,* from *trux,* fierce.

turpitude

It was a fairly scandalous year, but not distinguished for *turpitude* alone.

turpitude—disgraceful conduct, shameless behavior, depravity. In the days before sexual permissiveness, the word could be applied to traveling with a lady not one's wife. Long ago, the British philosopher Bertrand Russell was turned away from our shores by immigration boards because of "moral turpitude" (surely the word *moral* here is an example of redundancy, tautology, pleonasm). In the 1920's, when Hollywood was known as "Sodom by the Sea" because of the Fatty Arbuckle, Wallace Reid, and William Desmond Taylor cases, and the movie industry hired Will H. Hays to create a new image of decency, pressure was brought on stars to avoid public scandals by holding them to a "moral turpitude clause" in their studio contracts.

vector

Through most of the world, the stray dog is the most important *vector* of rabies.

vector—carrier is the meaning as used in biology and in the excerpt; it has a highly technical meaning in mathematics (from L. *vectus,* p.p. of *vehere,* to carry, convey, transport).

Also: *vehicle; inveigh,* to make a violent verbal attack, "to sail into," and its noun *invective; vehement,* violent, fervent, impassioned.

vertiginous

He *vertiginously* keeps crossing the border between genuine paranoia and justified terror.

vertiginous—to say that this is the adjective form of *vertigo,* the sensation of dizziness, also a confused or disoriented state of mind, is to define it (from L. *vertigo, vertiginis,* turning, wheeling, dizziness).

vicarious

> Most of them are nonstudents, he said, getting a *vicarious* kick out of living in the shadow of a great university.

vicarious—shared in or experienced by imaginary participation in someone else's experience in a story, novel, film, or play (from L. *vicarius, vicis,* change, interchange). Most of the ordinary person's experiences are vicarious or fantasized. That's why it is used here with the word "kick" (more often, "thrill").

Also: *vicar; vicissitudes,* changes, ups and downs; *viceroy; vice president,* etc., where it means in place of.

vitiate

> If Mr. Gierek, head of the Polish Communist Party, opens union elections to an unlimited number of candidates from the rank and file, would that not tend to *vitiate* the Party's control?

vitiate—corrupt, spoil, invalidate, render ineffective (from L. *vitiare* from *vitium,* fault, vice).

Also: *vicious.*

watershed

> Beethoven, in fact, is the Great Divide, the *watershed* between a time when music was composed and performed for princes of church and state and a time—a time in which we still live—when music had to please an ever-widening circle of cultural strivers and parvenus.

watershed—an extensive stretch of high ground from each side of which the river systems of a continent flow in opposite directions, ultimately finding their way to open waters. It's much used today as a metaphor for a significant or crucial turning point in history, in science, or in the arts. It has replaced *turning point.*

3. Taking a Turn for the Worse— Pejoratives

Little wonder then that President Carter pounced on the American petroleum industry last week, using more *pejorative* terms in one press conference than he has uttered in the 38 weeks of his White House residence— strong words like "profiteering" and "ripoff" and "grabbing (for) gross profits"—and pointing like a district attorney to the oil lobby as the would-be assassin of his legislative proposals on energy.

Those words used by the President were probably always pejorative. Most of the words in this chapter, however, were once respectable. They have come to a bad end; now they are certainly pejorative or uncomplimentary.

Take *parochial* and *provincial,* for example, once unexceptionable words. Used in a geographic or religious sense, they are still neutral descriptive terms. But used in sophisticated society, they mean "narrow," "limited in outlook," "not fashionable."

That's what has happened, with time, to other "rural" words. The city mouse scorned the country mouse, remember?

The snobbism of townsfolk toward their country cousins has downgraded all words having to do with rural areas, while at the same time upgrading words connected with city life (*urbane, civil, civility, courtly, courtesy*). The German word *bauer,* farmer, and the Dutch word *boer,* which also means countryman, give us the far from respectable *boor* and *boorish.* Then we have words like *heathen* (from *heath*), *savage* (from L. *silva,* forest), *villain* (from *villa,* a country home), and *peasant,* a word you wouldn't use about our midwestern farmers. Yet *peasant* not only does not have a pejorative meaning in European countries, but once was a proud appellation. Oliver Goldsmith, deploring the migration of villagers to the large cities, wrote:

> "Princes and lords may flourish, or may fade;
> A breath can make them, as a breath has made;
> But a bold peasantry, their country's pride,
> When once destroy'd, can never be supplied."
> *The Deserted Village*

The same fate has befallen words connected with the olfactory sense. *Smell, aroma, odor,* even *stink** and *reek,* once had neutral or even favorable meanings.

Shakespeare's use of *reeks,* in Sonnet 130, seems humorous today because the word has gone way down on the scale of smells. This is the sonnet beginning "My mistress' eyes are nothing like the sun," in which he shows how fed up he was with the extravagant love sonnets of his contemporaries, with their shopworn stock of eyes like sapphires, teeth like pearls, lips like rubies, cheeks like roses, hair like spun gold, etc. The temptation is to quote his sonnet in its entirety, but I quote only the quatrain that is pertinent:

> "I have seen roses damask'd,† red and white,
> But no such roses see I in her cheeks;
> And in some perfumes is there more delight
> Than in the breath that from my mistress reeks."

---

*The OED's second entry for *stink* is dated c. 1000, "*Ic stince swote*" (sweet).

† damask'd: deep pink.

To return to *boorish,* the broken-down descendant of honest farm stock: one of the synonyms for it is *gauche,* the French word for the left hand, and so we are on the trail of another prejudice. Our word *sinister* (L. *sinistra,* left hand; Italian *sinistra*) testifies to that. On the other hand, the French word *droit,* right, gives us *adroit* (and its opposite, *maladroit; mal,* bad). Latin adds its weight with *dexter,* right, yielding dexterity, dextrous, and *ambidextrous,* two right hands! In our national pastime, at least, this wrong is being redressed. Left-handed batters and left-handed pitchers are at a premium and are paid accordingly.

So here are some words that have taken a turn for the worse, and also some that began life as pejoratives and still retain their derogatory meaning.

What makes the study of pejoratives especially interesting is that they are cultural and historical signposts. Prejudice, intolerance, arrogance have all left their mark—and so has history. In the second entry, see what Munich did to *appeasement!*

animadversion

Large numbers of experts on animal behavior have been deeply skeptical of these claims, but their *animadversions* have appeared only in technical journals.

animadversion—generally adverse criticism. From L. *animus,* mind, anger, hostility (note *animus, animosity*) + *ad,* to + *versus,* p.p. of *vertere,* turn. *Adverse* by itself means turned against.

appease, appeasement, pacify

For better or worse, "Munich" has become one of the most evocative words in the discussion of international politics, and statesmen embarking on reasonable policies of conciliation have to find other labels for them than "*appeasement,*" a word that the Munich conference made irrevocably pejorative.

appease—originally meant only to make peace, but as the excerpt shows, the noun *appeasement* has forever been assigned a derogatory force.

baroque, rococo, romantic

> In his studio, he showed intricate abstractions laced with *baroque* wrought-iron complexities.

> The great motion picture palaces of the twenties and thirties with their *rococo* grandeur have been destroyed as cultural tastes, population and life styles have shifted.

> Why was this innocent, seemingly popular novelist, Marie Corelli, even if "*romantic*" in the pejorative sense, so disliked in the literary world that a critic of stature, 32 years after her death, informed his readers that she was both "unbearable" and "unreadable"? (*TLS*)

baroque, rococo, and *romantic*—in their original setting in the arts, these are merely descriptive terms of different styles in various periods of the world's artistic history. Today there must be millions of music lovers who prefer programs of *baroque* music (1550–1700), and as many tourists who travel widely searching out examples of *baroque* and *rococo* art and architecture. *Rococo* art, which immediately followed the *baroque*, was considered an extreme form of *baroque*, being too elaborate, intricate, and ornate. Therefore, *rococo* almost by definition had a built-in pejorative sense.

The *romantic* period in English literature, ushered in by "Lyrical Ballads" in 1798, was marked by the attempt to bring back imagination and emotion to poetry, a reaction against the intellectualism of the classical school of Dryden and Pope. The *romantic* poets Wordsworth and Coleridge were soon followed by Shelley, Keats, and Byron.

All three words can be used disparagingly today. If we were to compare them, as we do adjectives, in the order of pejoration, the sequence would undoubtedly be *romantic, baroque, rococo.*

bathetic

> Then comes the *bathetic* finale in which boy and girl
> walk off hand in hand into the sunset and disappear up
> their own psyches. (*TLS*)

bathetic—emotionally jumping off the deep end, insincere,
overdone, anticlimactic (from Gr. *bathos*, depth).
> Also: *bathysphere,* a diving bell.

bathos

> It does slop over into *bathos* with increasing frequency
> near the end, but each time it recovers itself.

bathos—overdone pathos; a sudden descent "from the sub-
lime to the ridiculous."

bibulous

> A Saudi in Cairo for a respite from the land that made
> him rich but where nothing more *bibulous* than fruit
> juice is allowed was drinking the best Scotch.

bibulous—intoxicating; addicted to or fond of alcoholic drinks
(from L. *bibere*, to drink).
> Also: *imbibe.*

chic

> He was part of the radical *chic* bandwagon, which ran
> out of steam once the Vietnam War ended.

chic—currently fashionable, trendy. However, when it describes
someone's appearance, dress, or manner, it is not pejorative: it
means elegant and sophisticated. The French "*un chic type*" is
idiomatic for a good fellow, a decent sort.

co-opt

> Edward Gierek, the Polish party leader, will be under
> pressure to retrieve most of the concessions to the

unions. He can be expected to try to divide, or *co-opt* the worker leadership.

co-opt—as it is frequently used, it means to appropriate or absorb for one's own purpose (from L. *optare,* to choose).

cretinous

Traditionally, it is with young Arthur's ascension to the throne, after the reign of his *cretinous* father Uther Pendragon, that the do-good principles of chivalry are introduced into sixth-century England.

cretinous—describing a person of marked mental deficiency. From Fr. *crétin,* ultimately from L. *christianus,* a Christian, through a desire to indicate that such people are, after all, human beings.

diatribe

While incoherent most of the time, his *diatribe* is at least democratic in that he tramples roughshod without discrimination over the Carter Administration, the Soviet Union, Cuba and, as a grand finale, Nigeria.

diatribe—from the Greek *diatribe,* a short ethical discourse. It now means only a long abusive or bitter speech.

didactic

The play is incessantly *didactic,* and the lessons are of a vast and obvious ordinariness.

didactic—coming from a Greek word meaning *taught,* means teaching a lesson or pointing a moral. However, it is often used, especially in literary criticism, to mean overburdened with moral emphasis, therefore dull, pompous. An autodidact is a self-taught person.

disingenuous

To argue in the nuclear age that cheap foreign steel or expensive oil are as threatening as hostile missiles is *disingenuous,* to say the least, yet it serves to underpin (weakly) the innocent general view that military strength has lost some of its importance.

disingenuous—pretending to be innocent, naive, not candid or frank. *Ingenuous* has no pejorative shading; it means genuinely innocent or naive. *Naïve,* feminine of *naif,* via French, from L. *nativus.*

dissemble, dissimulate

It is all very well for the writer to *dissemble* her love of pomposities.

dissemble—to pretend, to feign, to conceal one's true feelings through deception. From L. *dis,* not + *similis,* similar, giving us *dissimulate,* synonym of *dissemble.*

doctrinaire, indoctrination

Some of Ibsen's champions, G.B. Shaw included, tended to make him far more *doctrinaire* than he actually was. (Ibsen denied that he had intended *A Doll's House* as a tract on women's rights.)

His wholly undocumented assertion that teaching in American colleges is just ideological *indoctrination* is ignorant slander of teachers and students.

doctrinaire—related to L. *doctrina,* learning, has come to mean maintaining a stubborn attitude toward one's own views. From the same root, *indoctrination* is now equated with "brainwashing." So suspicious is human nature that we assume that one indoctrinates only partisan or subversive views.

elitist, elitism

If the editor ever left the Georgetown cocktail set where he and his arrogant *elitist* buddies dine on third-hand information, gossip and rumor, he would discover the real America.

elitist, elitism—the above is an attack not only on the editor but on the word *elitist*, which also means, as it used to, "the elected, the chosen few," as here:

> The work of the scholar, the composer, the performer, must always be *elitist* in the sense that it can only be done well by a very few in each generation.

However, notice that *elitist* is qualified by "in the sense that."

epigones

> The modern espionage agent has to a large extent become as formalized as the private eye. The le Carré *epigones* give us a miserable and unhappy man as the spy.

epigones or *epigoni*—followers who are less gifted, lesser lights, inferior imitators (from the Greek word for to be born + *epi*, after).

The *epigones* or *epigoni* were the descendants of the seven heroes who perished before Thebes. Ten years later, they marched against Thebes and razed it to the ground. Now *epigones* is used only pejoratively, on the supposition that all followers are a sorry lot. (See **janissaries, myrmidons, minions,** and **satrap**.)

epithet

> At this point, Mr. Sadat roared with laughter as Mrs. Meir neatly pinned him with one of his own *epithets*. "You always called me an old lady, Mr. President," she said.

> Threats and *epithets* have been hurled at the patrollers along with an occasional can or bottle.

epithet—though still used as a descriptive term, a name added,* it is more often used as an abusive characterization. A strong verb like *shouted* or *hurled* is used with the word *epithet*.

---

*Like the epithet "Iron Lady" for Margaret Thatcher, Prime Minister of the United Kingdom.

erudite, erudition

> Ali, our politically *erudite* heavyweight, is now bring-
> ing back a startling revelation from Russia and will
> attempt to sell it to those not familiar with the Russian
> system.

erudite, erudition—used in both a favorable and an unfavorable way. A learned man, a scholar, can be praised for his
erudition, his great knowledge. Erudite may be used sarcastically, as above. It may be used in a derogatory way to mean
bookish, devoted to very specialized learning, knowing more
and more about less and less. From L. *rudis,* untutored,
ignorant—"rude" in the sense used by Thomas Gray when he
referred to the "rude forefathers" who sleep in the village
cemetery. The prefix *e* removes the ignorance.
     Also: *rudiments,* the elementary, basic principles or
skills; *rudimentary,* elementary, basic, fundamental.

farrago

> They persist in compounding the original error, if that
> is what it was, with a *farrago* of falsehoods.

farrago—one of many words used to describe a mixture of
diverse objects. From the Latin word for mixed fodder for
cattle, related to *farina* and *farinaceous.* Other words for this
kind of *mishmash* (which see) are: *hodgepodge, gallimaufry,
olio, potpourri, goulash, salmagundi, pastiche, omnium ga-
therum* (itself a mixture), and even *minestrone.*

fulsome

> Among the younger generation of Soviet ballerinas,
> Nadezhda Pavlova receives *fulsome* praise—"miracle,"
> "amazing gifts," "mastery"—even "the hope of Soviet
> ballet" (Nadezhda = hope; pun intended).

fulsome—frequently misused; it no longer means full or abun-
dant; it now has only the unfavorable meaning of excessive or
overdone to the point of being in bad taste or even at times
nauseating.

fustian

It would be easy to dismiss the flow of *fustian* in his play as a novelist's mistaken notion of what the stage is all about. On a stage people can talk and talk and talk to the point of self-indulgence and well beyond, can't they?

fustian—pompousness, pretentiousness; also, a strong cotton or linen fabric. *Fustian* as a reference to a poetic style appears in a famous couplet:

"And he, whose *fustian's* so sublimely bad,
It is not poetry, but prose run mad."
Alexander Pope, "Epistle to Dr. Arbuthnot"

A synonym for *fustian* is *bombast* or *bombastic.* The noun *bombast* was a soft material used for padding. As a description of style in writing and speaking, *bombastic* characterizes the use of inflated language. (See **rodomontade,** which adds bluster and boast.)

gratuitous

Depicting of murder and mayhem that had no dramatic relevance was described as *gratuitous* violence, the kind that is a cheap shot, exploitative.

gratuitous—once meaning (like *gratis*) "given freely," it is only occasionally so used today. The more frequent meaning is unwarranted, unnecessarily intrusive, meddlesome, uncalled for (a who-needs-it, who-asked-you-to word).

hedonism

From being the most repressed country in Europe, Spain is becoming the wildest—though, one assumes, the current *hedonism* is a passing phenomenon.

hedonism—the ethical doctrine that regards pleasure or happiness as the goal of the good life (from Gr. *hedone,* pleasure). In the excerpt the word becomes almost a synonym for *orgy.*

impute

> While we *impute* to them the most malicious and opportunistic intentions, we fail to see how aggressive our own so-claimed defensive measures are.

impute—to put thoughts into someone else's mind; to attribute views or motives to someone else, invariably bad ones (from L. *putare,* to think + *im,* into). Nobody evidently imputes praiseworthy motives to others.

　　Also: *disputatious; putative; compute; reputable; deputation.*

> "Nor you, ye Proud, impute to these the fault,
> If Memory o'er their tombs no trophies raise."
> Thomas Gray, "Elegy Written in a Country Churchyard"

ineffable

> Who has forgotten the *ineffable* imperiousness with which Charles Laughton, as Captain Bligh, called "M-i-s-t-e-r Christian" in the film *Mutiny on the Bounty?*

ineffable—though in religious contexts, and sometimes in others, it means unable to be spoken, inexpressible in an awesome sense ("the *ineffable* name of the Deity"), it is often used with a strong derogatory meaning, as though there were no words vile or low enough to express one's loathing.

ingratiate

> The P.L.O., looking for ways to *ingratiate* itself in Western opinion, volunteered to try to persuade the Ayatollah to be merciful.

ingratiate—to work oneself into another's favor, often for self-serving reasons (from L. *gratia,* grace, favor). Also used favorably: She gave an ingratiating performance.

　　Also: *grateful; ingrate (in,* not); *gratuity; gratify; congratulate.*

innuendo

> The likeliest explanation is that nobody [no candidate] is coming up with any good ideas, new or old, to deal with substantive problems, so bluster and *innuendo* are being used to veil the vacuum.

innuendo—occasionally used to mean a hint, suggestion, a nuance (from L. *innuere,* to nod). But again the meaning has been perverted, so that the hinting generally refers to a sly insinuation, a veiled remark, something thrown in with malice aforethought.

invidious

> *Invidious* as it may be to single out one object from the more than 300 in the show, it could be argued that its highest point is reached in the statue of "Aphrodite with Priapus" which embellished one of the houses of pleasure that abounded in Pompeii.

invidious—likely to cause ill will, envy, discontent, resentment—all derogatory meanings. The word *envious* comes from L. *invidiosus,* meaning exactly that.

janissaries

> Unsurprisingly, the governor's *janissaries* tend to talk like the governor, and this includes his Chief of Staff.

janissaries—originally a famous militia of the Ottoman empire; now used to describe any loyal, submissive followers or supporters. "Yes-men" is sometimes implied: "The playwrights and other free spirits imported from the East Coast were uncomfortable dinner partners of Louis B. Mayer's homegrown Hollywood *janissaries.*"

lucubration

> The *lucubrations* of this popular philosopher are offsprings of the marriage between the pseudoscience of Marxism and the pseudoscience of Freud.

lucubration—literally from the Latin word that means "to work by candle or lamplight" (from L. *lux, lucis,* light, akin to *lucere,* to shine). Our expression is "to burn the midnight oil," suggesting pretentious, laborious study.

Also: *lucid; pellucid (pel* for *per,* thoroughly); *translucent.*

mandarin

> Although it is not a book without substance, it is surely all style—the writing is mannered and *mandarin,* and the language is shaped and fashioned like a bar of silver in the hands of a Cellini.

mandarin—an elegant, overrefined style, marked by polished, ornate complexity in use of language. But when spelled with a capital, *Mandarin* is the chief dialect of China. It is now undergoing a process of representing each sound of the language with a single symbol. In imperial China, a mandarin was any one of the nine highest ranks of public officials.

minions

> Why do you sit with them and their *minions* instead of with your friends?

minions—obsequious followers, favorites, especially servile and fawning followers (from Fr. *mignon,* darling, pretty).

niggling

> These, though, are *niggling* questions to ask of a film that is the most imaginative, most intelligent, and most original of the year in every other way.

niggling—finicky, fussy, giving attention to petty details.

obsequious

> Ordinary Cambodian citizens now resent being forced to serve *obsequiously* such new overlords.

obsequious—once meant prompt, obedient, dutiful but, having acquired a surfeit of these qualities, is now used to mean fawning, servile, subservient, sycophantic.

offal

> Variety meats (tongue, liver, and other *offals*) are now among America's leading exports to France.

offal—waste parts, entrails, rubbish. The word is a combination of *off* + *fall*. Figurative use: the offal that passes for our daily mail.

> Hamlet, upbraiding himself for his inaction against his uncle, says:

> "Or ere this
> I should have fatted all the region kites
> With this slave's offal."

pharisaical

> In this handbook for Scrabble players there is even a chapter on how to cheat, *pharisaically* disguised as the honest player's defense against corruption: turning over a tile to make a false blank can be extremely rewarding and carries only a small penalty if detected. (*TLS*)

pharisaical—the Pharisees were a sect (the name comes from a Hebrew name meaning apart) who were extremely devout and scrupulously exact in their religious observances. In modern usage, *pharisaical* describes persons of rigid adherence to outward forms and rituals instead of to the true spirit. In the passage above, the word is used tongue in cheek to suggest *hypocritical*; other synonyms are *self-righteous, sanctimonious*.

philistine, philistinism

> Those who fear we have become a nation of *Philistines*, so lost in material pursuits that we trample on

culture, may take some comfort from the reports of the
book publishing industry that this will be their biggest
year.

philistine, philistinism—the Philistines were the natives of
Philistia in the ancient world. Today a *philistine* is one who
looks down on intellectual and cultural activities, being concerned only with material values. Matthew Arnold first used the
word in this sense:

> *Philistine* must have originally meant, in the mind of
> those who invented the nickname, a strong, dogged,
> unenlightened opponent of . . . the children of light.

In *Essays in Criticism*, Arnold wrote: "*Philistinism!*—We have
not the expression in English. Perhaps we have not the word
because we have so much of the thing."

plastic

> "Your Show of Shows" or "The Mary Tyler Moore
> Show" or the early efforts of Norman Lear look like
> enduring works of genius compared with the *plastic*
> juvenile concoctions dominating the current rating
> risks.

plastic—as an adjective, has come to mean not genuine, artificial, phony, in general a word of disapproval. The noun is
used in the same way.

poetaster

> The *poetaster* Clement Moore, in his immensely popu-
> lar "A Visit from St. Nicholas," multiplied the single
> reindeer into a team of eight.

poetaster—the addition of *aster* to a word has almost the same
force as putting *pseudo* in front of it. So *poetaster* is a word
describing a second-rate poet, a mere rhymester. The attach-
able *-aster* cuts words down in size and quality. A *criticaster* is
an inferior critic. A *pilaster* is a false pillar or column that is part
of the wall, a projection of it made to look like a column.

The French word *cinéaste* is now used by one American film critic to disparage the qualifications or opinions of another American film critic; it has not worn as well as the words *nouvelle vague* and *auteur*.

prolix

This is a wordy play, a little *prolix,* and the playwright is not afraid to make the same point twice.

prolix—verbose, repetitious, protracted, unduly prolonged, long-winded (from L. *pro,* forth + *lix* from *liquere,* to flow, pour forth).

puerile

Worse, almost, is the fact that his novel is so wretchedly written, and that his observations are so invariably *puerile.*

puerile—from L. *puer,* boy, can mean boyish, but now almost exclusively means childish, immature, unworthy of an adult. It is a useful word for critics who prefer not to come right out and say a writer's style is atrocious.

pundit, punditry

Week after week, his column of 800 words manages to avoid the twin perils that beset the Washington correspondent, of gossip and trivia on the one hand and *punditry* on the other.

pundit, punditry—like other words for teacher or teaching, *punditry* is often used in a derogatory sense, especially in literary criticism, of someone who makes pronouncements authoritatively and pompously, or sententiously (which see).

rhetoric

If Mr. Carter is to move beyond *rhetoric* in the human-rights area, therefore, his only valid course is to ban the

> export of all arms, equipment and training to the
> security forces of authoritarian forces abroad.

rhetoric—once a respected and prestigious subject taught in
the universities until the early twentieth century, *rhetoric* is
now almost exclusively used as just talk, mere words, or words
propelled by "hot air."

sanctimonious

> In South America, our *sanctimonious* sermonizing
> about human rights has made us unpopular.

sanctimonious—from L. *sanctus,* holy, now describes someone who is hypocritically so. A *sanctuary* is a holy place, as well
as a haven or refuge. Something *sacrosanct* is doubly holy.
Shakespeare used *sanctimonious* in the derogatory sense in
Measure for Measure, describing "The sanctimonious pirate,
that went to sea with the Ten Commandments, but scraped
one out of the table."

scholastic(ism)

> The current pronunciamentos of the experts are suf-
> fused with a sickly *scholasticism* as they hand down
> computer printouts from their academic ivory towers.
> (G.W. Ball)

scholasticism—the dominant philosophical and theological
system of scholars in medieval universities. In their discussions
they often engaged in such subtleties of logic and hair-splitting
quibbles that the word *scholasticism*—except historically—has
become a synonym for pedantry.

Indeed, one of the leading scholars, John Duns Scotus
(the Scotsman), will always be rememberd—in dictionaries—
as the source of the word *dunce* (Duns, dunse, dunce).

sciolist

> It displays the mysterious anger a *sciolist* reserves for
> pseudo-problems.

sciolist—one who pretends to scholarship or knowledge (from L. root *sci,* know), it has always had a pejorative meaning.

Also: *omniscient,* all-knowing; *nescient,* not-knowing, ignorant, agnostic; *prescient,* knowing beforehand; *science,* "knowledge"; all the *conscious* words; *conscience,* an awareness of right and wrong; *unconscionable,* not guided or restrained by conscience, hence unreasonable, unscrupulous, outrageous.

screed

> His *screed* on the Oct. 6 Op-Ed page is disquieting. He has been to Lebanon and seen the terrible devastations there. However, his most damaging remarks are left for Israel, which he has not visited.

screed—a lengthy discourse, usually used to describe opinions expressed in an uncomplimentary way.

sententious

> It is as preachy as any of the sermons that the 18th century used to put out as children's books. But it is more than *sententious*; it verges on the grotesque.

sententious—meaning full of maxims and sayings even to the extent of being terse and pithy, has degenerated so that it often means the very opposite—wordy, verbose, ponderously trite, excessively moralizing.

sexism, sexist

> A bastion of *sexism* has fallen to the times: hurricanes will no longer be exclusively named for women.

sexism, sexist—*sexism* is a new word meaning prejudice or discrimination based on sex (what the ERA is all about). *Sexist* follows the pattern of *racist, speciesist.*

(sic)

> In the Hollywood column written by an admirer, he was referred to as "the reknowned (sic) plastic surgeon."

sic—a Latin word meaning thus or so. In English it always comes wrapped in parentheses or brackets when tossed into a quoted passage. The (sic) points an accusing finger at the word immediately before it and says, "This is the way it appeared in the original. Don't hold me responsible for this misspelling or misusage. I know better." When a writer really wants to rub it in, he adds an exclamation mark after sic, thus (sic!).

simplistic

> The Domino theory of Communist expansion, while discarded as simplistic by many in the West, is still taken seriously in many non-Communist Asian countries, and nowhere more so than in Thailand.

simplistic—should always be used pejoratively, since it does not mean simple, but oversimplified, making a complex, intricate problem unrealistically simple.

> Heard on a TV news program: "In Pearl Harbor, a simplistic (sic) monument has been erected over the U.S.S. Arizona." The word here is simple, and a beautiful word when so used.

sophistry

> Supporters of the tax credit brush aside the distinction, noting that only a modest amount of it would go to the truly affluent. But that is sophistry; the only reason few rich people would be helped by the tax credit is that there aren't very many rich people.

sophistry—from Greek sophos, wise. The Sophists or Wise Men were a group of teachers who achieved great fame in Greece in the fifth century B.C. Although they had many good educational ideas, they acquired a bad reputation because they accepted pay and because they used subtle methods of argumentation. Some of them were also accused of making the weaker or worse reason appear to be the stronger or better reason. Hence the word *sophistry* has an unfavorable connotation and means arguing deceitfully, attempting to turn a poor case into a good one by means of clever but specious reasoning.

> "Destroy his fib or sophistry—in vain!
> The creature's at his dirty work again."
> Alexander Pope, "Epistle to Dr. Arbuthnot"

It was Francis Bacon who wrote: "Universities incline wits to sophistry and affectation."

speciesist

> Paradoxically, the public tends to be *"speciesist"* in its reaction to animal experimentation: For many people, a test is permissible when it inflicts pain on a "lower" animal like a hamster, but not when the victim is a dog.

No comment necessary.

specious

> Our society should not be deluded into accepting the dangerous and *specious* notion that limited nuclear war may stay limited to small nuclear bombs and to military targets alone and that society may survive such conflict.

specious—once meaning pleasing in appearance, is now almost always used to mean deceptively so, as in *specious reasoning*.

stricture

> "He will read in these pages some harsh words about some of his rulers, their policies, their agents; and he

> may feel that some of these *strictures* fall gratuitously upon himself as citizen voter in a democratic state."
> (Begin)

stricture—generally means today an adverse criticism or remark, censure. However, in its nonpejorative sense, it can be used to mean something that restricts, limits, or restrains—as this quotation from Robert Louis Stevenson illustrates:

> These are my politics: to change what we can; to better what we can; but still to bear in mind that man is but a devil weakly fettered by some generous beliefs and impositions; and for no word however sounding, and no cause however just and pious, to relax the *stricture* of these bonds.
> "Epilogue of the Cigar Divan"

From L. *strictura*, compression, contraction, from *strictus*, strict, the p.p. of *stringere*, to draw tight, to contract.

Also: *stringent; stringency; strict; restrict; constrict.* In medicine, a pathological condition, an abnormal narrowing of a passage or a duct, is called a *stricture.*

tendentious

> It is unfortunate that the Mayor's request for an objective review was accompanied by his *tendentious* statement that "recent studies have shown that the quality of education" in the city has declined. What recent studies have shown is that achievement in certain areas has declined in schools across the country.

tendentious—promoting a particular view or tendency; hence, biased, not impartial.

tirade

> Ayatollah Khomeini in a *tirade* upbraided the Pope, called President Carter "an enemy of humanity" and challenged the United States to use economic or military force to free the hostages being held at the American Embassy in Teheran.

tirade—a long, vehement speech characterized by intemperate, sometimes violent language; harangue; a speech of denunciation (from Fr. *tirer,* to shoot, to fire).

trendy

> Film scholarship has become a flourishing surrogate for a liberal arts education. The film department has in fact become to academe in the 1970's what the psychology department was in the 50's—a way to legitimize *trendy* mediocrity with a bachelor's degree.

trendy—not yet in all the dictionaries but much used, means following the trend, doing what at the time is very fashionable, up-to-date. (See **chic**)

virago

> We don't know exactly why they've separated, but by the time she's begged him for help, turned into a screeching *virago* on the spot, hurled the phone halfway across the room, upended the coffee table and begun to howl like a dog, the possible causes of a rift begin to suggest themselves.

virago—originally meaning a woman of great size, strength, and courage, is now almost entirely a synonym for a scold, a shrew, or a termagant (from L. *vir,* man).

> Also: *virile, triumvirate.*

4. Pretentious? Moi?

A teacher's dedication to the subject he is teaching is generally commendable, but the newsletter of the Modern Language Association of America has learned of a teacher of French in Copenhagen who may have gone a bit far. He urged his class to make a special effort to learn a certain word because it was so rare that they might never see it again.

Some words are rare but not quite that rare. But rare or just unusual they are welcomed in this chapter. Call them pretentious words, call them snob words, call them what Coleridge did: "dictionary words," but they are interesting words, words you will be sure to face (or maybe contend with) in your reading.

These are words you are not likely to use in conversation, unless you are like William F. Buckley, Jr., who can without any self-consciousness casually inject such words as *anfractuous* and *appoggiatura* into an informal interview. Or if you are like Woody Allen and Diane Keaton, who in a philosophical discussion in "Love and Death," play Ping-Pong with the word *hermeneutics* without a raised eyebrow or a quivering lip.

In short, these are words you may come upon, for the most part, in your reading, as I have. Some people have an addiction for polysyllabic or esoteric words. In Robert Graves' memorable autobiography covering his World War I experiences (*Goodbye to All That**), he has an amusing anecdote about one of his professors:

> Professor Edgeworth of All Souls' avoided conversational English, persistently using words and phrases that one expects to meet only in books. One evening, Lawrence [the famous Lawrence of Arabia] returned from a visit to London, and Edgeworth met him at the gate. "Was it very caliginous in the metropolis?"
>
> "Somewhat caliginous, but not altogether inspissated," Lawrence replied gravely.

Some critics admire this kind of word. In reviewing Mr. Buckley's *The Controversial Arts,* Walter Goodman concludes his review with:

> And who can hold a grudge against a writer who brings to the page such rare adornments of the language as "concinnity," "energumen," "paralepsis," and "synecdoche," and uses them correctly?

Some are not enthusiastic and fault the writer. This from the *Times Literary Supplement:*

> He can write powerfully and evocatively, especially on Milton. He does harbour nevertheless a fatal inclination for words like "iconicity", "logocentric", "metamorphical", "volatilization", and phrases like "daemonic matrix", "ontological bivalence", "theophanic utterance".†

So in this chapter your slightest velleity to dazzle or be dazzled will be fulfilled. Occasionally, some more familiar words will be included—to offer relaxation.

---

*Reprinted by permission of Curtis Brown Ltd. Copyright © 1929 by Robert Graves.

†Notice the British use of the commas and the period outside the quotation marks, where we would tuck them safely inside. The British, however, do use the period inside if a complete sentence is quoted.

abulia

> He defines the present state of Europe as "*abulia*" and defines that as a paralysis of the will that human beings could exert to master their own destiny.

abulia—inability to make a decision, or impairment or loss of ability to exercise will power (from Gr. *a,* without + *boule,* will). The prefix *a* or *an* before a vowel sound is called the alpha privative; meaning "not" or "without," it changes the word it precedes to a negative. It is a most dependable prefix, not as fickle (or versatile) as Latin *in,* which may mean "not," "into," or "against" and may even be an intensive (it had to be dropped from *inflammable).*

adventitious

> There has been no catalogue raisonné and no fat monograph. There have been no delirious prices at auction, and no scandals, financial or emotional, to bring this artist *adventitious* publicity.

adventitious—accidental, added by chance. This is one of those cases where the derivation helps *after* you know the meaning of the word. From L. *ventus,* having come + *ad,* to, something additional, therefore accidental, supplemental.

aerobics

> Dr. Cooper is the chief apostle of "*aerobics,*" a credo which holds that life can be prolonged by systematic exercise that stimulates the heart, lungs, and blood vessels.

aerobics—from Gr. *aero-,* air + *bios,* life.

afflatus

> I need the *afflatus* of a novelistic idea—a knowledge of a whole before I can give a part.

afflatus—inspiration, powerful impulse, supernatural or over-mastering urge (from L. *flatus,* p.p. of *flare,* to blow).
Also: *deflation; inflation; flatulence.*

aleatory

Miss Musgrave's music has a good deal of *aleatory* and plenty of dissonance. Yet it is anything but avant-garde. She constantly tries for melody.

aleatory—depending on the throw of the dice; music resulting from purely random succession of notes, a characteristic of avant-garde music; dicey (from L. *aleator,* gambler, *alea,* dice game).
Julius Caesar, when he took the irrevocable step of crossing the Rubicon, used the proverb often heard from those who enter upon bold attempts: "The die is cast," *Iacta alea est.*

algolagnia

The author treated English *algolagnia* as a mere variant of universal romantic *algolagnia.*

algolagnia—pleasure derived from inflicting pain on oneself or others, suggesting in one word both masochism and sadism (from Gr. *algos* + *lagneia,* pain).
Also: *nostalgia,* a longing for a return home (*nostos*), in memory or actuality, to former times or haunts (a sentimental pain); *analgesic,* a drug that leaves one without (*an*) pain.

alliumphobe, -phile

The subject of the miracle- and taste-values of garlic is charged with emotion, especially among those known as "*alliumphiles,*" who love garlic, and those known as "*alliumphobes,*" who detest it.

alliumphobe, -phile—included for those who, like the author, detest garlic, and also to introduce the Greek combining forms

-*phobe,* fear, and -*phile,* love, which can be plugged into almost any noun. From the Gr. *allium,* garlic. The *Allium* genus includes such plants of strong odor as the onion, the leek, the chive, and the shallot, as well as the more controversial garlic.

amaranthine

> The talents of Poe's self-elected rival were small potatoes, with no *amaranthine* flowers such as may be found in the unfading, undying works of Poe.

amaranthine—for this lovely word the excerpt gives a definition. From Gr. *a,* not + *marantos,* withering, wasting, dying away. The *h* crept in because *amaranth* is the name of an actual flower as well as the name of an imaginary flower that never fades or dies, *anthos* being Greek for flower, as in *anthology,* literally a collection of flowers.

> "There are no fields of amaranth
> On this side of the grave."
> Walter Savage Landor

ambrosia

ambrosia and *nectar*—the food and drink of the Roman and Greek gods, assuring them of immortality. *Ambrosia* comes from Gr. *am,* not + *brosos,* mortal; the etymological meaning of *nectar* is "overcoming death" (see internecine).

> Also: *nectarine.*

anaphora

> Senator Kennedy's electrifying and moving speech at the Democratic Convention showed again how effective *anaphora* is in political oratory.

anaphora—an effective rhetorical device of repeating the first words of sentences or clauses. The most famous modern example is probably Martin Luther King, Jr.'s "I have a dream . . . , I have a dream . . . , etc." The clue to the meaning is in the Greek prefix *ana,* again.

anfractuous

> In an interview on "The Firing Line," Mr. Buckley tossed off the word *anfractuous.* Being asked what it meant, he said, with an appropriate gesture, "Oh, winding, tortuous."

anfractuous—and that's what it means. From *ambi,* for *an* + *fractus,* p.p. of *frangere,* to break. The knowledge that *an* is here an abbreviation for *ambi,* around, tells it all—winding about, tortuous, full of intricate turnings.

animism

> Most of the people live in rural communities, and 60 percent practice *animism,* 35 percent are Christians and 5 percent are Moslems.

animism—the doctrine that all living organisms have souls separable from bodies; the belief in the existence of spirits and demons. From L. *anima,* soul (as the principle of life) as opposed to *animus* (the principle of thought and feeling).

anodynic, anodyne

> In the circumstances, a fairly *anodynic* European stand is emerging, at least for the time being, . . . calling for further "Euro-Arab dialogue" between the representatives of the Community and the Arab League.

anodynic—painless, soothing; the form usually seen is *anodyne* (from Gr. *an,* without + *odyne,* pain).

anomie, anomy

> *Anomie,* that dislocation of spirit someone—or, indeed, an entire society—arrives at with the breakdown of familiar and supportive norms, is very much with and in us today.

anomie—add to the definition helpfully given in the excerpt: the state of society or individual in which ordinary norms and standards of conduct and beliefs are lacking (from Gr. word *anomia*, lawlessness: *a* without + *nomos*, law).

Also: *astronomy; gastronomy; economy;* and many more words with *nomy.*

anorexia

There is surely no medical problem more symptomatic of the affluent late twentieth-century Western world than *anorexia nervosa,* a sometimes fatal disorder in which individuals, usually adolescent girls, systematically starve themselves to lose weight.

anorexia—without any desire to eat; chronic loss of appetite (from Gr. *an*, without + *orexis*, appetite). *Anorexia nervosa* is a voluntary starvation diet.

anthropophagy

Anthropophagy, or cannibalism, has become the center of popular anthropological attention.

anthropophagy—cannibalism (from Gr. *anthropos*, man (kind) + *phagein*, to eat). Also: *sarcophagos,* flesh-eating limestone coffin used by the ancient Greeks.

> "The Cannibals that each other eat,
> The Anthropophagi, and men whose heads
> Do grow beneath their shoulders."
> Shakespeare, *Othello*

antinomy

One of the placards carried in an anti-draft demonstration at Princeton University reads, "There Is Nothing Worth Dying For." The old *antinomy* of the philosophers can now be updated: Is it worth dying in defense

of the proposition There is nothing worth dying for?
(From a letter in *The N.Y. Times* by Roy A. Rosenberg)

The theorem is a variation on the only well-remembered
line of the Cretan poet Epimenides, who said, "All
Cretans are liars." Another version of the same *antinomy* is more succinct and more troublesome; it reads,
"This sentence is false."

antinomy—an inconsistency, or built-in contradiction; opposition of one law to another (from Gr. *anti*, against + *nomos*,
law). See **anomie.** Not to be confused with *antimony*, one of
the metallic elements.

aphasic

I was led to the notion when my hostess on an internal
flight, *aphasic*, jet-lagged, her ankles swollen, lost her
bearings and her final nouns.

aphasic—from *aphasia*, loss or impairment of power to speak
(from Gr. *a*, without + *phasis*, speech).
     Also: *dysphasia*, loss of power to speak or understand
language: *dys*, bad.

apodictic

I must strongly protest his *apodictic* statement that
only Schliemann's "second career is the sole justifi-
cation for yet another biography, or indeed any biography, of the man." (*NYRB*)

apodictic—absolutely certain or necessarily true; uncontest-
able.

apopemptic

Men as intelligent as Scott (the Antarctic explorer
Robert Falcon Scott, 1868–1912) were, 70 years ago,

most extraordinarily articulate. Alongside them, most of our scientists and executives, even assuming they would dream of writing *apopemptic* communications from a canvas igloo while dying, would sound like Western Union operators. (From a book review by William F. Buckley in *The N.Y. Times*)

apopemptic—valedictory to one departing; farewell or leave-taking. Gr. prefix, *apo,* away from, tells us something and is an often-met prefix, useful to know.

Apopemptic is exactly the right word here, since Scott died on this mission. He reached the South Pole on January 18, 1912, but died on the return. His careful diary was found on his frozen body in a tiny tent only a few miles short of a supply cairn containing food and fuel. Most people remember the note in his journal just before the end, "For God's sake look after our people."

apo(ph)thegm

A long time ago Tom Paine warned in an *apothegm* that "We must take care to guard even our enemies against injustice."

apothegm—like *aphorism,* this is a concise formulation of a truth, a maxim, adage, and (after a long period of use) a proverb.

aposiopesis

The story as a whole is a rumor of a time, a place and a people. It is a vague accusation, an *aposiopesis,* or breaking off for dramatic effect.

aposiopesis—a sudden breaking off, as of a thought in the middle of a sentence or a break in the middle of a dramatic sequence.

apotheosis

> It was then that the so-called Renaissance occurred, which produced the outburst of art, literature, and humanistic study that is still popularly conceived as an *apotheosis* of Western culture.

apotheosis—most easily defined by its Latin twin, *deification*. In its general nonreligious sense it means an exalted position, highest development, quintessential or ultimate fulfillment (from Gr. *theos*, god; L. *deus*).

Also: *monotheism; pantheon* (from *pan*, all). Some like to say, "I won't put *him* in my pantheon."

apposite

> This novel's significance continues to grow when the problems raised by its own temporal and political context may seem no longer *apposite*.

apposite—appropriate, fitting, apt, suitable (from L. *posit*, placed + *ap* from *ad*, next to).

arpeggiate

> Unlike many pianists who play Scarlatti, she did not *arpeggiate* or otherwise break up chords in a guitar style, so that her playing had an unusual crispness.

arpeggiate—the clue to this word is *arpa*, Italian for harp; hence, it means to play a distributive chord on the piano as it would have to be played on a harp, notes following each other in a swinging arc.

autochthonous

> There are still frequent charges of arbitrary arrest, torture, and disregard for the welfare of the *autochthonous* Indian population.

autochthonous—native, aboriginal, indigenous (from Gr. *auto,* self + *chthonos,* earth, sprung from the earth itself). *Aboriginal: ab,* from + *origine,* the beginning.

basilisk

> Dorothy Hamill's routines are far freer and more imaginative than the ones she was permitted to use when performing under the *basilisk* eyes of the Olympic judges.

basilisk—a special kind of snake, a fabulous serpent whose look and breath were thought to be fatal. From Gr. *basileus,* king, because of the crest that some of these mythical creatures had on their backs and tails.

bedight

> "GAILY *BEDIGHT,* a gallant knight
> In Sunshine and in shadow. . . ."
>
> Edgar Allan Poe, "El Dorado"

bedight—clad, arrayed. This archaic word is listed here not only because it occurs in the first two lines of a well-known poem but also because one candidate for a license to teach English, dazzled and fooled by the capitalizing of the first two words, concluded his teaching of the poem with: "Oh, boys and girls, I forgot to tell you something. The name of the knight was Gaily Bedight," thus joining Alexander Pope's "Lo, the poor Indian!"

belletrists

> The author spearheads the clique of British *belletrists* who would place Wodehouse between Homer and Dante in the pantheon of world literature.

belletrists—writers interested in literature (poetry, drama, novel) as such, to the neglect of more practical and informative literature. From Fr. *belles lettres*, literally "beautiful letters" and therefore fine literature.

bicephalous

> In the totalitarian states, they are trapped in the talons of the *bicephalous* eagle.

bicephalous—two-headed (the ruling dictator and the KGB or Savak or whatever names the secret police are given). From Gr. *bi*, two + *kephale*, head.
> Also: *acephalous* (*a*, without), without a leader or head of state.

bloviate

> Politicians everywhere are noted for their windiness. But nowhere, to use H. L. Mencken's word, do they *bloviate* so relentlessly as in the Supreme Soviet.

bloviate—to deliver an oration that is verbose or windy. Probably from *blow* + *ate*.

borborygmic

> I lay in the huge, impersonal dormitory known as The Jungle, surrounded by 150 snoring, grunting, *borborygmic* men, and thought of the intimate, incense-laden hush of my bedroom at home.

borborygmic—referring to stomach growlings, involuntary intestinal rumbling noises; an onomatopoeic word, imitative of the sounds made.

caesura

> Subtly altered *caesuras* invade his speech.

caesura—pause (see **alexandrine**).

cachination

> Swinburne's eldritch screams of laughter (the wild *cachinations* that Henry Adams described) would ring out to alarm the company.

cachination—a loud laugh. Another onomatopoeic word. Associate this word with *cackle* and you'll have a clue not only to its meaning but also to its pronunciation.

carapace

> She hums and sighs with a taut delicacy, making her deliberation a stone *carapace* over her unruly heart.

carapace—hard, bony covering, turtle's shell.

carceral

> In his new book he gives us a new pejorative description of the modern world: we live in a "disciplined" or a "surveillance" or a "*carceral*" society.

carceral—imprisoning (from L. *carcer,* prison).
     Also: *incarcerate*.

catamite

> On this peep-show, porn-movie street, some make eye contact with the lurking *catamites*.

catamite—a boy used in pederasty; a boy kept for sexual purposes. Though much changed, *catamite* ultimately comes from Greek mythology: Ganymede (from Etruscan *Catmite,* from Greek *Ganymedes*), most beautiful of all mortals, was carried up by the gods to be Zeus's cupbearer. Astronomers placed *Ganymede* among the stars under the name of *Aquarius.*

cenacle

> No one, not even in the most benighted high-school English classroom in Dubuque, can still believe that

the celebrated circle of smart alecks who lunched together at the Algonquin between the wars were an
important literary *cenacle.*

cenacle—a small dining room where a literary or philosophic
group eats and talks. In a religious context the room is the one
in which The Last Supper took place (from L. *cena,* dinner).
When a doctor prescribes medication to be taken *p.c.,* the *p.c.*
stands for *post cenam,* after a meal. The Greek-derived *sym-
posium* is a companion word for *cenacle,* emphasizing drinking: *sym,* together + *posis,* a drinking.

chiasmus, chiastic

It is not what the President has done for the hostages
but rather what the hostages have done for the President.

chiasmus, chiastic—the above only partially illustrates a *chiasmus,* which means a complete inversion in the second part of a
sentence, as for example: He flew to Mexico; to the Greek
islands fled she. From the Greek letter *X* (*chi* or *khi,* according
to the present trend in transliterating). The meaning is suggested by the shape of the letter X. In Xmas, the X stands for
the letter *chi,* which stands for *Christos.*

chiliastic

It is worth asking why an American author whose
Dostoyevskyan preoccupations are with the messianic,
the apocalyptic, and the *chiliastic* should be popular in
the U.S.S.R. today.

chiliastic—the exact equivalent of the Latin-derived word *mil-
lennial; chiliad* (from Gr. *chilioi,* thousand) is more easily
recognized in the combining form *kilo-,* as in *kilometer, kilo-
gram,* or *kilowatts. Millennium* or *chiliad* may be used literally
to mean a thousand years, but more often it is used to mean
some far-off year when people will have remolded "this sorry
scheme of things entire . . . nearer to the heart's desire."

chrestomathy

> The book contained a resumé of *The Lord of the Rings*
> and the usual appendices: genealogical tables and
> notes on the *chrestomathy* of elvish names. (*TLS*)

chrestomathy—a collection of literary passages, especially
useful in studying a language. From Gr. *chrestos,* useful +
mathein, to learn.
     Also: *polymath,* someone very learned in many (*poly*)
fields.

clerestory

> Both buildings are brick boxes; one is simple and
> banal, while the other has *clerestory* windows and a
> high tower.

clerestory—the upper part of the nave, transepts, and choir of
a church, containing windows; any similar windowed con-
struction used for light and ventilation (from Middle English
clere, lighted). Pronounced "clear story."

comity

> The white attitudes toward black Americans measured
> in this Times/CBS News Poll offered other, though
> less insistent evidence of recession's threat to *comity.*

comity—courteous behavior, politeness, civility—usually found
in the expression *the comity of nations* (from Gr. *komis,*
polite).

costiveness

> Can so regular a flow of novels, stories, poetry and
> criticism all be in the first class? Of course they can.
> *Costiveness* is not necessarily a literary virtue.

costiveness—constipation. From Latin via French, *constipare*, which can be reduced, if you look carefully at the consonants *c*, *st*, *v* (*v* = *p*), to *costive*, same meaning as *constipated*.

crapulous

> Celine did not enjoy Africa, apart from the solitude it offered him. There were too many mosquitoes and too many *crapulous* whites. (*TLS*)

crapulous—sick from drink (from L. *crapula*, intoxication).

crenellations

> The tourists stare up at the *crenellated* walls of the 13th-century princely abode on a cliff 350 feet above the bazaar-like main street of Vaduz.

crenellations—notches on battlement walls or towers in medieval fortresses, through which weapons could be fired or lethal weapons dropped (seen in such movies as *Ivanhoe* and *Beau Geste*). From Latin *crena*, notch, groove. Another word that means pretty much the same as *crenellations* is *machicolations*, openings in roof or parapet from which missiles can be hurled on assailants below.

crepuscular

> He used the Conte crayon, achieving blacks like no others in the history of drawing, blacks that are themselves a form of light—velvety, shimmering, *crepuscular* and ghostly.

crepuscular—a beautiful word referring to dusk, twilight; sometimes shady in a wicked sense: "crepuscular sexual practices and tastes" (from L. *crepusculum*, twilight, from *creper*, dusky, dark).

cybernetics

> More than a generation ago, Gregory Bateson was among the founders of *cybernetics*, the study of behavior-controlling mechanisms in human beings and computers and other advanced machines.

cybernetics—well defined in the excerpt. The dictionary definition may add a little more clarification: a science dealing with the comparative study of the operations of complex electronics computers and the human nervous system. At any rate, the word was coined by Norbert Wiener in 1948, from the Greek word *kybernan,* to steer, guide, govern. In the consonants you can see *k* (= g), *b* (= v), *rn,* forming the word *govern.*

diffract

> Michael Higgins and Lindsay Crouse, as father and daughter, are hard and precise as two diamond chips, and *diffract* as many darting colors.

diffract—to break up a ray of light into colors (from L. *dif* [*dis*] + *fractus,* p.p. of *frangere,* to break).

> "Heaven's light forever shines, earth's shadows fly;
> Life, like a dome of many-coloured glass,
> Stains the white radiance of eternity."
>
> Shelley, "Adonais"

disquisition

> A number of important *disquisitions* have appeared on the preservation, or wanton destruction, of historic buildings.

disquisition—formal discussion, discourse. Despite the formal aspect of disquisition, it is usually modified by such adjectives as *learned, academic, important.*

dithyramb, dithyrambic

> In his humility before the idea that each of us has a chance at happiness, he sometimes grows rather too *dithyrambic.*

dithyramb—choric hymn sung in Ancient Greece at the festival of Dionysus to the accompaniment of music; any wild, frenzied, or emotional speech or writing.

dyslexia

> The author makes clear what *dyslexia* is (not a reading disability alone, but a dysfunction which causes one).

dyslexia—impairment of ability to read (from *dys,* bad + *lexis,* reading, speaking). The prefix *dys* is widely used to name medical malfunctionings. *Alexia, a,* not + *lexis,* reading, means word blindness, loss of ability to read.
> Also: *lexicon.*

dystopia

> He knows that when he sees the future, it will not work—he will automatically be creating a "*dystopia*" (no one creates utopias any more: even the utopias of the past look like dystopias to us).

dystopia—not in all dictionaries, but it obviously means a bad, an unsuccessful, or a failed utopia. *Utopia* itself, which literally means "no place" (Gr. *ou,* no + *topos,* place), conveys an expectation of failure. True also of Samuel Butler's *Erewhon,* which is *nowhere* spelled backwards.
> Also: *topography; topiary.*

echthyic

> Why does the noble trout stand in so many anglers' imaginations above its *echthyic* fellows?

echthyic—characteristic of fish. The better-known word is *ichthyology,* study of fish as a science.

eldritch

> The void atmosphere is that of Paul Nash's sinister
> evocations of the Western Front. But one of the draw-
> ings is different: a small dark wood, *eldritch,* menacing.
> (*TLS*)

eldritch—eerie, strange, weird, or unearthly; much used in
horror stories. (Cf. *cachination* excerpt for another example of
the use of *eldritch.*)

enchiridion

> "How to Make It in a Man's World" is an *enchiridion*
> for young women who don't want to deposit their
> brains in the sugar canister.

enchiridion—this is one to surprise your friends with (if not to
endear them to you). It means *hand*book, *man*ual, guide book.
From Gr. *en* (in) + *chir-,* hand + *idion,* diminutive suffix,
equals something small that can be held in the hand.
     Also: *chiromancy,* palmistry (exact equivalent); *chiro-
practor*; *chiropodist* (hand and foot).

endorphin and enkephalin

> Analysis of spinal fluid before and after acupuncture
> has shown a marked rise in opiate-like substances
> (*endorphins* and *enkephalins,* for example) recently
> identified as the body's natural defenses against pain.
> Acupuncture may stimulate their production.

endorphin—a newly coined word explained in the passage
(made up of Gr. *endo,* within + *morphine*). Medical science is
working on what can be even more of an analgesic or anodyne
through study of the fluid of the brain, to produce *enkephalins*
(*en* + *kephalos,* head + *morphine*).

enjambment

> The rhythms are precisely consonant in their complex
> line-lengths, *enjambments,* phrasings and patterns of
> accented sound.

enjambment—in poetry, one line running into the next, so that words closely related syntactically appear in the following line, unlike Pope's closed heroic couplets:

> "A little learning is a dangerous thing;
> Drink deep or taste not the Pierian spring."

Compare these couplets with Browning's in "My Last Duchess":

> "Oh sir, she smiled, no doubt,
> Whenever I passed her; but who passed without
> Much the same smile? This grew; I gave commands;
> Then all smiles stopped together. There she stands
> As if alive."

Some time reread "My Last Duchess" in its entirety. What may surprise you is that it is written in rhymed couplets with end words that generally run into the next line (enjambment), thus deemphasizing the rhyme but retaining its music.

entrammeled and untrammeled

This is a reaction against the kind of literary criticism that became too easily *entrammeled* with social and moral concerns.

None support an *untrammeled* power of the President to annul any treaty he wishes.

entrammeled—enmeshed in, entangled. *Untrammeled*: unconfined, unlimited.

entropy

In science, religion, social life, and art, dogmatism is the *entropy* of thought; what has been dogmatized no longer inflames, it is merely warm—and soon it is to be cold.

entropy—the concept of entropy is defined in the Second Law of Thermodynamics as being the equivalent of inertia. This law predicts that every organized system must eventually break down. As used figuratively, as it is in most nonscientific contexts, it means a gradual slowing down, a cooling off. Part of another news clip asks: "Should art whistle happily as the universe approaches inertness and mankind makes its way into final darkness?"

epicene

> The actor plays Hal initially as an indolent, sulky, slightly *epicene* presence. But he never manages Hal's growth into valor and exuberance; he remains a pale and hesitant figure.

epicene—effeminate, unmanly. This is the word that some writers and speakers should use instead of *effete* (which see).

epistemology

> The problem in focusing on some measure of rationality is not going to be solved by teaching courses in logic, *epistemology,* and the philosophy of science.

epistemology—the origin of the study of knowledge: how people know, what they know, and how much they can know; i.e., the nature, the methods, and the limits of knowledge (from Gr. *episteme,* knowledge).

eponym, eponymous

> In the novel *Anna Karenina,* the *eponymous* heroine and her tragedy take second place in Tolstoy's scale of importance. The true protagonist is Levin, a self-portrait of the novelist.

eponymous—from the book of the same name, from the Greek root *onyma* (and its variants *onoma* and *onomata*), name + *epi*, after = named after.
Also: *antonym; synonym; pseudonym; anonymous* (*an*, not or without); *onomatopoeia; paronomasia* (which see); *onomastics* (study of names).

eristic

> In the matter of the Salt talks, Mr. Kennan feels that all the talk and fuss about weapon systems is a kind of *eristic* militarism that prevents us from the fruitful explorations we should be undertaking.

eristic—provoking strife or controversy or discord. Eris, the Greek goddess of discord, was actually the fomenter of the Greco-Trojan War. In mythology, it was Eris who rolled the golden apple into the assembly of the gods—the golden apple on which was inscribed "To the fairest." Zeus took the easy way out—a mythological cop-out—by passing the choice to Paris, son of Priam, King of Troy. Paris, being young, chose Aphrodite, who had promised him Helen, the most beautiful girl in the world. The rest is history, almost, and one of the masterpieces of all time, Homer's *Iliad*.

erythrophobia

> There can surely be no doubt that the Victorians were deeply ashamed about sex and this shame revealed itself in widespread *erythrophobia*. *(TLS)*

erythrophobia—the fear of reddening or blushing (from Gr. *erythro-*, red + *phobia*, fear of). Also *erythromycin*, a much-prescribed, broad-spectrum antibiotic, usually a blushing pink or red (from Gr. *mykes*, a fungus). One who studies mushrooms and other fungi is a *mycologist*; in medicine, *mycosis* is a fungous growth in the body or a disease caused by a fungous growth. Note that *fungus, callus, mucus* are nouns. The corresponding *ous* forms are adjectives.

esurient

> In those days he was a lean and *esurient* actor.

esurient—hungry. From L. p.p. *esus* from *edere,* to eat; *esurire,* to want food (*esca*). Latin *pugnos edere,* a phrase meaning "to eat fists," is a figure of speech for "to get a good beating."
Also: *esculent,* edible; *inedible; comestible; obese.*

ethos

> The whole *ethos* of ancient Egypt was the denial of death.

ethos—a term with wide meaning: character; disposition; fundamental outlook; the spirit that animates the customs and moral values of a people. Aristotle used it to mean the character of man in the struggle between passion and moderation; in Greek tragedy it refers to an element of character that determines what a man does in contrast to what he thinks.

Ethical is, of course, derived from *ethos*. The Romans had the word *mores* for the same idea as *ethos*, but *ethos* has deeper implications and is a much stronger word.

etiolated

> I exploit every drop of sunlight to improve my *etiolated* city skin.

etiolated—bleached, whitened, blanched.

etiology

> The daily life of the election is thick with the crisis of inflation; its *etiology* and prospects.

etiology—the study of causes, especially in medical research, which seeks the causes of diseases in order to deal effectively with them.

exegesis

> In its time, T.S. Eliot's "The Cocktail Party" became a cocktail party conundrum, with theatergoers and critics wrestling for *exegesis*.

exegesis—critical explanation or interpretation of passages in the Bible, Shakespeare, James Joyce, Samuel Beckett, Vladimir Nabokov, etc. (See **hermeneutics**).

fictive

Diaries are often tedious and unreliable—tedious because the detailed record of drunken excess must be
so, unreliable because of a natural tendency to confer
fictive point and shape on facts even at the moment of
setting them down in the diary.

fictive—giving the truth a narrative treatment; fictitious; imaginary.

flagitious

"That," shouted the witness, "is a cowardly, dastardly,
contemptible, and *flagitious* insinuation."

flagitious—outrageous, flagrantly wicked, scandalous, vicious
(remember it by the rhyme).

fleering

The peremptoriness, the rancor, the tone of malice
and disdain and *fleering* sarcasm—these were all
present in his review.

fleering—jeering, sneering (rhymes again). In the excerpt, the
words preceding *sarcasm* give you a clue to the climactic use of
fleering. The verb *fleer* pops up in crossword puzzles.

floccipaucinihilipilification

When a reporter brought up Mayor Koch's austerity
budget, Senator Moynihan was ready. "I'm glad you
asked me that," he said, and added, "The floccipaucinihilipilification problem is not behind us."

floccipaucinihilipilification—the action of estimating as worthless. The word is formed from the statement of a rule in the
Eton Latin Grammar illustrating a use of the genitive (posses-
sive) case. The examples cited—*flocci, pauci* (or *nauci*), *nihili,*

pili—all mean "of little value." Scott and Southey used it. It is listed in the *Guinness Book of Records* as the longest word in the *Oxford English Dictionary*.

florilegium

> The professor of English literature at a British university has collected some of her flowers in a *florilegium* of 113 leaves. (*TLS*)

florilegium—anthology, both words meaning "a gathering of poems." This is one of the few cases where the Latin-derived word is rarer than its Greek twin (Gr. *anthos,* flower; L. *flos, floris,* flower = anthology). The Greek poet Meleager is reputed to have compiled the first anthology and to have coined the word for what he called a garland of songs. He included only a very few of Sappho's, "a few but those few—roses."

fulgurant

> Of the 13 books she has published, some have moved readers and critics to *fulgurant* praise.

fulgurant—shining, dazzling (from L. *fulgur,* lightning, brightness). A beautiful French word *foudroyant* (from same L. source, found in our desk dictionaries) means dazzling, stunning.

    Also: *effulgent,* shining forth (*ef* for *ex*); *refulgent,* shining radiantly.

fungible

> The reason gold has shot up to $700 an ounce is that paper money is in the last analysis paper and gold is as *fungible* as grain. (Heard on TV)

fungible—interchangeable, like gold or grain, any unit of which can be replaced by another unit (from L. *functus,* p.p. of *fungor,* to perform).

    Also: *defunct* (*de,* down, out); *functionary; perfunctory* (*per,* getting through with), performed in a routine manner.

gnathic

> His face was big, *gnathic*, with spectacles that slid down his nose.

gnathic—related to the jaw (from L. *gnathos*, jaw).

Also: *prognathous*, having a jaw that protrudes forward (*pro*) to a considerable degree; identifying feature of the royal family of Hapsburg, especially the Spanish branch, which Velasquez did nothing to conceal.

gnome

> In these poems, he plays with epigram, *gnome*, riddle, rune, and meditation.

gnome—pithy saying of a fundamental truth, maxim, adage, aphorism, apothegm (from Gr. *gnome*, maxim, judgment; *gnosis*, knowledge). In *The Bible as Literature*, the subtitle of The Book of Proverbs is "An Anthology of Gnomic Poetry." This *gnome* has nothing to do with those *gnomes*, the dwarfs of folklore, who guarded treasure.

Also: *gnostic; agnostic; prognosis; diagnosis*

gravamen

> They soon began to abuse what they were reading, and each was reading some part of some novel of my own. The *gravamen* of their complaint lay in the fact that I reintroduced the same characters so often.

gravamen—the weightiest part of an accusation; the essential part of a grievance or complaint (from L. *gravis*, heavy, weighty, serious). Pronounced *gra-vay'-min*. The word is found in current use, though the illustration above is from Anthony Trollope's *Autobiography*. After he heard the complaint of the two clergymen in the Athenaeum Club in London, he went home and disposed of one of his (and many others') favorite characters: "It was with many misgivings that I killed my old friend Mrs. Proudie."

Also: *gravid,* "heavy with child," pregnant; *aggravate,* the exact opposite of *alleviate,* to make lighter; *gravity; grave,* serious. The mortally wounded Mercutio (in *Romeo and Juliet*) puns on the word in one of his last speeches: ". . . ask for me tomorrow and you shall find me a grave man."

haruspex

A dark, ageless figure [sits] at the hearth, part historian, part *haruspex.*

haruspex—a sort of lower-echelon soothsayer, who looks (L. *specere*) at the entrails of an animal on which to base his predictions. From L. *auspex, auspicis,* a soothsayer who used the flight of birds (*avis,* bird) to make prognostications.

hebdomadal

This leaves a *hebdomadal* deficit of $33,000.

hebdomadal—weekly, every seven days (from Gr. *hepta,* L. *septum,* seven). The word was once more frequently used, especially for the weekly publications in which a novel might run serially. Dickens's novels were first published in this way. Visiting New York, he was met at dockside by readers who pleaded with him not to let Little Nell die.

hermeneutics

Back and forth went the discussions about Shakespeare, from traditional analysis to the latest *hermeneutic* news.

hermeneutics—the science and methodology of interpretation.

heuristic

In denigrating reductionism, he fails to appreciate that the search for simple mechanisms has been, and almost surely will continue to be, an important *heuristic* tool for the scientist.

heuristic—helping to discover or learn; helping students to discover or learn for themselves. From Gr. *heuriskein,* to discover—but easily remembered when you annex it to *eureka,* which comes from the same root. "Eureka (I have found it)"—is what Archimedes is said to have shouted as he ran unclothed out of the public baths in Syracuse, Sicily, after having made the discovery of how to find the exact weight of the gold in a king's crown.

A related word in meaning is *maieutic,* the method used by Socrates to help his students "give birth" to ideas, for the word *maieutic* ultimately comes from Gr. *maia,* midwife.

holism

> Recently, officials of the Carter Administration have had some carefully measured good words to say about *holistic* health. Thanks to the spiraling costs of medical health care and popular resentment over the impersonality of the medical establishment, *holism* is fast gathering a wide following across the country.

holism—sometimes *wholism,* is a move away from technology and toward the view that the body, mind, and spirit can be kept healthy with minimal use of drugs or surgery; the belief that an organic or integrated whole has a reality independent of and greater than its parts. From Gr. *holos,* whole.

Also: *hologram; holograph; holocaust.*

indurated

> He was, when threatened, obtuse, *indurated,* ferocious.

indurated—obstinate, hardened, unyielding, made unfeeling (from L. *in* [intensive] + *durus,* hard).

Also: *during; endure; durable; duress; obdurate,* which has much the same meaning as *indurated;* and *dour.*

inspissated

> Writing poetry remains in a sense my major commitment, even if for a time the poems were inspirited and *inspissated* with political excitement. (*TLS*)

inspissated—thickened, heavy, intense.

irenic

He was an ecumenical and *irenic* figure.

irenic—promoting peace, conciliatory, pacific. Irēnē (three syllables), called Pax by the Romans, was the Greek goddess of peace.

An interesting use of the word appeared in *The Times Literary Supplement:* "After using many pseudonyms, and having won some recognition, he found his way back to his own *irenic* full name, William Makepeace Thackeray."

karmic

Nonrational powerful forces fascinate many Americans currently—witchcraft, ancestral curses, *karmic* accidents, demonic possession, and extraordinary psychic abilities.

karmic—having to do, in the Buddhist faith, with a person's action which will determine his destiny in his *next* existence. You can see that it fits right in with the forces that "fascinate so many Americans." The noun *karma*, loosely, means destiny.

labile

Every time I got a report card or a personality report, they always put down that I was *labile*, a common German psychological term, East and West, suggesting someone who is unstable and easily influenced.

labile—unstable, liable (an anagram for *labile*) to change; sometimes used of blood pressure that fluctuates (from L. *labi, lapsus*, slip).

Also: *Lapsus linguae*, a slip of the tongue.

lagniappe

One of the Philadelphia players castigated the manager for benching Luzinski, Garry Maddox and Bob

Boone late in the season. As *lagniappe,* he called the
Philadelphia fans "the worst in baseball."

lagniappe—something extra, something for good measure.
Pronounced *lan-yap.* This word was born in the United States
among the Creole population of Louisiana. Its original meaning is seen in this sentence written by a traveler in 1893 in
Harper's Magazine:

> "Take that for a lagniappe," says a storekeeper in New
> Orleans as he folds a pretty calendar into the bundle of
> stationery you have purchased.

lambent

> The merriest time of all is being had by the real spoke
> of the party wheel, the silver-haired figure in the dark
> blue suit wearing a *lambent* ear-to-ear grin.

lambent—gently glowing or flickering; softly radiant; flitting
over subjects with effortless brilliance ("a *lambent* wit"); lumi-
nous ("soft and *lambent* eyes"). Associate the word with an old
type of *lamp,* a word that may have a similar origin.

litotes

> Auden was fond of constructing anagrams. For T.S.
> Eliot, Auden liked "*litotes,*" a rhetorical figure of
> speech: "a not untalented poet." For Wystan Hugh
> Auden, he suggested an anagram: "Hug a shady wet
> nun."

litotes—its use is an example of two negatives making a positive. "Not bad" is the most usual.

littoral

> The rest of Europe has been hesitant about extending
> membership to Greece and other less affluent nations
> on the Mediterranean *littoral.*

littoral—coastal or seashore region.

logomachy

> The high medieval synthesis of patristic Christianity and Hellenic philosophy had broken down into a *logomachy* among various schools of Realism and Nominalism.

logomachy—strife with words only (from Gr. *logos*, word + *mache*, fight, battle).
Also: *neologism* (*neo-*, new, hence a coined word).

lustrum

> During these three *lustrums*, Samuel Johnson produced most of his great works, including his epoch-making dictionary, which he compiled virtually single-handed. And yet during these fifteen years he was dogged by poverty and ill health.

lustrum—the meaning is given in the second sentence—clear to anyone who can divide 15 by 3; a quinquennium; half a decade; in ancient Rome, a purification of all the people by means of ceremonies held every five years, after the census.

machicolations (See crenellations)

maieutic (See heuristic)

marcescence

> He was past 50 when the mysterious *marcescence* set in which was finally to end in death.

marcescence—a beginning to wither or droop. In botany it is used in the sense of withering but not dropping off (from L. *marcere*, to wither). Note: the suffix combining form *-escent*, *-escence* slows up the adjective and noun so that they carry the idea of becoming or growing. Compare *obsolescent* with *obsolete, adolescence* with *adulthood, senescence* with *senile*.

masticable

> Plenty of people want some sort of "spiritual nourishment," but find art, music, science, and philosophy not *masticable*.

masticate—to chew (food). From L. *masticare,* from Gr. *mastikhan,* to gnash one's teeth.

> Some books are to be tasted, others to be swallowed, and some few to be chewed and digested; that is, some books are to be read only in parts; others to be read but not curiously; and some few to be read wholly, and with diligence and attention.
>
> Francis Bacon, "Of Studies"

metempsychosis

> Is it amnesia? Or a psychotically split personality? Or a genuine case of *metempsychosis,* of transmigration of the soul?

metempsychosis—a theory held by the Greek philosopher Pythagoras that the soul at death passes into another body, human or animal. From Gr. *meta,* over + *em,* into + *psyche,* soul; L. *trans,* over + *migratus,* p.p. of *migrare,* to migrate; *transmigration.*

> "Ah, Pythagoras' metempsychosis, were that true
> The soul should fly from me and I be changed
> Into some brutish beast."
>
> Marlowe, *Doctor Faustus*

metonymy, synecdoche

> James Thurber, in his delightful character sketch of his old English teacher, recalls how Mrs. Groby loved *all* figures of speech but doted on *metonymy*.

metonymy, synecdoche—some confusion exists about just which is which. In general terms *metonymy* (from Gr. *-onymy,* name) is the name of one thing for that of something else with which one associates it; for example: the Kremlin for the USSR; the Oval office for the President; and the Hill for Congress. (*The Oval office proposal is likely to meet strong opposition when it gets to the Hill.*)

Synecdoche is usually characterized as using the part for the whole or the material for the thing made; for example: *canvases* for paintings at an art exhibit; *pigskin* for football.

mimesis, mimetic

The New York City subway map is a model of naturalism. Water is blue, parks are green. Rapid transit cartography has now joined the current trend of conservatism in the arts—the abandonment of abstraction of *mimesis*.

mimetic—characterized by mimicry or imitation; imitative (from Gr. *mimos*, a mime or actor, imitator).
Also: *pantomime* (*panto-*, all); *mimicry*.

mirific

His own remarkable adventures have a quality of the *mirific*.

mirific—wonderful, causing wonder (from L. *mirare*, to wonder, to look).
Also: *miracle; admire; mirage*.

modality

They have agreed on the *modalities* whereby they will negotiate the remaining issues.

modality—method, manner, procedure, the how and what of something (from L. *modus*, manner).

modular

"Expensive and unproductive gimmickry"—open classrooms, *modular* scheduling, and other reforms—simply contributing to mediocrity instead of producing academic excellence.

modular—relating to a unit of measurement; a space word: capable of being easily detached from or joined to or arranged with other units.

moiety

He tells us that as a young man among the *moiety* of Czechs—"the more dynamic, the more intelligent, the better half"—he cheered the accession of the Communists to power in February 1948 but that he was soon disillusioned by the harsh oppression of the new regime.

moiety—one of two equal portions; half. (Pronounced *moy.*) It's hard to believe, but *moiety* finally goes back to L. *medius,* middle, *la moitié*, the French word for half, being the mediator.

mystagogical

We've heard a lot of *mystagogical* nonsense recently about the superiority of the right hemisphere [of the brain].

mystagogical—tending to disseminate mystical doctrine. From Gr. *mystes,* initiator into occult rites + *agogos,* leader, as in *pedagogue (pais, paidos,* child). *Pedagogue* once meant a slave who led a child to school and cared for him at home.

mythomaniac

The young man was characterized as a *mythomaniac,* or compulsive liar.

mythomaniac—no further comment necessary (Gr. derivation obvious: *mythomania* is a mania for making up myths). A much weaker word is *prevaricator*: literally, one who straddles.

nattering

> This was the result of years of *nattering* about the evils of private enterprise.

nattering—grumbling, fault-finding, idle chatter. In one of "his" speeches (written by William Safire), Spiro Agnew dazzled the press with the alliterative "nattering nabobs of negativism."

neoteny

> He wants to prove that the cranial angles support the theory of *neoteny*, that human development is a case of retardation, of the retention of previously juvenile characteristics.

neoteny—retention of juvenile characteristics in the adult (from Gr. *neo-*, new + *teinein*, to stretch).

nimiety

Excess, redundancy, superfluity, pleonasm (from L. *nimius*). (See **plethora**)

nous

> *Bad Boys* is directed by Susumu Hani with considerable Freudian *nous.*

nous—from Gr. *nous*, mind, this is a word that is coming into vogue, meaning the highest form of intellect, sometimes with the additional idea of expertise. Pronounced *noose*.
    Also: *noetic* (adj.); *noology*, study of the mind; *paranoia; noumenal*, concerning things that are not knowable to the sense but are conceivable by reason.

nugatory

> National respect for the courts is not achieved by rendering them *nugatory* by the interposition of subterfuges.

nugatory—worthless, trifling, of no consequence (from L. *nugae*, trifles, jokes).

numinous

> The Bible was almost the only book Rembrandt read and he saw it as a drama that was simultaneously human, historical, and *numinous*.

numinous—as used today, most often means filled with a divine presence; like a god, or goddess. Another one of the beautiful words.

oenologist

> About 200 vintners, *oenologists,* and wine merchants sniffed, swirled, sipped, and spit their way through 32 wines drawn directly from barrels and splashed into tastevins, the shallow silver tasting cups whose bowls are molded to reflect the light.

oenologist—with newspapers regularly featuring columns on wines, no definition is needed (from Gr. *oinos,* wine).

> "I wonder often what the Vintners buy
> One half so precious as the goods they sell."
> > Fitzgerald, "The Rubaiyat of Omar Khayyam"

oneiric

> Such a vision works best when left a bit dreamlike, and her first books have a marvelously disturbing, *oneiric* resonance.

oneiric—having to do with dreams (from Gr. *oneiros,* dream).
Also: *oneiromancy,* use of dreams to forecast the future.

ontogeny

> In one form or another, the idea that "*ontogeny* re-
> capitulates *phylogeny*" has exerted its force since an-
> tiquity; the belief in recapitulation in the latter half of
> the 19th century was the dominant viewpoint in
> evolutionary biology.

ontogeny—life cycle of a single organism, as opposed to *phylogeny,* development of the race. For a long time, the warcry of
evolutionary biology was "*Ontogeny* recapitulates *phylogeny,*"
that is, the individual organism in its early stages goes through
a development similar to those evolutionary stages the human
race has gone through. From Gr. *onto-,* organism + *-geny,*
origin, development; *phylo-,* race, tribe.

ontology

> For most Americans, being liked is almost a subdi-
> vision of *ontology.* We need it, as if to establish our
> existence.

ontology—the study of what it means for something to exist;
branch of philosophy that deals with the nature of being. Adjective: *ontological.*

otiose

> Britain was right to terror-bomb German cities in 1942
> because survival was at stake (to continue to do so, in
> 1945, in Dresden, however, was *otiose*; it was no
> longer "necessary" for survival).

otiose—futile, functionless, sterile, idle (from L. *otium,* ease,
leisure). To *negotiate* is to not (*neg*) be at leisure, to be busy

doing something. When a piece of writing or a portion of it is said to be *otiose,* the implication is that it serves no purpose, performs no useful function.

palimpsest

> His accounts were a *palimpsest* of debts wiped clean only by fortuitous shipments of booty from Peru.

palimpsest—a parchment written upon several times with earlier text not altogether erased, leaving some original writing visible. Some major literary works of antiquity were recovered in this way. In the excerpt the word is used figuratively. (From Gr. *palimpsestos,* rubbed or scraped again: *palin,* again.)

Also: *palindrome* (which see).

paramnesia (See déjà vu)

paranomasia

This is a word used by those who don't want to use the three-letter word *pun.* One usually "perpetrates" a pun, so low is it in the scale of humor. A famous sophisticated pun by Sydney Smith, the well-known nineteenth-century British wit, deals with two women, living on opposite sides of a street, who engaged in loud daily disputes as they leaned out of their windows. It was Sydney Smith's reasoned conclusion that they would never come to any agreement because they were "arguing from different premises."

The more outrageous the pun the more it is frowned upon, at the same time as it is admired, especially if it introduces a literary reference. For example, a college student who cut her class in philosophy to go horseback riding ran into her professor when she was still in her riding clothes. "Uh-uh," he said, shaking his head, "You should put Descartes before the horse." Or, after viewing Hawaiians in a short film, enjoying their favorite sport, you come out with the killing remark, "He also surfs who only stands and wades." If you have suppressed a groan so far, one last example will give it free play: on seeing a Miro print in the dining area: "You know, that's no place to hang your Miro. It should be in the library opposite *Thus Spake Zarathustra.* Then you can hold the Miro up to Nietzsche."

Puns rarely hold up when repeated. The *mise en scène* and spontaneity are missing; only the groan survives.

parsec

A number of such explosions in the past have occurred closer than *ten parsecs* (32.6 light years).

parsec—a unit of astronomical length (a measurement for interstellar space) based on the distance from earth at which stellar parallax is one second of arc and equal to 3.258 light years, or 19.2 trillion miles. The word is an acronym made up of *par*allax + a *sec*ond (of time).

peripeteia

The Greek drama that the author had made of his life demanded a *peripeteia,* some dramatic incident to salvage the slow decline of his career.

peripeteia—a sudden, unexpected reversal of circumstances in a literary work; a similar change in actual affairs. (Both definitions are relevant in the passage above.)

pettifoggery

The result of such *pettifoggery* (barring Soviet scientists from professional meetings in the United States) can only be to keep away from America all significant international meetings, leaving Americans who are curious about Communist advances to beg for admission to Communist countries.

pettifoggery—quibbling over petty details (from Fr. *petit*, small). *Pettifogger* is also someone who engages in legal chicanery.

phatic

> She seems never to have heard of what linguists call *phatic* speech, the kind of sentences that merely make a friendly noise, like "Have a nice day."

phatic—establishing an atmosphere of sociability rather than communicating ideas (from Gr. *phatos*, spoken). (See **buzz words**.) Some amateur neologist has come up with the word: to *havernize*.

phylogeny (See ontogeny)

plangency, plangent

> .   The English poems lack the significant sound-play, the frequent *plangency* of the Hebrew originals.

plangency—lamentation, wailing (from L. *plangere*, to lament, weep, beat one's breast). Rigoletto, father of the abducted Gilda, feeling guilt as well as unbearable grief, can express himself only by beating his breast and wailing, *"Piangi, piangi"* (weep, weep).

English words that begin with *pl, bl, cl, chl,* or *fl* invariably appear in Italian as *pi,* as above; *bi,* as in *bianco,* blank, white; *chiaro,* clear; *fiore,* flower, etc.

polity

> The Government has always identified itself as an Islamic *polity,* dedicated to the service of Islam's holy places, its adherents, its ideals, its achievements, and its final authority in men's affairs.

polity—a politically organized unit, a nation.

prolegomenon

His book is too short for its purpose, and must be regarded as no more than a suggestive *prolegomenon* to its important theme. (*TLS*)

prolegomenon—a long introductory essay (from Gr. *pro*, beforehand + *logein*, to say). A *proem* is a short introduction or preface, from Gr. *pro* + *oime*, song.

proleptic, prolepsis

The poem Lord Alfred Douglas wrote was entitled "De Profundis," a *proleptic* irony: its tenor is that he has a love but cannot say, because of its nature, who his love is. (*TLS*)

proleptic—dealing with an event before it could have taken place; anticipatory. In the poem by Lord Alfred Douglas referred to above, the irony was *proleptic* because Oscar Wilde was still to write *his* famous *De Profundis* after his imprisonment.

psephologist

France provides the latest example of the danger of using polls. France has just said a very resounding no to the left-wing would-be government, confounding all the opinion polls and all the *psephologists*.

psephologist—one who by use of statistics evaluates election returns. From Gr. *psephos*, pebble, used in voting, just as Gr. *ostrakon*, shell, was used when voting to *ostracize* an official.

psychotropic

He helped conduct a survey regarding the use by psychiatrists and doctors on the medical staff of *psychotropic*, or mind-altering, drugs.

psychotropic—defined in the passage. From Gr. *psycho-*, mind + *trop*, turning.

Also: *heliotrope,* turning toward the sun (*helios*); *tropism; entropy.*

pullulate

It sets the tone for a picture that fairly *pullulates* with cheap melodrama and sickening violence.

pullulate—teem, swarm.

rebarbative

He was immersed in the *rebarbative* and cheerless fiction of Dreiser.

rebarbative—grim, unattractive, forbidding, repellent. From Fr. *rébarbatif: faire face à l'ennemi* (L. *barba,* beard), to face beard to beard, which suggests some sort of antagonism.

reify, reification

The intensity of prose needed to *reify* this message could not have been sustained through a long career.

reify—literally, "to make a thing," give definite, concrete form to something that is abstract (from L. *res,* thing). Latin phrases in English: *in re* (in the matter of), *in medias res* (in the midst of things).
Also: *real; realize; rebus.*

revenant

She made her literary debut in 1974 with an extraordinary, poetic novel about a library staffed with eccentrics and haunted by *revenants.*

revenant—ghost, specter, wraith. From Fr. p.p. of *revenire,* from *re,* back + *venire,* come: come back from the dead.

riven

> The Syrians must be laughing all the way back to Beirut—or what's left of that wracked, *riven* city.

riven—torn apart. *Rive* means to tear apart, as in the old ballad "Johnny Campbell":

> "Saddled and bridled and gallant rade he:
> Hame cam his guid horse, but never cam he,
> Out cam his auld mither greeting fu sair,*
> And out cam his bonnie bride riving her hair."

rubric

> The author points to another element that we can loosely put under the *rubric* "plot."

rubric—before the invention of printing, the monks who copied by hand the works of ancient authors or set down the services and holy books of the Church illuminated their own manuscripts. Following the practice of the Roman scribes, the monks used red ink for the headings and parts of chapters. Such a heading, or initial letter, in red was called a *rubric* (from L. *ruber,* red). Since the heading often gave instructions, the word *rubric* came to mean a directive or rule of conduct, as well as a heading. The meaning of *rubric* has been extended still further so that we meet it today in the sense of a special motto, pet phrase, category, classification, settled custom, even shibboleth.

scholiast

> It is true that he used such outmoded slang words as "dumbbell," "lounge lizard," "for crying out loud," "the once-over," "the cat's meow." And no matter what innumerable *scholiasts* of humor contend, it was to him that we owe the immortal simile, "As busy as a one-armed paperhanger with the hives."

*weeping full sore

scholiast—annotator, commentator (from Gr. *scholion,* a marginal note), not to be confused with *scholastic* or *scholasticism.*

sec

As Ko-Ko, his *sec* style, his way with the lines and his ability to dominate the stage showed that he long since had made the part his own.

sec—dry. When describing a wine, it means, of course, not sweet. From Fr. *sec,* dry (L. *siccus,* dry: that's why *desiccated* has two *c*'s). In Shakespeare's time, his characters drank a deal of *sack,* which was any variety of strong *dry* wine from Spain or the Canary Islands. However, the Duke of Clarence in *Richard III* was drowned in a butt of Malmsey, which was a *sweet* fortified white wine, originally from Greece.

Also: *siccative,* causing to dry, and (when used as a noun) a substance that promotes drying as an additive in paints; *exsiccate,* to dry up.

semiotics

The book offers a splendidly original theory about art as a system of signs that foreshadows modern *semiotics.*

semiotics—a general theory of signs and symbols (from Gr. *sema,* mark, sign). In medicine, *semiotics* relates to symptomology.

Also: *semaphore; semiology,* the science of signs in general. *Semiology* now ranks high among vogue words in cinema criticism and analysis, as can be seen from the latest titles of British Film Institute publications.

sesquipedalia

The gem *reprioritization* (seven syllables and 16 letters) is a worthy entrant in the *Sesquipedalian* Sweepstakes.

sesquipedalia—words a foot (*ped*) and a half (*sesqui*-) long.
Also: *sesquicentennial.*

shaman

More than just his formidable intellect, he had an uncanny impact upon people. Whether or not he resembled a *shaman*, his former friend has claimed he did have an aura of one who possessed more than ordinary wisdom.

shaman—a priest of a primitive form of religion (*shamanism*). Followers believe that events are controlled by good and evil spirits who can be influenced or propitiated by a witch doctor or *shaman*. More often used figuratively as an adjective: *shamanistic.*

simulacra

In common with Vladimir Nabokov, Mr. Stoppard can make the English language do handstands and pratfalls, merrily strewing his script with a plethora of puns, a surfeit of *simulacra*—and a high proportion of them are vintage Stoppard.

simulacra—images (from L. *simulare*, to imitate).
Also: *simulate; simultaneous; verisimilitude.*

superfetation

His enormous range of reference, the *superfetation* of tags, allusions, educated winking in at least five languages, has made his name a watchword among all who believe that ostentation is an infallible sign of intellect.

superfetation—teeming production (from L. *super*, above, extra + *fetere*, to bring forth, from *fetus*, offspring).
Also: *effete (ef for ex, out + fetus)*, worn out, exhausted).

surcease

She has turned to music lessons for *surcease* from a breakneck pace.

surcease—a temporary respite or end to; cessation. Macbeth, in one of the great soliloquies, ponders the question of where murder ends:

> "If it were done when 'tis done, then 'twere well
> It were done quickly: if the assassination
> Could trammel up the consequence, and catch
> With his surcease success; that but this blow
> Might be the be-all and the end-all here,
> But here, upon this bank and shoal of time,
> We'd jump the life to come."
>
> Shakespeare, *Macbeth*

susurrus

> For weeks there has been a low, persistent *susurrus* of the kind that promises some major event in the city. (*N.Y.*)

susurrus—a low whisper, as suggested by the sound of the word, an example of onomatopoeia.

synecdoche (See **metonymy**)

syllepsis (See **zeugma**)

synergy

> Scientists who knew both winners of the Nobel Prize well unequivocally agree that *synergy* was at work, despite attempts to distinguish between the nature of their separate contributions.

synergy—cooperation, teamwork (from Gr. *syn*, together + *ergon*, work.

Also: *erg*, a unit of *energy*. Also all words like metal-*lurgy*; drama*turgy*; thauma*turg*ist, a magician, one who works miracles (Gr. *thauma*, wonder, miracle).

syzygy

> When an alignment of the earth, moon, and sun,
> known as *syzygy,* occurs at about the same time as
> *perigee,* the moon is pulled even closer to the earth
> and creates even higher tides.

syzygy—the near alignment of three celestial bodies. The word
is a curiosity: a six-letter word with three *y*'s. It also means a
pair of things, especially opposites. From Gr. *syn,* together +
zygon, a yoke.

tabescent

> He poured tea with great delicacy, his long and
> *tabescent* fingers clasping the handle of the silver
> teapot. (*TLS*)

tabescent—referring to progressive wasting or withering away
(from L. *tabere,* to waste away). (See **marcescence**)

taxonomy

> *The Murder of Roger Ackroyd* provided *taxonomists*
> of the detective story with the adjective *acroidal,* used
> to denote that sub-species narrated by the character
> [who is] eventually revealed as the murderer.

taxonomy—the science of classification. Europe's great tax-
onomists of the eighteenth and nineteenth centuries were
Linnaeus (Swedish), Cuvier, and Lamarck (French). Linnaeus,
a botanist, was the originator of taxonomic classification.

A friend, after reading a student's Ph.D. thesis, asked
her why she had used *taxonomy* when *classification* would
have been more suitable. Her reply: "*Taxonomy* has an aura
about it. In some kinds of writing, words have to be dressed in
evening clothes."

Also: *taxon* (plural *taxa*), large categories of species.

teleology, telic

If you have seen any movies made in Greece, you know that the word ΤΕΔΟΣ (TELOS) means "The End." Therefore, *teleology* means study of final causes, and *telic* means purposive, denoting an end or purpose.

tenebrous

> This country is a terrible police state, as brutal, *tenebrous,* calculating, vicious, and somber as any other South American dictatorship.

tenebrous—gloomy, dark. *Tenebrism* is a style of painting specifically associated with Caravaggio (1565–1609) and his followers, who hid most of the figures in shadow while strikingly illuminating others. In Italian these painters are referred to as *Tenebrosi,* "the somber ones."

tergiversation

> Those of us who try to function under the windblown umbrella of the humanities cannot deny that given the *tergiversations* of certain colleagues, we do not need enemies today.

tergiversation—changing of sides, desertion of a cause, apostasy, going one way and then another. From L. *tergum,* back + *versare,* to turn (literally to turn one's back on).
> Also: *versatile, traverse.*

theophany

> Since the problem here is *theophany,* knowledge of the infinite, the author plies us with passionate yearnings that overpower his plot and overwhelm his sentences.

theophany—divine manifestation; visible appearance of a deity (from Gr. *theo-,* God + *phanein,* to show).
> Also: *epiphany.*

threnody

> In that production, the play seemed to be a *threnody* to lost, spent youth.

threnody—a song of lamentation, funeral song, *dirge*, which, by the way, is a contraction of the first word of a Latin funeral service that begins: *Dirige, Domine, Deus meus, in conspectu Tuo viam* (O Lord, my God, direct my way in Thy Sight). This is based on Psalms 5:8, "... make Thy way straight before my face."

tocsin

> With her usual sensitivity to potential threats to the city's livability, Ada Louise Huxtable has been sounding the *tocsin* for more stringent regulation of building in the increasingly more congested heart of Manhattan.

tocsin—an alarm sounded on a bell; a warning bell.

> "That all-softening, overpowering knell,
> The tocsin of the soul—the dinner bell."
> Byron, "Don Juan"

traduce

> Dozens of writers and public figures have found themselves *traduced* in fiction while they were still around to read it.

traduce—slander, malign, vilify, defame, calumniate (from L. *trans,* across + *ducere,* lead [down the garden path]). This word was gradually come to be used as a synonym for betray. (See **traduttore-traditore**)

transmogrifications

> Throughout much of our human history, the old, whether numerous or few, have been treated with

respect. They have held positions of privilege, as so many of our honorific words imply—senator, veteran, guru, alderman, seigneur, presbyter—all *transmogrifications* of the words for "old."

transmogrifications—ordinarily means changes into grotesque or humorous forms or shapes; in the above excerpt it means transformations with no pejorative overtones—a switch!

troglodyte

The author is nothing if not fair-minded, and I cannot think of anyone better equipped to describe the *troglodyte* face of Yassir Arafat.

troglodyte—prehistoric cavedweller, or one who wishes to live that way (from Gr. *trogle,* hole). Not complimentary.

trope

He has been engaged with mystical texts for many years, deriving from them the main figures [of speech] and *tropes.*

If sometimes he substitutes fanciful *tropes* for the facts of the matter, well, that is poetic license, and what is politics if not another form of heroic verse?

trope—a figure of speech; use of a word in a figurative or metaphoric sense (from Gr. *tropos,* a turn [of phrase]).

> "For rhetoric, he could not ope
> His mouth, but out there flew a trope."
> "Hudibras," Samuel Butler

During the progress of the play with which Hamlet plans to "catch the conscience of the king," the alarmed Claudius asks, "What do you call the play?" to which Hamlet answers, "The Mouse-trap. Marry, how? Trōpically."

ululate

> The ceremony was held at a cemetery overlooking the
> sky-blue waters of the Mediterranean. As women
> keened and sobbed and *ululated,* high-flying friendly
> jets could be heard rumbling overhead.

ululate—wail, howl, lament loudly (from L. *ululare,* to howl).

vatic

> He brought out all this with ever-increasing confidence,
> until for the last hour of his talk it was as a case of *vatic*
> possession, almost, that he confronted us.

vatic—prophetic (from L. *vates,* a prophet).
  Also: *vaticinate,* to foretell, prophesy.

velleity

> The author is also not averse to distorting history a
> little when it suits a *velleity.*

velleity—the slightest wish; lowest form or degree of volition; a
mere wish that does not lead to action. Associate *velleity* with
words akin to *will*: the German *wollen* or the French *voulez.*

venery

> There is the fervor to establish, amid the swirl of self-
> seeking, *venery,* greed, sloth, deception, and sheer
> ignorance, a more edifying and redeeming proposition
> for the conduct of human affairs.

venery—the pursuit of sexual pleasure or indulgence (from L.
venus, veneris, desire, love). Another word *venery* means the
act of hunting, the pursuit of game (from L. *venari,* to hunt).
From the first meaning we get *venereal*; from the second,
venison.

veridical

> Even Ian Fleming has proved susceptible to literary analysis, but le Carré and Len Deighton remain ingenious, *veridical*, documentary rather than imaginative.

veridical—speaking the truth; corresponding to reality (from L. *verus*, truth + *dicere*, to speak).
Also: *verities; veracity; very; verisimilitude* (simul; resembling the truth).

wittol

> On the evidence, her husband was a born cuckold (or, to be precise, a *wittol*).

wittol—a man who knows of his wife's infidelity and tolerates it (from *wit*, related to German *wissen*, to know + cuckold).

zeugma, syllepsis

> Recently in reviewing William Buckley's latest novel, Christopher Lehmann-Haupt got into a good-natured hassle about the difference between *zeugma* and *syllepsis*.

zeugma, syllepsis—even dictionaries and linguists find it difficult to agree on which is which. They agree only that what is generally involved is a verb (or some other part of speech) that is doing *double duty*. In one case there's a syntactical problem; in the other, a verb has two or more objects yoked together, objects that are not compatible, since for each the verb is used in a different sense; for example: *He took his hat and his departure.*

I learned long ago that such a coupling was called a *zeugma*. It is an engaging device, since it is often amusing, as in the TV commercial slogan of Aer Lingus which informs the listener that "We serve eleven cities and Irish ale." Witty, attention-getting, and easy to remember.

In one of his delightful fables in verse, "The Sycophantic Fox and the Gullible Raven," Guy Wetmore Carryl
(1875–1904) uses a zeugma in stanza 3. The fox is speaking:

"Sweet fowl," he said, "I understand
    You're more than merely natty;
I hear you sing to beat the band
    And Adelina Patti.
Pray render with your liquid tongue
A bit from 'Götterdämmerung.' "

Here, "to beat" does double duty with amusing results.
If there are any who want to argue with you that this is a
syllepsis and not a zeugma, be tolerant. It's sure to be a draw.

ziggurat

The proposed new zoning does not envision an ideal
building configuration like the traditional *ziggurat,* or
wedding cake, of 1916 or the slab of 1961.

ziggurat—a temple of Assyrians and Babylonians, a terraced
pyramid with each elevation narrower than the one below.
Used figuratively in the vivid passage quoted.

5. Triple Threat (For Relaxation)

In this chapter we will play a game with synonyms stemming from the three main sources of English words: Anglo-Saxon (used here to include all words of Germanic origin), Latin, and Greek. Synonyms do not always have *exactly* the same meaning. Indeed, *Merriam-Webster's New Collegiate Dictionary* defines a synonym as "one of two or more words of the same language having the same or *nearly* the same essential meaning in all or *some* of its senses." (Emphasis added.)

Since we are dealing with three of a kind (one of them to be supplied by you) it will be easy, by looking at the two synonyms already given, to discover which of the meanings is called for. When a person says he is cool, calm, and collected, he is playing this game, for he is using synonyms in a collective sense (*cool* has several meanings, as has *collected*), and he has also tapped the three main sources of our language: cool (Anglo-Saxon), calm (Greek), collected (Latin).

It may seem a little surprising to learn that *calm* has a Greek ancestry. Actually, it comes from the Greek word *kauma,* which means great heat, the heat of noonday, when people rested from their work and tried to relax and be calm!

Example:

Anglo-Saxon	Latin	Greek
foretell	predict	_ _ _ _ _ _ _ _

The answer is *prophesy*. The word *prognosticate*—from the Greek, too—would also be correct except that a word of only eight letters is called for. On the other hand, although the word *forecast* would fit the number of letters called for, it would be in the wrong column, since it is Anglo-Saxon, not Greek, in origin.

In case you would like to know how well you have done in playing TRIPLE THREAT, here are my suggestions for scorekeeping. There is a total of 98 correct answers. If, out of this total, you missed:

0–5	You are *sui generis*
6–10	You're some kind of genius
11–20	You are top echelon
21–30	You have no mean linguistic talent
31–40	You're doing all right
Over 40	You're human

From time to time I have given hints by supplying the initial letters of the missing synonym. You will find the answers at the end of this chapter.

GAME A

Anglo-Saxon	Latin	Greek
1. _ _ _ _ _	humorous	comical
2. teacher	_ _ _ _ _	mentor
3. ape	imitate	_ _ _ _ _
4. _ _ _	adversary	antagonist
5. madman	_ _ _ _ _ _ _	maniac

Anglo-Saxon	Latin	Greek
6. worship	adore	i_____
7. ___	antique	archaic
8. alike	_____	analogous
9. talk	conversation	_____
10. l___	tabulate	catalogue
11. angry	_____	choleric
12. smell	scent	a____
13. ____	volume	tome
14. top	_____	acme
15. wordbook	dictionary	_____
16. r__	circumference	perimeter
17. true	g_____	authentic
18. forgiveness	pardon	a_____
19. ___	convulsion	paroxysm
20. freedom	_____	autonomy
21. springiness	resilience	e_____

GAME B

Anglo-Saxon	Latin	Greek
1. w_____	sorcery	magic
2. forecast	p_____	prognosticate
3. fiendish	infernal	d_____
4. p____	succinct	laconic

Anglo-Saxon	Latin	Greek
5. gear	e _ _ _ _ _ _ _ _	paraphernalia
6. sluggish	torpid	l _ _ _ _ _ _ _
7. c _ _ _ _	reprimand	criticize
8. saw (saying)	a _ _ _ _	apothegm
9. narrow	provincial	p _ _ _ _ _ _ _
10. s _ _ _ _ _ _	suffocate	asphyxiate
11. thrifty	f _ _ _ _ _	economical
12. fleeting	evanescent	e _ _ _ _ _ _ _
13. p _ _ _ _ _	predicament	dilemma
14. wandering	m _ _ _ _ _ _ _ _	nomadic
15. gift	aptitude	t _ _ _ _ _
16. _ _ _	clamor	pandemonium
17. edge	margin	p _ _ _ _ _ _ _
18. s _ _ _ _ _	salacious	pornographic
19. guileless	i _ _ _ _ _ _ _ _	unsophisticated
20. tiny	minuscule	m _ _ _ _ _ _ _ _ _

GAME C

One might call the triplets in this section identical triplets because in almost every case the meaning of the roots of the three source languages is the same.

Anglo-Saxon	Latin	Greek
1. b _ _ _ _ _	corporeal	somatic
2. heavenly	c _ _ _ _ _ _ _ _	ethereal

Anglo-Saxon	Latin	Greek
3. unfeeling	impassive	a_ _ _ _ _ _ _ _
4. h_ _ _ _ _	occult	cryptic
5. fellow-feeling	c_ _ _ _ _ _ _ _ _	sympathy
6. healthful	sanitary	h_ _ _ _ _ _ _
7. f_ _ _ _ _ _	incendiary	pyromaniac
8. baneful	p_ _ _ _ _ _ _ _	toxic
9. many-tongued	multilingual	p_ _ _ _ _ _ _
10. t_ _ _ _ _ _ _ _	serfdom	helotry
11. cleansing	p_ _ _ _ _ _ _ _	catharsis
12. shapeless	formless	a_ _ _ _ _ _ _ _
13. s_ _ _ _ _ _ _ _	dispersion	diaspora
14. teamwork	c_ _ _ _ _ _ _ _ _ _	synergy
15. manlike	hominid	a_ _ _ _ _ _ _ _ _
16. h_ _ _ _ _ _ _	manual	enchiridion
17. reshape	t_ _ _ _ _ _ _ _	metamorphose
18. overfullness	profusion	p_ _ _ _ _ _ _

GAME D

These triplets are a little bit different, too, in that one of them may be more intensive or different in degree than the other two. For example:

Anglo-Saxon	Latin	Greek
meeting	convention	synod

(*Synod* is obviously a higher-level word than the other two.)

1. _ _ _ _	enormous	colossal
2. guess	c_ _ _ _ _ _ _ _ _	hypothesis

Anglo-Saxon	Latin	Greek
3. sorrowful	doleful	m _ _ _ _ _ _ _ _
4. t _ _ _ _	torment	tantalize
5. world	u _ _ _ _ _ _ _	cosmos
6. muddle	confusion	c _ _ _ _
7. b _ _ _ _ _	mordant	sarcastic
8. friend	c _ _ _ _ _ _ _	crony
9. kinds	classes	c _ _ _ _ _ _ _ _
10. t _ _ _ _ _ _	securely	hermetically
11. talkfest	c _ _ _ _ _ _ _ _ _	symposium
12. carousal	revelry	_ _ _ _
13. b _ _ _ _	rapture	ecstasy
14. curse	m _ _ _ _ _ _ _ _ _ _	anathema
15. gap	hiatus	c _ _ _ _

GAME E

Anglo-Saxon	Latin	Greek
1. w _ _ _	tittle	iota
2. hit-or-miss	d _ _ _ _ _ _ _ _	unsystematic
3. toadyism	obsequiousness	s _ _ _ _ _ _ _ _
4. d _ _ _ _	homunculus	pygmy
5. haven	s _ _ _ _ _ _ _	asylum
6. swearing	profanity	b _ _ _ _ _ _ _
7. a _ _ _	an inebriate	a dipsomaniac
8. riddle	c _ _ _ _ _ _ _	enigma

Anglo-Saxon	Latin	Greek
9. harmful	injurious	d _ _ _ _ _ _ _ _ _ _
10. y _ _ _ _ _ _ _ _	standard	criterion
11. sheer	t _ _ _ _ _ _ _ _ _	diaphanous
12. scattered	occasional	s _ _ _ _ _ _ _
13. b _ _ _ _	origin	genesis
14. beginner	n _ _ _ _ _	neophyte
15. ghost	apparition	p _ _ _ _ _ _
16. f _ _ _ _ _ _ _	preface	proem
17. womanish	e _ _ _ _ _ _ _ _ _	epicene
18. byword	proverb	a _ _ _ _ _ _ _
19. w _ _ _ _	verbose	pleonastic
20. undying	i _ _ _ _ _ _ _	amaranthine
21. forsaker	defector	a _ _ _ _ _ _ _
22. f _ _ _ _ _	intermittent	spasmodic
23. odd	e _ _ _ _ _ _ _ _	idiosyncratic
24. rift	division	s _ _ _ _ _

Answers to Triple Threat

(A) 1 funny, 2 tutor, 3 mimic, 4 foe, 5 lunatic, 6 idolize,
7 old, 8 similar, 9 dialogue, 10 list, 11 irate, 12 aroma,
13 book, 14 summit, 15 lexicon, 16 rim, 17 genuine,
18 amnesty, 19 fit, 20 independence, 21 elasticity

(B) 1 witchcraft, 2 presage or predict, 3 diabolical, 4 pithy,
5 equipment, 6 lethargic, 7 chide, 8 adage, 9 parochial,
10 smother, 11 frugal, 12 ephemeral, 13 plight, 14 mi-
gratory, 15 talent, 16 din, 17 periphery, perimeter,
18 smutty, 19 ingenuous, 20 microscopic

(C) 1 bodily, 2 celestial, 3 apathetic, 4 hidden, 5 compassion, 6 hygienic, 7 firebug, 8 poisonous, 9 polyglot, 10 thralldom, 11 purgation, 12 amorphous, 13 scattering, 14 cooperation, 15 anthropoid, 16 handbook, 17 transform, 18 plethora

(D) 1 huge, 2 conjecture, 3 melancholy, 4 tease, 5 universe, 6 chaos, 7 biting, 8 companion, 9 categories, 10 tightly, 11 conference, 12 orgy, 13 bliss, 14 malediction, 15 chasm

(E) 1 whit, 2 desultory, 3 sycophancy, 4 dwarf, 5 sanctuary, 6 blasphemy, 7 sot, 8 conundrum, 9 deleterious, 10 yardstick, 11 transparent, 12 sporadic, 13 birth, 14 novice, 15 phantom, 16 foreword, 17 effeminate, 18 aphorism *or* apothegm, 19 wordy, 20 immortal, 21 apostate, 22 fitful, 23 eccentric, 24 schism

6. Around the World in Many Languages

> Foreign words and phrases such as *cul de sac, ancien régime, deus ex machina, mutatis mutandis, status quo, gleichschaltung, weltanschauung,* are used to give an air of culture and elegance. Except for the useful abbreviations *i.e., e.g.,* and *etc.*, there is no real need for any of the hundreds of foreign phrases now current in English.
>
> George Orwell, "Politics and the English Language" (1946)*

Words recognize no barriers; they respect no immigration laws. That's why no matter how hard a nation such as France may try, through its Académie Française†, to keep the French language pure by keeping English words out, it had to yield, grudgingly, to the importation of the word *pipeline* ‡, but only

---

*Reprinted with permission from H. B. Jovanovich, Inc.
†In 1980, for the first time since its inception in 1634, that organization broke with tradition to elect a woman, Marguerite Yourcenar, to membership.
‡The word the Académie Française wanted used was *oléoduc,* patterned on the word *aqueduc (aqueduct).*

154

provided it was pronounced "peep-lean." Despite the frown of that august body, the number of importations is swollen unofficially by such words as *le veekend, le queek lunch, un flashback, le wait-and-see, le drug store,* and many others.

Japan, on the other hand, holds its doors wide open. The importation of English words is enormous, but with pronunciations that Americans might find difficulty in recognizing—*shiyopingu senta* and *resutoranto,* for instance. Some alarmed linguists say that the language is becoming so swamped with foreign words that Japanese is in danger of losing its identity.

There are no barriers of containment either. The Soviet Union with its KGB has not been able to refuse exit visas to such words as *samizdat* and *gulag.*

Now let's go back to George Orwell's remarks at the head of this chapter. I suppose the English language could survive without importing foreign words, just as we could survive without coffee, tea, cinnamon, Dover sole, ginger, Brie, and caviar. There are always bread and American cheese and coke. But without these foreign words, English would not be the rich and colorful language it is.

They do something. Sometimes a foreign word cuts through and cuts down on verbiage. With only one Spanish word, *incomunicado,* you are saying "held without being permitted to communicate in any way with the outside world." *Détente* is certainly more succinct than "relaxation of tensions." It's prettier, too.

Sometimes we have no equivalent for a foreign word. *Schadenfreude,* a German word, means "the joy (*Freude*) we get from the mishaps or hurt (*Schade*) of others." We could say "the sadistic pleasure we take in the misfortune of others," but even these ten words fall a little short of what is compressed into the one German word.

Sometimes the foreign word or expression is more vivid and picturesque. *Esprit d'escalier,* literally "wit of the staircase," means all the witty things you neglected to say that evening at the party, the bright and brilliant things you thought of on the way home.

And then there's that Yiddish word that has been almost worked to death—*chutzpah*; you could instead use "unmitigated gall" or "nerve" or "raw cheek" and still not get the essence of it. Heywood Broun once said that *chutzpah* could not be defined: an example of it had to be given. His was "When a young man on trial for the murder of his parents pleads for clemency on the grounds that he is an orphan." That's *chutzpah*.

One might ask what is gained by using *cela va sans dire* instead of its literal equivalent, "that goes without saying," in the following:

> Quentin Crisp has his heroes; Gertrude Stein, Tallulah Bankhead, Salvador Dali, Oscar Wilde (*cela va sans dire*), Norman Mailer, Marlene Dietrich, Mae West.

Well, for one thing, *cela va sans dire* is suited to its placement alongside the mention of Oscar Wilde. Then perhaps the writer wanted to soften the cliché overtones of "that goes without saying." The French words, it must be admitted, do add a touch of *je ne sais quoi*, a *soupçon* of elegance.

At any rate, as the world becomes smaller, through satellite comunication there will be more importations everywhere, enriching the languages of all nations.

The listing of languages is alphabetical.

ARABIC AND RELATED MOSLEM LANGUAGES

It is obvious that with the Moslem world in crisis, Arabic words have had to slip into English through sheer repetition, if only to give us names for things we don't have or use, like *chador* or *keffiyeh*.

However, during the Dark Ages, the Arabs were the preservers and transmitters of Greek and Roman learning. Arabs (Moors) ruled over part of Spain for several hundred years, beginning in the early eighth century A.D., and from that period our legacy of words includes: albatross, alchemy, alcohol, alembic, algebra, assassin, burnoose (a long hooded cloak), elixir (a cure-all), cipher, magazine, mattress, minaret, mohair, lute, myrrh, nadir and zenith, saffron, salaam (like the Hebrew *shalom*), sherbet, talcum, talisman, tarboosh (a kind of cap worn by men), tariff, and—perhaps the greatest contribution—zero. The preponderance of words begin with *al,* a prefix meaning *the.*

The contemporary words that follow, since they are new to us, are generally defined in the newspaper item.

ayatollah

The highest title a mullah can hold is that of *ayatollah,* or "reflection of Allah." There are approximately 1,200 ayatollahs in the Shiite world today, and of them six men hold the title of grand ayatollah.

chador

Among the Kurds the women, dressed in a rainbow of colors, rarely wear the *chador,* the head-to-ankle shawl that conceals all but the eyes and hands.

fellah

Yet Dayan's patriotism is that of a *fellah.* He seems to know all about the domestication of camels, about sheep and old-fashioned plows and hoes and pitchforks and the habits of mules and donkeys in the fields and the planting seasons and the proper humidity of soils prior to seeding.

fellah—a peasant or agricultural worker in Arabian-speaking countries. Don't confuse with *fedayeen* (*een* is the plural), commandos.

hajj, also hajji, hadjj, hadjji

Today, the King left on a *hajj,* or Moslem pilgrimage to Mecca, during which he is expected to talk with leaders of Saudi Arabia and perhaps other nearby nations.

hajj—the four spellings above are given as a special service for Scrabble players who engage in logomachy.

hegira

The Islamic new year, starting Islam's 15th century, marks the Hegira, or flight of Mohammed from Mecca to Medina in A.D. 622.

hegira—as a common noun it means a mass migration, an exodus, a trek.

imam

Among Shiite Moslems, an *imam* is a representative of Mohammed on earth, and though officially there is no Iranian *imam* at present, a growing number of Ayatollah Khomeini's followers are calling him *imam*.

jihad

Such a struggle, the Ayatollah said, would be, "in general terms, a *jihad*." *Jihad*, an Arabic word, is the term for Islamic holy war.

keffiyeh

The tribesmen, in their white *keffiyeh* headgear, carried themselves with the deportment of seasoned diplomats.

keffiyeh—a headdress worn against dust and heat.

mullah

Masoud surveyed the small crowd crammed into his shop where he sells tape cassettes and said, "I wish those *mullahs* would come here to see just how thirsty the people are for music."

mullah—a religious leader.

FRENCH

auteur

The French invented this word and it means "author." And their theory is that the director of a film is the real author of a film. However, while in Cannes I learned that they made the important qualification that only very great directors can claim the title *"auteur."*

auteur—well defined above. The *"auteur* theory" of film criticism is usually said to date from an article written by François Truffaut in *Cahiers du Cinéma* in 1954.

bête noire

His *bêtes noires* are scientists who insist that man is "nothing but" a killer ape, or a stimulus-response machine, or a bundle of neuroses, or the product of purely random mutation.

bête noire—literally, black (*noire*) + beast (*bête*); pet aversion.

brouhaha

When the Ministry of Education, in error, sends a girls' boarding school, St. Swithin's, to share accommodations with a boys' boarding school, Nutbourne, the resulting *brouhaha* defies description.

brouhaha—commotion, hubbub, uproar.

cinéma vérité

The two men spent more than a year with the neo-Nazis before cameras were allowed to record families and rituals. The style is *cinéma vérité*, using no narration, as the subjects speak for themselves.

cinéma vérité—a much abused and misused *cinéaste* term for what ordinary mortals call candid camera; it amounts to using a hand-held camera to record life and people "as they are," with natural sound and the minimum of rehearsal and editing. It attempts to bring to movies the freer reporting technique of TV and relies strongly on the interview.

coup de grâce

> Gene Garber threw wildly past first base trying to pick off Lopes, who went to second, and Bill Russell followed with a single to center for the *coup de grâce*.

coup de grâce—although the *p* is silent, the *c* in *grace* is pronounced strongly. One Sunday, viewing and listening to a blow-by-blow account of the final moments of a golf tournament, I heard the commentator say, "Trevino, now leading the field at ten under par, is ready for his approach shot. Here it comes. The ball is rolling toward the hole—and drops in—for a birdie. Well, that's the *coup de grah!*" Like many others, the commentator has the mistaken notion that in French every final consonant is silent. Not so. If an *e* follows, the consonant is pronounced firmly. Other similar mispronunciations I've heard on TV include *vichyswah* for *vichysoisse* (*swahz*) and *détahn* for *détente* (*tahnt*)!

Oh, *coup de grâce* means "blow of mercy"; the name given to the blow with which a knight dispatched his vanquished opponent. It is also applied to the final stroke with which a bullfighter ends the bull's agony or to the final action of an executioner. Hence, in its broadest implication a *coup de grâce* is a final, decisive stroke.

cul de sac

> The Norwalk police said the *cul de sac*, 150 yards from the Westport town line, had been used as a lovers' lane for the last 15 years.

cul de sac—literally, bottom (*cul*) + of (*de*), a sack (*sac*); blind alley; place of no exit; dead-end street; impasse.

déjà vu

> What troubles them is a sense of *déjà vu*: once again, the American press seems to be engaged in "breaking" a President; again, the President is firing his closest aide while claiming that aide is the best public servant he has known.

déjà vu—much used (literal meaning "already seen") and sometimes mispronounced as *déjà voo*. The French *u* is made by forming one's lips to say *oo* and saying *ee*. The word is defined in *Merriam-Webster's Collegiate Dictionary* as *paramnesia*: the illusion of remembering scenes and events when experienced for the first time—which is exactly what *déjà vu* means, except that it is used a little loosely, as in the passage quoted. *Paramnesia* is from Gr. *para-*, almost + *-mnesia*, remember (also: *amnesia*—*a*, not; *amnesty*—equivalent to "let's forget it").

Déjà lu, "already read," a feeling that one has already read something, is an interesting addition:

> All these stories are new—copyright 1978—and the unwary reader is thereby spared the nagging sense of *déjà lu* that one gets from many anthologies. (*TLS*)

démarche

> A *démarche* or protest by the Western nations on behalf of Cambodia might have some effect.

démarche—a move, countermove, or maneuver in diplomatic relations. Pronounced *day-marsh'*.

éminence grise

> Tohamy is President Sadat's closest confidant, his *éminence grise*.

éminence grise—literally, "gray eminence"; an intimate counselor who works in the shade.

engagé

It was commonplace then for the *engagé* philosopher to peek in on trade-union meetings, expose present and foreseeable evils, and dash off letters to statesmen in times of national crisis.

engagé—much used in the sense of involved in or committed to a cause.

épater le bourgeois

The document issues from a cabaret spirit, one strand of which has been an impulse to *épater le bourgeois.* But beneath the mockery a great deal is revealed about the subject.

épater le bourgeois—to shock the middle classes.

Bourgeois . . . is an epithet which the riff-raff apply to what is respectable, and the aristocracy to what is decent.
Anthony Hope (1863–1933), *The Dolly Dialogues*

(The amusement known as *épater le bourgeois,* so popular with the "Lost Generation" in the twenties, is revived whenever youth is moved to shock the prevalent mores.)

esprit d'escalier

The French call it *"esprit d'escalier."* The translation is "staircase wit," the bon mot, the clever phrase that comes to mind as one is descending the staircase after a party—the frustration that thinking of a brilliant witticism comes 10 minutes or 4 hours after it could have been uttered.

esprit d'escalier—but all is not lost. Such brilliant afterthoughts can be recycled in a recital of that evening's events, generally introduced by "And then I said. . . ."

It was Ambrose Bierce who carried this bit of cynicism a quantum leap further in his entry in *The Devil's Dictionary*:

> *to remember: to recall with additional details something that never happened.* *

faute de mieux

> With his bench depleted by injuries, the skipper sent in an untried rookie *faute de mieux,* and luckily the youngster delivered.

faute de mieux—for want of something better.

fin de siecle

> In the story one becomes aware of the insistent repetition of such words as cloak, lover, passion, darkness, lilies, silk and wind. Good heavens—these words evoke the mood of the *fin de siècle*—and not the *fin* of this century of ours, now on the way down and out.

fin de siècle—"end of century"; referring specifically to the nineteenth century, whose closing years are characterized in literature as decadent, sophisticated, world-weary, devoted to escapism, extreme estheticism, and fashionable despair. Here we see again why such foreign phrases are used: all these ideas are evoked by three little words!

---

*That's how I remembered the entry. But when I checked with Bierce I found instead:

> *to recollect: to recall with additions something not previously known.*
Since this was my recollection of what Bierce wrote, I decided to let it stand to emphasize the point made about the fickle goddess Mnemosyne.

frisson

> But the shiver down the spine—the *frisson* for its own sake—never inspired Dickens. His *frisson* was that of indignation and pity at all the suffering and injustice of the world.
>
> Edgar Johnson, NYRB

frisson—a shudder or shiver as of excitement, fear, pleasure, or thrill; a chill up (and down) your spine.

lèse majesté

> For many years it was *lèse majesté* to discuss Eliot's first marriage—a conspiracy of silence was kept up, and "The Waste Land" was taught as an exercise in mythology.

lèse majesté—offense against a ruler; any such action against a person to whom deference is due; any affront to another's dignity.

longueurs

> Berlioz' "Roméo et Juliette" is full of brilliant and original concepts, but it also has its moments of *longueurs*.

longueurs—dullness; arid stretches.

louche

> The biographer is content to paraphrase Isherwood's own published accounts of events, with the addition of a few *louche* new anecdotes. (*TLS*)

louche—shady; of questionable character; phony; improper; disreputable. The French means "squint-eyed." From L. *luscus*, one-eyed.

métier

> He found his *métier* in journalism, and particularly in that kind of frontier reporting in which he almost always worked alone.

métier—the work one is particularly suited for. Why not use the English word *job, work, profession, trade*? Because to get the full meaning of *métier*, these words need a modifying adjective, like *chosen, true, most suited,* etc. (In the passage above, "his" *métier* suggests the one most suited to him.) *Métier* has all these overtones in one word. We can see it again in the cynical remark attributed to Heinrich Heine on his deathbed: "Dieu me pardonnera; c'est son métier."

noblesse oblige

> In the tradition of Acheson, Cyrus Vance was urbane, and he served out of a sense of *noblesse oblige.*

noblesse oblige—"nobility obliges, or has its obligations." This French maxim was anticipated by Euripides in an extant fragment of *Alcmene*: "The nobly born must nobly meet his fate."

Just as the code of chivalry prescribed honorable conduct for a knight, so noble birth imposed the obligation of noble actions. Those who consider themselves the upper level of society must act in a supposedly superior manner; or, as Emerson put it (*Progress of Culture*): "*Noblesse oblige*; or, superior advantages bind you to larger generosity."

As used today, *noblesse oblige* implies that more is expected from certain persons in keeping with their background, office, or position.

parti pris

> Once past Tolstoy's *parti pris,* there remains a literary masterpiece of awesome scope.

parti pris—"having taken a side": preconceived opinion, a settled policy, bias, prejudice.

rechauffé

His book is a strong and cleverly prepared counter-attack in the name of science in the Great American Literary Sex War (though served to us, four years after the American version, somewhat *rechauffé*). (*TLS*)

rechauffé—literally, "warmed over"; rehashed; any used or old literary material worked up in a new form.

roman à clef

He served in the Kennedy and Johnson administrations and was Jimmy Carter's speechwriter in 1976. So that it is no surprise that "First Family" is a *roman à clef*, and the *clef* fits several locks.

roman à clef—"novel with a key"; a novel in which real characters and events figure under a disguise. They become recognizable if the reader has a "key" to their identity.

sans-culottism

The most lamentable effect of this mind-body split has been literature of sexual explicitness which has degenerated this year into a lucrative new *sans-culottism*.

sans-culottism—literally, "without trousers or breeches." A term of contempt, *sans-culottes* was used by the French aristocrats for the poorly dressed revolutionists, who wore pantaloons instead of knee-breeches. Now *sans-culottism* refers to any extreme radical or revolutionary movement.

trompe l'oeil

But is it a case perhaps of *trompe l'oeil* painting? I can soon settle that.

trompe l'oeil—used chiefly in art for a painting that tricks (*trompe*) the eye (*l'oeil*), making one for a moment believe that parts of the painting seem to come out of the canvas toward the viewer.

vespasiennes

> In the years after World War I there were more than 1,200 *vespasiennes* in Paris.... According to the mayor's count, there are just 103 today.

vespasiennes—kiosk-like public conveniences (long ago called *chalets de nécessité* by Parisians) named after the Emperor Vespasian, who was not the first to install them in Rome but was the first to impose a tax on their use.* History does not say whether that was the reason these facilities were so named.

GERMAN

Having the same parentage as English, German has many words similar to ours, but the same word may have different though related meaings: *Kraft* in German means strength; in English, *craft* is a particular kind of strength; the cognate of *sterben,* to die, is *starve,* a particular kind of dying.

German Pronunciation

In German words some of the consonants have sounds different from ours: $v = f$, $w = v$ as in *Volkswagen*; initial $s = z$, as in *sagen*, to say; initial $z = ts$, as in *Zeitung,* newspaper; initial *st* and *sp* are pronounced *scht, schp.* Fortunately, the vowels are fairly well stabilized: *a* is always the *a* in *father;* *e* is either *bet* or *bait*; *o* is often as in *go*; *u* is as in *boot.* Umlaut *ü* is very much the same as French *u*; form your lips to say *oo* and let your tongue say *ee*.

---

*Suetonius, *The Twelve Caesars.*

Capitalization

In German all nouns are written with a capital first letter. I will use a lower case initial letter, treating the borrowed German word as an English word. However, where the writer of the excerpt has kept the capital, it is retained.

angst

> In their *angst* over finances, college presidents who are abandoning colleagues for age-old reasons are in this instance abandoning sense.

angst—this excerpt gives the literal meaning of *angst*—anxiety, fear. However, the word is more often used in a wider sense. *The Reader's Encyclopedia* quotes the German philosopher Martin Heidegger: "Human existence is characterized by personal consciousness and accompanied by feelings of insecurity and dread. *Angst* is not fear of anything specific but a dread of nothingness."

Since many contemporary writers plumb the sense of metaphysical anguish in their works—dramatists particularly (Beckett is the supreme example)—*angst* is a recurrent word in literary criticism.

bildungsroman

> But the English title [*The Education of a True Believer*] has a special validity of its own. The book is much like a *Bildungsroman,* the story of a character's education in the broadest sense of becoming.

bildungsroman—a novel (*roman*) that deals with the development or education or maturation of the main character. *Hochgebildet* means highly educated.

doppelgänger

> When a long lost painting by Dieric Bouts, a 15th century Flemish master, was sold at auction for

$3,740,000, Derek John, a specialist in art discoveries, said, "I saw the two [paintings] were by the same hand. It was like seeing the *doppelgänger* of the picture I had found."

doppelgänger—doppel, double + *gänger,* goer, a person's ghostly counterpart and companion or just a "double" as here. In *The Secret Sharer,* Conrad tells of a young captain who takes on board, hides, and saves a murderer who is psychologically and physically his "double." The symbolism becomes obvious in the following:

"But for the grace of God there goes John Bradford." Said by Bradford on seeing some criminals taken to be executed.

echt

Not a mirror-image of the author, Susanna is *echt* Hollywood royalty, the granddaughter of a First Tycoon, modeled on the entrepreneurs who founded the great studios and ran them as their personal fiefdoms.

echt—genuine, authentic, the McCoy.

gemütlichkeit

He sees today's Germans as vacillating between the abstractions of phenomenology* and the *Gemütlichkeit* of old drinking songs.

gemütlich, gemütlichkeit—agreeable, agreeableness; congeniality.

gestalt

Perhaps his most trenchant insight was that *Gestalt* perception—the capacity to discern an underlying

---

phenomenology: The theory that limits knowledge to phenomena only (things known only through the senses).

pattern across seemingly diverse data—underlies not only recognition of the same object under various conditions but also the formulation of enduring scientific generalizations.

gestalt—configuration; perception of the whole (best defined in the excerpt). What the great chess masters have: they don't see individual pieces; they see the pattern made by those pieces.

kaput

Skylab is falling. The huge satellite is wobbling about up there like a drunk at a NASA Christmas party, and one of these days its orbit will go *kaput* and Skylab will come tumbling down.

kaput—broken, wrecked, incapacitated, destroyed; *gehen kaput,* go to pieces.

kitsch

The Alchemist, also directed by him, was a very different kettle of *kitsch.*

kitsch—this increasingly popular word comes from a verb meaning to slap a work of art together. In critical and literary circles, *kitsch* contemptuously characterizes sensational, slushy, slick writing or art designed for popular appeal. Synonyms: *trash, rubbish.*

luftmensch

Then there is the second or semi-public persona, the one who has made enemies and alienated people. He is a thinker who never has an unspoken thought, the huckstering *Luftmensch* who invariably lands on his feet.

luftmensch—someone with his head in the clouds (*luft,* air + *mensch,* man). Also: *Luftwaffe,* air force; *Lufthansa.*

realpolitik

> *How Long Will South Africa Survive* provides the general reader with a scholar's insights into the amoral world of international *realpolitik* as it impinges on the fate of southern Africa.

realpolitik—practical politics; a euphemism for power politics.

schadenfreude

> Although he had a tendency to describe his charac-ters with a touch of irreverence and cruelty—his comedy is pure *Schadenfreude*—"the joy of damage."

schadenfreude—"harm" + "joy"; a feeling of enjoyment de-rived from the misfortunes of others; a sort of Aristotelian catharsis of the lower emotions.

> In the misfortune of our best friends, we find some-thing that is not exactly displeasing.
> François, Duc de la Rouchefoucauld
> (1613–1680), *Maximes supprimées*

> I am convinced that we have a degree of delight, and that no small one, in the real misfortunes and pains of others.
> Edmund Burke (1729–1797),
> *On the Sublime and the Beautiful*

schmaltz, schmalts

> Changing from one fur coat to another, from one sequin suit to another, the performer plays classical music and popular songs, all in his inimitable style of shameless *schmaltz*.

schmaltz, schmalts—something stickily sentimental, banal. Ap-parently not derived from Yiddish, in which it means only "rendered fat."

GREEK

Ancient Greek has contributed to the formation of thousands upon thousands of English words, often by way of Latin, and is continuing increasingly to do so as words have to be coined to keep pace with advances made in medicine, psychology, and the sciences or to provide names for new discoveries and inventions. The following list may therefore seem rather brief, but many Greek words already firmly established (*hubris, psyche, eureka,* for example) are recorded in the body of the book.

The tendency of some translators today is to go back to classical Greek orthography rather than to use the more familiar spellings of Greek names as filtered through Latin. In a contemporary and beautiful translation of Homer's *Odyssey* by Robert Fitzgerald, we meet the enchantresses Kirkè and Kalypso, the heroes Akhilleus and Aias (Ajax), and the fearsome couple Skylla and Kharybdis.*

Greek Plurals

There are a few words taken over from Greek (and Latin) that still retain their original plurals. In some cases we can use either. However, one must take care: *phenomena,* for example, is plural and not singular as some think and write.

In Greek, words ending in *is* form their plurals by changing *is* to *es* (pronounced *eez*): analysis, analyses; crisis, crises; hypothesis, hypotheses; oasis, oases; synopsis, synopses. Words ending in *on* form their plurals by changing *on* to *a*: criterion, criteria; phenomenon, phenomena.

So here are a few of the less familiar words from Greek—the language of wisdom, as George Bernard Shaw called it—that you may come across in your reading.

---

*The *kh* represents (or transliterates) the Greek X (*chi* or *khi*), a sound made by pronouncing the letter *h* far back in the throat as if one were clearing it or gagging.

agape

Now more than ever, what we need in this troubled world is the application and practice of what the Greeks called "*agape*."

agape—pronounced with three syllables: *ah-ga-pay.* Spiritual love or unselfish love as contrasted with *eros* (erotic), physical love.

Byron used the corresponding verb *agapo,* I love, as part of the refrain of a charming poem, "Maid of Athens, Ere We Part":

"Maid of Athens, ere we part,
Give, oh, give me back my heart!
Or, since that has left my breast,
Keep it now, and take the rest!
Hear my vow before I go,
Ζωη μον, δας αγα πω.
(Zoë moo, sahs agapo.)*"

hetaīra (also hetaēra)

In the upper reaches of society, women clearly had more scope for exercising their special gifts, though evidence is sadly lacking. One did not have to be a *hetaira,* like Pericles' mistress Aspasia, to achieve this.

hetaira, hetaera—plural, *hetairi* or *hetaerae.* A highly cultivated courtesan of a special class in ancient Greece; a female companion.

hoi polloi

But an added emphasis is being placed on "sizes," or larger gem diamonds, the kind that will not adorn the bodies of *hoi polloi,* but will be found wherever the cognoscenti gather to flaunt their affluence.

---

*My life, I love thee.

hoi polloi—the masses; the common people; literally, *hoi*, the + *poly*, many. Therefore, to say or write "*the* hoi polloi" is inelegant and tautologous.

koine

> Italian dialects are disappearing at great speed. Their demise must satisfy the ghost of Mussolini, the arch-enemy of dialectal culture and advocate of a uniform *koine* with grandiose Mediterranean aspirations.

koine—pronounced *coy-nay* or *-knee.* A regional dialect or language that has become the common language of a larger area (from Gr. *koine,* common). At the time of Alexander the Great in the fourth century B.C., three of the four languages spoken in the Peloponnese were gradually blended into "koine," the common Greek tongue. (See **lingua franca**)

HEBREW

The Hebrew of the Bible (Old Testament) is the language spoken by the Israelis, supplemented necessarily by the adoption and adaptation of modern words, generally English. However, just as in France, such invasions are frowned upon by the Academy of the Hebrew Language, as indicated in the headline:

> ISRAEL APPLYING
> THE "BRAKESIM"
> TO FOREIGNISMS.

(Hebrew words are usually accented on the last syllable; since *im,* pronounced *eem,* at the end of a word is the plural form, the word *brakesim* is a double plural.)

aliya

> To encourage a sizable *aliya,* emissaries are stationed in every urban center with a significant Jewish community.

aliya—the Hebrew term for immigration to Israel; literally, "ascent."

behemoth

> These corporate *behemoths*—General Electric, Standard Oil and the like—became so complex that chains of managerial responsibility have effectively diluted control from the top.

behemoth—some authorities think that the colossal creature referred to is the hippopotamus; at any rate *behemoth* is used to denote a large massive animal, the size of the mammoth or mastodon. Figuratively, the term is used to describe anything huge. The increasing number of conglomerates are sometimes called *behemoths,* and the bass fiddle is called the *behemoth* of musical instruments.

kibbutz (plural, kibbutzim)

> The communities—some of them moshavim, or cooperatives, others *kibbutzim,* or communal settlements—consist on the average of several hundred Israelis each.

kibbutz—"gathering"; specifically, a collective farm or settlement under communal ownership and management in modern Israel. *Moshavim* are cooperatives.

minyan

> In Dorohol, barely 10 miles from the Soviet border, 650 Jews, the last of 8,000 who survived the war, are carrying on the shtetl tradition. For them life goes on as always, and if the Jewish community of Rumania has its way, it will go on until the last of them can no longer assemble the 10 adult males for the daily *minyan* for prayer.

minyan—a quorum, constituting 10 males over 13 years of

age, necessary for public prayers. There is a movement, characteristic of our time, to allow women to be eligible to be counted in a *minyan.*

pilpul

> This is the heart of the so-called but grievously misnamed "race–I.Q. controversy." The rest is *pilpul.*

pilpul—serious discussion or argument over points of interpretation of holy writings, especially of the Talmud. The use of the thumb in its gyration down and then up to suggest the different possibilities or points of view is of the gravest importance. The syllables *pil* and *pul* somehow suggest the movement of the thumb down and then up. As an English acquisition *pilpul* is used to suggest subtle argumentation about complex points, intricately arrived at.

sabra

> Those in line represented a cross section of Israel. They included concentration-camp survivors, young *Sabras* (native-born Israelis), people from Oriental countries.

sabra—actually of Aramaic or Arabic origin. It is the name of an edible cactus flourishing in the Negev (the desert region of southern Israel) that is hard and tough on the outside but soft and sweet on the inside, like the prickly pear. *Sabra* is a descriptive name affectionately applied to native-born Israelis. The ä in *sabra* is pronounced like the *ä in father.*

tohubohu

> Not in Alfred Nobel's time, but in our own era, has mankind become capable of destroying itself and returning the earth to "*tohubohu*," primordial chaos.

tohubohu—from *tohu,* confusion + *bohu,* emptiness = chaos.

W3 quotes Walter Lippman: "bringing order out of the tohu-bohu of human relations." *Tohubohu* was French before it was English, having been used by Rabelais some 50 years before it appeared in English. The Hebrew *tohu v'vohu* is found at the beginning of the Book of Genesis:

> "And the earth was *without form,* and *void,* and darkness was on the face of the deep."
>
> (King James Version)

INDIAN (Sanskrit)

ashram

Hindu *ashrams* across the country are regularly attended by people who graft the teachings of gurus onto their Christian heritage without abandoning the church.

ashram—a secluded place of worship, a religious retreat.

dhoti

Like most leaders of the movement, he does have a shaved head, a saffron-colored flowing garment called a *dhoti,* and streaks of Ganges River mud on his forehead.

dhoti—a Hindi word. "A flowing garment" is what it says in the passage quoted, but my three desk dictionaries call it "a loin cloth worn by Hindu men." So do W2 and W3. Also *dhooti.*

mantra

Indira Gandhi gravely listened as Allen Ginsberg, palms reverently pressed together, chanted *mantras* at her.

mantra—a sacred, often secret word or formula chanted or intoned; a passport to nirvana.

nirvana

nirvana (often *Nirvana*)—a state of oblivion to the care or pain of the external world; a condition of great peace or bliss; inner peace. In both Buddhism, where the state of absolute blessedness is characterized by release from the cycle of reincarnations, and Hinduism, where it is characterized by reunion with Brahma, *nirvana* is attained through the suppression of desire, the extinction of the self and of individual existence.

yoga, yogi

Yoga is an Eastern discipline normally identified with Hinduism. It aims at mental tranquility through postures, breathing exercises, meditation and other practices.

yoga (often *Yoga*)—the discipline aimed at mental tranquility through a system of exercises. *Yogi* is a person who practices yoga.

ITALIAN

To indicate tempo and mood in musical compositions, Italian words are almost exclusively used. Almost—for sometimes, especially in the cases of Gustav Mahler and Claude Debussy, the language of the composers is also used. Here is a sampler:

	German	*Italian*	*French*
lively	*lebhaft*	*vivace*	*vif* or *animé*
slow	*langsam*	*adagio*	*lentement*
slowing down	*zurückhaltend*	*rallentando*	*retenu*

(My favorite notation is the German *nicht schleppen*, don't drag.)

Perhaps a few words on pronunciation may help those unfamiliar with Italian: *chi* = key; *ci* = tshee; *ce* = tshay; *sci* = she; *sce* = shay. In the *gn* or *gl* combination, the *g* sound is not heard. It has actually disappeared in *conoscenti.* No *dig* in Modigliani, just *modilyani*; imbroglio = *imbrolyo.*

ben trovato

There are hundreds of anecdotes about Hašek, which Sir Cecil says are more *ben trovato* than true, but the book would have been dull if they were all omitted. (*TLS*)

ben trovato—ben(e), well + *trovato*, found (as in French *trouvé*, or English treasure *trove*). In short, *ben trovato* means well found (appropriate to the situation) but not well founded.

bravura

Whatever it is that we value in great letter writers—a new voice, rapid shiftings of tone, sudden flares of *bravura*, keen notice of the surrounding world—is only occasionally present in Wilson's letters.

bravura—"bravery, bravado," a bold attempt or display of dash, daring brilliance; in music, a performance that deserves the accolade of *"Bravo!"* If you are a shouter at operas, use *brava* for a diva or a prima donna, and *bravi* for the sextette from *Lucia.*

brio

How he prepared for and undertook his mission is handled by the authors with an unfailing *brio* and constantly mounting suspense.

brio—animation, spirit, vivacity, liveliness, sprightliness.

chiaroscuro

> The late Mr. Trilling taught me that the occasional ugliness of American life is part of the *chiaroscuro,* so to speak, of our eccentricity, of our starred and striped individuality.

chiaroscuro—chiaro, clear, light + *oscuro,* dark, shadowy; a sharp contrast, interplay of light and shade to produce the illusion of depth or dramatic effect. Rembrandt's painting "Night Watch" is a famous example in art. The word is often used figuratively, as in the quoted passage.

ciao

This familiar Italian word (pronounced *chow*), which is used when meeting or leaving friends, has an interesting history. It goes back to Latin *sclavus,* slave, then appears in Italian as *schiavo* (I am your), slave, and finally becomes, in Italian dialect, the much reduced *ciao.* Of course, *I am your slave* has no such meaning in this context, any more than did Samuel Johnson's use of the "complimentary" close in his scathing letter to Lord Chesterfield, who on the eve of the publication of Johnson's famous dictionary had offered to become his patron. ("Is not a Patron, my Lord, one who looks with unconcern on a man struggling for life in the water, and when he has reached ground, encumbers him with help?") To this Johnson signed himself:

> My Lord,
> Your Lordship's most humble
> Most obedient servant,
>   Sam. Johnson

cognoscenti

> So the audience he addresses is perforce one of *cognoscenti*—not only those readers acquainted with the large body of Milton's writing but also those on intimate terms with British poets.

cognoscenti—it means "the knowing ones"; this plural form is given because the singular, *cognoscente,* is rarely met. *Cognoscenti* (now written *conoscenti* in Italian) are those who have expert knowledge, or expertise. The French equivalent of *cognoscente* is *connoisseur*; the Yiddish, *maven.*

commedia dell'arte

> There is his *commedia dell'arte* period—masks and harlequins and fanciful creatures in the crazy patterns of what he calls the "theater of life."

commedia dell'arte—a type of popular Italian comedy which had its greatest vogue in the sixteenth and seventeenth centuries. It was performed by specially trained troupes of actors who improvised from standard plots involving a group of familiar formalized characters such as Arlecchino (Harlequin), Pulcinella, Pantaloon, Columbine, and Pierrot. Though it died out in mid-eighteenth century, it founded a tradition of mime (Jean-Louis Barrault, Marcel Marceau, Charlie Chaplin), influenced Molière and Marivaux, and has its echoes in English pantomime, harlequinade, and Punch-and-Judy shows, not to mention countless other theatrical descendants, including Beckett's *Waiting for Godot.*

lingua franca

> This project would open the world of competent, confident and joyous reading not only to our American children but to those in the 90 other nations for whom English is a required course. English is, in fact, the *lingua franca* of the modern world.

lingua franca—"the Frankish language"; name given to a mixture of Italian, French, Spanish, Greek, and Arabic spoken in Mediterranean ports. Any hybrid language used by peoples of different speech to enable them to understand each other; a common language. (See **koine**)

paparazzi

> Mia Farrow, co-starring with Anthony Perkins, became frightened and distraught at one point, when a phalanx of *paparazzi* popped dozens of flash bulbs all around her.

paparazzi—Italian dialect, plural of *paparazzo*, "a buzzing insect"; photographers, especially free-lancers, who pursue sensational scoops for magazines and newspapers, taking candid shots as they swarm around celebrities.

sotto voce

> The steel-drum combos, the walking stereos, the businessman boasting *sotto voce,* "I have a hook-up from here to California"—we liked the drama of the urban scene.

sotto voce—"under the voice"; privately, aside, in an undertone or whisper.

traduttore-traditore

> It is high time for translators to quit trying to inherit the earth by succumbing meekly to that tired old *traduttore-traditore* cliché, or the maybe-malice-made mot of Frost's that poetry is that which gets lost in translation.

traduttore-traditore—"translator" + "traitor," expresses the notion that poetry cannot be translated, that something is lost in trying to achieve the rhythms and emotional effect as well as the thought of the original. But sometimes something may be gained: Edward Fitzgerald's "The Rubaiyat of Omar Khayyam" and the King James translation of the Bible come to mind.

verismo

> Nobody in American crime fiction so captured the imagination as Dashiell Hammett and none so established the convention of the *verismo* school of crime writing.

verismo—"truth"; the doctrine of reality; realism confronting the hard facts of life and depicting life faithfully.

In Italy near the end of the nineteenth century a competition that attracted 70 contestants was held for the best one-act opera. The winner, as every opera buff knows, was Pietro Mascagni. His *Cavalleria Rusticana,* performed in 1890, made opera history, launching not only Mascagni but the whole new trend in opera known as *"verismo."* The blood-and-thunder themes of grandiose historical dramas so long in vogue gave way to naturalistic themes, to characters and situations closer to the audience, and the music, too, was more concerned with human appeal.

JAPANESE

Headline in the *Times:*

> JAPANESE? EASY
> AS "APPARU PAI"

haiku

> Mallarmé wrote her [Misia Sert, a great beauty, friend of artists and poets] a *haiku* on a paper fan every New Year's Day. Verlaine read her his poems and wept into his absinthe.

haiku—a form of Japanese lyric poetry consisting of a single stanza of seventeen syllables in three lines: five in the first and third lines, and seven in the second. So popular is the *haiku* that hundreds of thousands of new haiku are published every year in Japanese newspapers and magazines.

kabuki

> *Kabuki,* the traditional popular theatre of Japan, is an all-encompassing theatre art as evidenced by the name itself.

kabuki—popular Japanese theatre, using highly stylized movement, singing, and dancing. The word can be divided into three separate parts, each a different performing art: *Ka,* music or song + *Bu,* dance + *Ki,* acting.

kamikaze

Other members of Congress see themselves as prudent promoters of new energy supplies and, in turn, regard the first group of Congressmen as *kamikazes,* willing to sacrifice all in their Populist zeal.

kamikaze—a fighter who makes a suicidal crash on a target; an airplane doing the same thing.

samurai

Pre-1600 *samurai* are thought of differently, as being practical warriors, engaged in actual rather than theoretical warfare, ruthless if necessary, but human or even humane on occasion. (*TLS*)

samurai—warrior aristocracy of Japan; those practicing the chivalric code of Bushido.

sayonara

The other day, 2,200 people attended a farewell service for Lan Lan, a panda, at Tokyo's zoo. The First Secretary of the Chinese Embassy read a memorial address, as the specially composed sentimental tune "*Sayonara,* Lan Lan" played in the background.

sayonara—farewell.

shogun

In the 1850's the fearful feudal *shogun* set the village of Yokohama as the site for a foreign settlement.

shogun—literally, "leader of an army"; originally the title of military governors. Associated with this word is *tycoon,* from a Japanese word meaning great lord. *Tycoon* has passed into English to describe an industrial magnate, a man of great power and wealth in the world of business.

LATIN

> We were standing at the first tee waiting our turn. It was one of those rare Adirondack days. In a sudden burst of euphoria, one of our foursome began to declaim the opening lines of the "Aeneid": "Arma virumque cano, Troiae qui primus ab oris...," at which point his son Joel (age 6), tugging at his father's sleeve, interrupted to say, "No secrets, Daddy. No secrets."
>
> from "Memoirs of J. C. M."

Certainly to educated Englishmen, even up to the 18th century, Latin was no secret language. In his "English Social History" (1944), George Macaulay Trevelyan writes:

> Grammar school boys, even out of school hours, were not allowed to speak anything but Latin. They were spied on and flogged. During the 1400's, 1500's, 1600's, and as late as the 1700's, Latin was the second language in England.

In the United States rules were not so stringent, but I do remember reading somewhere that long ago at Harvard, students, while on the college grounds, had to converse in Latin. If this is true, it must have been quiet on campus.

Pronunciation of Latin words is a matter of choice. Those who have studied any Latin tend to pronounce it as they did in school. The dictionaries often give an Anglicized pronunciation as well, or a mixed one.

There are a few words taken over from Latin that still retain their original plurals. In some cases we can use either form. *Formulas* is seen more often than *formulae,* but *addenda* and *stimuli* are found more often than *addendums* and *stimuluses.* However, one must exercise some care to distinguish between the singular and plural form. The returning alumnus who greeted a former professor with, "Don't you remember me? I'm an alumni," was properly put in his place when the professor rejoined with, "How singular!"

It's a touchy business. Many think that *media, strata,* and *bacteria* are singular. They aren't. By sheer force of usage, *agenda* and *insignia* have become singular. *Data,* a plural, is used both ways.

How touchy a business it is may be illustrated by *The Andromeda Strain,* where I came upon these two sentences within six pages of each other:

> Perhaps it [intelligent life on a distant planet] was no larger than a *bacterium.* (p. 127, paperback edition)

> Take up a harmless *bacteria* and bring it back in a new form virulent and unexpected. (p. 133)

So there you are! And here, if you're interested, are some singular and plural forms of Latin words often used in English (an *i* ending is pronounced *eye;* an *ae* ending, *ee*):

algae (plural, pronounced *aljee*); *bacillus, bacilli; dictum, dicta; effluvium, effluvia; erratum, errata; medium* (a means of mass communication), *media; stimulus, stimuli; stratum, strata.*

The following have the normal English plural as well as the Latin: Those ending in *us* have the *i* plural; those ending in *um* have the *a* plural:

cactus, fungus (*j* sound in *fungi*), *nucleus; curriculum, memorandum, addendum.*

a priori, a posteriori

> The General Theorists fill the void of ignorance with convenient assumptions and, by ingenious deductions, lead inexorably to what was, *a priori,* to be proved.

a priori—deductive; refers to conclusions derived by reasoning from self-evident propositions, without support of a body of facts; whereas *a posteriori* is inductive, conclusions being based on observed facts and arrived at after (*post*) a study of these facts.

caveat

> In her letter, she is concerned with the possible divisive effect of "teaching the Holocaust." She might also recall the *caveat* of George Santayana that those who forget the past are doomed to repeat it.

caveat—"let (him) beware"; a warning. *Caveat emptor*: "Let the buyer beware."

deus (or dea) ex machina

> Quality education will be determined not by a mayor acting as a *deus ex machina* but by creating better morale in the school system and by better meeting problems in our city.

deus ex machina—"a god from the machine." A god or goddess appearing in a Greek tragedy was brought into view by a crane or derrick. His or her special duty was to ordain the ritual of the tragedy or to bring the action to a quiet close. The appearance (*epiphany*) of the god was interpreted by some critics, like the Roman poet Horace, as proof that the dramatist (notably Euripides) had so piled up complications that he needed divine intervention to untangle the situation. Hence, a thing or person who solves a difficulty artificially and abruptly is called a *deus* or *dea ex machina*.

in flagrante delicto

> It involves the shaming of the tough coal miner who is caught *in flagrante delicto* with the pathetic widow of a recently killed fellow miner.

in flagrante delicto—"while the crime is blazing"; redhanded; in the very act.

in situ

I pledge to support positive labor legislation such as *in situ* picketing and labor law reform.

in situ—"on the site."

in vitro

The *in vitro* fertilization (in a petri dish) and embryo transfer that resulted in the birth of a British baby raises serious social issues and policy questions.

in vitro—"in glass."
Also: *vitreous,* consisting of or resembling glass.

ipso facto

The Mayor of New York is *ipso facto* a national figure; he symbolizes New York, for better or worse, to the nation or the world.

ipso facto—"by the fact itself"; by the very nature of the case. (See **solipsistic**)

lacuna

Naturally, there are *lacunae*; the correspondence between these two famous women must have had literary and political, as well as personal, interest.

lacuna—gap, hole, missing part (from L. *lacus,* lake). The most famous lacuna of modern times must surely be the 18½-minute gap in the Watergate tapes.

mea culpa

We live in a *mea culpa* society, in which we blame ourselves for *every* crime, and in this mood of guilt we both excuse the crime and indirectly encourage its repetition.

mea culpa—"my guilt"; the guilt is mine.
Also: *culprit; culpable; inculpate; exculpate; inculpatory; exculpatory.*

modus vivendi

Even as she and her husband reached a *modus vivendi* of some little distance in their personal arrangements, she became his indispensable adjunct in politics and reform.

modus vivendi—"manner of living"; a feasible arrangement; a way of getting along with another person despite basic differences; "peaceful coexistence."

mutatis mutandis

Mutatis mutandis, there appears to be no end to which hypocrisy, stupidity and prejudice can go to throw up the particular smokescreen which is in fad at the moment to obscure reality and to divert us from the real problems which confront the nation and the world.

mutatis mutandis—with the necessary changes having been made.
Also: *mutation, mutants, immutable, permutations,* all having to do with change; *mutare,* to change.

numerus clausus

The *numerus clausus* is itself a matter of angry contention between the authorities and the students who say that the constitutionally guaranteed right to study also means studying the subject of their choice.

numerus clausus—"number closed"; quota.

obiter dicta (singular, **dictum**)

> He offers us his current estimate of the artist's accomplishments, and in the course of this analysis he also scatters some of his characteristic *obiter dicta* about other artists, past and present.

obiter dicta—things said (*dicta*) in passing (*obiter*); incidental remarks.

pace

> About 11.5 million people were taken from Africa by the Atlantic trade, and most of them (*pace* Alex Haley) reached their destinations "because it was in the interest of the slaving captains to keep their human cargoes alive and in the best condition for the market."

pace—with due respect to; by leave; with apologies to; showing polite disagreement. Pronounced *pay-cee*.

> The Latin word *pax*, peace, as used in English often has a derogatory meaning. *Pax Romana* (or any other) means a peace achieved by force of arms with concomitant slaughter, a meaning the word *pacify* sometimes has.

pari passu

> The worst of it is that with literary senescence goes, *pari passu*, the ability to detect that deterioration.

pari passu—with equal (*par*) step (*passus*).

> Also: *mille passus* (a thousand steps), a Roman mile.

persona (plural, **personae**)

> Disguise was also essential to Hitchcock himself: His public *persona*—the merry, cynical extrovert—concealed severe insecurity and pessimism.

persona—generally, the social facade the individual assumes; the outer personality presented to others; or sometimes the character in a novel who represents the author (the hero and author's *persona*). Much used, sometimes instead of *image*. In Ingmar Bergman's award-winning 1967 film *Persona,* Liv Ullmann, an actress who loses the power to speak, and Bibi Andersson, her nurse-companion—who resemble each other physically—set off a process of mutual psychological identification. Critic John Simon asked: "Could the entire tale have taken place in Alma's (the actress's) mind—was there only one person all along, assuming various '*personae*,' i.e., actors' masks?"

A *persona non grata* is a person who is unacceptable or unwelcome; the term is generally applied in diplomatic situations.

prima facie

In the author's indictment of the network's longtime chairman, he makes at least a *prima facie* case for the chairman's cozy relationship with Presidents, particularly Republican ones, and his deep involvement in G.O.P. politics.

prima facie—"at first view"; plausible; valid at first impression; self-evident.

qua

The late Johnny Mercer was one of the few who were more interested in songs *qua* songs than in songs for musical shows.

qua—"as." Pronounced *kway*.

quidnunc

It seems odd that so useful a word as *quidnunc* should be unfamiliar to most Americans, considering our intense concern nowadays with the matter of privacy. It comes from the Latin *quid nunc*—what now?—and is defined in Webster's as "one who seeks to know all the latest gossip." There is a widespread belief that our own era is on the way to becoming the Quidnuncs' Golden Age.

quidnunc—the above portion of a paid advertisement in the *Times* says it all.

quid pro quo

Thus, monetary policy throttles fiscal policy, and the Administration's commitment to a balanced budget by 1981 becomes the *quid pro quo* for the business community's support.

quid pro quo—something for something; a trade-off.

recto

Not everybody knows that the "Morgan Master" is the name given by Oakeshott in 1945 to the anonymous artist who painted the *recto* of a separate leaf of the Winchester Bible, now in the Pierpont Morgan Museum in New York. (*TLS*)

recto—ablative of *rectus,* "on the right"; on the front side of a page. In printing, the right-hand side of the page, hence the odd-numbered page; *verso* is the "turned-over" page, even-numbered.

reductio ad absurdum

In 30, 50, or 100 years, we will have computers instead of hearts, the ultimate transplant, the *reductio ad absurdum* of cosmetic surgery.

reductio ad absurdum—"a reduction to the absurd"; a train of reasoning in which a proposition is proved false by arguing it to a false, ridiculous, or absurd conclusion; carrying an argument to logical extremes.

sic transit

> "What a man's work comes to! So he plans it,
> Performs it, perfects it, makes amends
> For the toiling and moiling, and then,
>   *sic transit!*"
>   Robert Browning, "Old Pictures in Florence"

sic transit (gloria mundi)—so passes away the glory of the world.

sine qua non

> The New York stamp of approval is no longer the *sine qua non* of a musical career.

sine qua non—"without which not"; an essential or indispensable ingredient.

sui generis

> The Russian intelligentsia of the 19th century were a phenomenon almost *sui generis* in the degree of their alienation from their society and their impact on it. (*TLS*)

sui generis—"of his, her, its own kind"; in a class by himself, etc.; nonpareil; a stronger word than *unique* if that's possible, and I think it is, because *unique* is thrown around rather loosely (very unique, more unique!).

tabula rasa

> The British empiricists maintained that the mind is a *tabula rasa* and that all knowledge derives from experience.

tabula rasa—a clean slate; the mind, supposed by some philosophers to be in a blank or empty state before receiving outside impressions.

tacet

> A *tacet* in music is not a silence; it's a suspension.
> Hear, hear. And I do wish that actors and directors in
> the legitimate theater would do some of the hearing.

tacet—"it is silent"; a "rest" in musical language. In a book on
English that I have before me I notice this advice on good
writing and good conversation: "Occasionally try to find words
that make your listener see as well as hear what you are saying.
And occasionally try to listen. It often shows a fine command of
language to·say nothing." Hear, hear!

> Also: *tacit*; *taciturn*; *reticent*.

vade mecum

> Her book should be a *vade mecum* for aspirant critics
> and, maybe most of all, for dance students.

vade mecum—"go with me"; as used today, *vade mecum*
designates a special kind of reference book, a handbook or
manual, something ready and close at hand; a guidebook.

> "All these things will be specified in time
> > With strict regard to Aristotle's rules,
> The *Vade Mecum* of the time sublime,
> > Which makes so many poets and more fools."
> > > > Byron, "Don Juan"

Byron was poking fun at the interpretation of Aristotle's
Poetics, which was the manual of later writers of epic and tragic
poetry.

vox populi

> Gladstone certainly did not believe that the *vox populi*
> was the voice of God.

vox populi—one-half of the expression "*Vox populi, vox Dei*"
(the voice of the people is the voice of God); further shortened
to *vox pop.*

PORTUGUESE

auto da fé

> It is perhaps difficult to work up sympathy for a man who went to an *auto-da-fé* as blithely as we go to a beauty pageant.

auto da fé—"act of the faith": the ceremony accompanying the pronouncement of judgment by the Inquisition, which was followed by the execution of the guilty by secular authorities; an execution; used figuratively to denote the punishment of an unorthodox person.

RUSSIAN

apparatchik

> The Soviet dissidents themselves are often as dogmatic and intolerant as the Communist Party *apparatchiks* with whom they went to school.

apparatchik—part of the apparatus of the government; secret agents. ("He became a tool of the Soviet *apparat*, parroting official doctrine, a figurehead for Soviet culture"—from a writer's description of a figure in contemporary Soviet life.)

blat

> According to one young composer, a Union member, only those "with enormous influence" (the Russian word for it is *blat*) can hope to obtain that copy of Shostakovich's "Testament."

blat—apparently a word like our "clout."

gulag

A point that ought to be borne home to the Soviet people is that European athletes, unlike their own, have the right to embarrass their governments without being flung into the *gulag*.

gulag—Soviet penal system of labor camps; a Russian acronym for Chief Administration of Corrective Labor Camps. Aleksandr Isayevich Solzhenitsyn's *The Gulag Archipelago* gave the word wide currency. These infamous torture camps were part of Stalinism.

khorosho, chorosho

"Is that correct?"
"Perfectly correct."
"*Khorosho!* You don't deny anything. You're a good man."

khorosho—correct; like O.K., or *d'accord* in French, or *d'accordo* in Italian.

samizdat

They were circulated from hand to hand in Moscow. This was the birth of *samizdat*—privately circulated manuscripts—as a force to be reckoned with.

samizdat—*sam,* self + *izdat,* printed. Underground mimeographed material circulated from hand to hand.
        Also: *samovar* (sam-, self + *varit,* boiled), a large metal urn with a spigot, used to boil water for tea; *samoyed*, Arctic dogs.

ukase

When he agreed to run the company, one of his *ukases* to the firm's investment banker was that neither of them could mention the price of the stock for two

years—a decree as Spartan as one between two newly-
weds not to discuss sex for two years.

ukase—edict, authoritative pronouncement (from Russian
ukaz).

zek

Solzhenitsyn's books were the vengeance of the *zeks*
("I belong to the convict world of Russia," as he says).

zek—Russian prison slang for convict, derived from *zaklyu-
chenny*, the Russian word for prisoner.

SPANISH

aficionado

For nearly 25 years, to the delight of *aficionados* of the
macabre, Edward Gorey has been crosshatching pictures like the one reproduced.

aficionado—fan, devotee, buff (as in opera buff).

barrio

From the doorways of their wooden shacks in the
crowded hillside *barrios*, the slum dwellers of Caracas
have an excellent view of executive jets landing at La
Carlota airport.

barrio—district, quarter of a city in Spanish-speaking countries, often associated, as in this excerpt, with *ghetto*.

bracero

President Carter has ruled out any new *"bracero"*
program to bring in Mexican field hands to work for

American growers, and his Administration is cracking down on aliens now holding jobs illegally in this country.

bracero—a Mexican laborer admitted to the United States for seasonal stay and work. Those who enter illegally are called "wetbacks," because many of them swim across the Rio Grande.

cacique

Cortez had already sent to the *cacique* the best that he had in the way of a whimsical gift.

cacique—in Latin America and Spain, the chief of a tribe, a local political boss.

converso

He explored in his talk the widely held theory that the author of *Don Quixote* was a "*converso*" (a former Jew), as indicated by Cervantes' preoccupation with caste problems in his writings.

converso—"the converted one." Different from *marranos,* Jews who underwent baptism, especially those who accepted conversion to escape persecution, though many practiced their own religion clandestinely. *Marrano* is believed to come from an Arabic word *muharram,* forbidden thing (in this case the eating of pork) + *ano,* Spanish ending. A converso publicly recanted his faith and adopted Christianity under pressure of the Spanish Inquisition.

enchilada

The recent resignation of Mr. Carter's "*big enchilada*" is inconsequential.

enchilada—figuratively, "the big cheese"; actually a tortilla rolled with a mixture of meat and cheese.

macho, machismo

> After Europe, American cars seem far too big and powerful, mad monuments to *macho*.

macho—masculinity, virility. The addition of *-ismo* is equivalent to the addition of *-ism* to an English noun. *Machismo* is pronounced *ma-cheese-mo*.

YIDDISH

> You don't have to be from Pinsk to know that the following terms offer a rich array of alternatives for the overused "jerk": nudnik, schlemiel, shlimazl, shmendrick, shmegegge, shnook and shmo. Please note that the spellings of this lode of invective are just one version, since phoneticization of Yiddish is as contentious as the language itself.
> William E. Farrell, *The N.Y. Times*, August 11, 1980

Yiddish, a language of High German origin, was spoken by the Jews of Eastern Europe, called Ashkenazim. Into the language have entered many Hebrew words as well as words picked up in the various countries where Jews have settled.

Where I had a choice of illustrative sentences, I selected those used by non-Jewish journalists or columnists, because so many of these words have found a permanent place in our written as well as spoken language. You may notice that very often the context is literary.

Since Yiddish is spelled phonetically and transliterated into English, there is only accidental uniformity in the spelling of some words, as Mr. Farrell suggests. There is a group called the Committee for the Implementation of the Standardized Yiddish Orthography, whose address is Columbia University, but theirs is a losing fight, I think, because the spellings now used in our books and newspapers have become so firmly rooted that one would probably hesitate before taking a bite into a *beygel* or would be somewhat puzzled when confronted by the word *khutspe*. *Bagel* and *chutzpah* are already in the mainstream of our language.

However, there *is* a reform that it is not too late to effect. German words never use *sh*; it's always *sch*. On the other hand, Yiddish should never use *sch*; it should always be *sh*. The *ch* will be retained as the *ch* sound found in the Scottish *loch* and *bricht nicht,* the *kh* sound in Russian, the sound of *j* and *x* in Spanish, the X in Greek, and the *khess* in Hebrew. This Yiddish *ch* = *kh* sound is the *h* made far back in the throat.

chutzpah

> One of the new proprietors is an Englishman who had the *chutzpah* to open a wine shop in Paris and, worse, to try to teach the French about their own product.

chutzpah—unmitigated effrontery, gall, nerve, etc. John J. O'Connor has evidently had his fill. In reviewing a new TV show, he writes:

> Enter André, the 10-year-old black kid who wants to work shining shoes in the restaurant. Jimmy keeps tossing him out, but is gradually won over by the boy's—you guessed it—"*chutzpah.*"

klutz, klutzish, klutzishness, klutzy

> Style is what the Grimm brothers preserved, gentle simpletons *klutzing* to glory.

> Her movements, said the *Times* critic, reflect "awkwardly endearing *klutzishness.*"

klutz—a clumsy, awkward person. From German *Klotz*, wooden block, clod, clump. The forms *klutzy, klutziness, klutzdom* also appear.

kvell (See **naches**)

kvetch

> It reflects the pervasive anxiety and endless *kvetching* of Manhattan overachievers. A bad case, in fact, of bottled-up old whine. (Tom Buckley)

kvetch—this can be a verb or a noun. *Kvetching* is habitually complaining, belly-aching, griping. A *kvetch* is one who's always complaining. From German *quetschen*, to squeeze.

macher

> The man who makes the difference is the team leader, the *macher*, the tough out in the last inning, the man who comes up with the big play when it counts.

macher—not related to *macho*; a woman can be a *macher*. A *macher* is a doer, the one who always does what's necessary in a difficult situation. From German *machen*, to make, to do. Often used sarcastically (the Yiddish is "*gantze macher*") in the way "big shot" is.

maven, mayvin

> Ted Williams, the former Red Sox slugger and batting *maven*, has always maintained that a hitter should be moved only by pitches thrown to certain high-percentage-yield areas of the strike zone.

maven, mayvin—expert, connoisseur. Pronounced *may-vin*.

megillah

> He read off the list of offenses as if he was reciting the *megillah*.

megillah—from a Hebrew word meaning scroll, especially the scroll of the Book of Esther read at the festival of Purim. In colloquial usage, *megillah* means a long and detailed story, usually with the implication that it is a boring tale.

mensh

President Carter, speaking from the steps of New York's City Hall last week before signing the government loan guarantee bill for the city, praised New York Governor Carey, saying he is "what we Southern Baptists call a real *mensh*."

mensh—a substantial human being: the highest praise to be given to a person. From German *mensch,* man.

Mme. Rosa (to the little Arab boy she has befriended): Be a mensh.
Momo: What's a mensh?
Mme. Rosa: Soi sage. Even a little boy can be a mensh.
French film, 1977, *Madame Rosa,* directed by Moshe Mizrahi

meshuga, meshuge

Mr. Houseman didn't need the panjandrums of show business; in the *meshuga* world of entertainment, his independence was the guarantee of being wanted.

meshuga, meshuge—crazy, strange.
Also: a *meshugeneh,* a person who behaves in a crazy, strange manner.

naches, kvell

Mike Douglas on his TV talk show one day said to his co-host: "I like the word *kvell,*" which he said meant, "to get *naches* from."

naches—variously defined as joy; dividends of pride (Edward O. Berkman); pleasurable pride, especially in another's or in one's own achievements.

kvell—to beam with pleasure at someone's accomplishments (especially a grandchild's).

nebbish, nebbich

He has been described as a Walter Mitty and he is nothing of the sort. This is no daydreaming *nebbish*.

nebbish—a poor, insignificant chap who never quite makes it, upon whom fortune never seems to smile, and who excites your pity. He becomes all the more pathetic when he is characterized by the diminutive, as in *a poor nebishl* (reformed spelling).

nudnik

When you meet a man who talks only about himself, you're bored stiff. The same is true in literature. When the writer becomes the center of his attention, he becomes a *nudnik*. And a *nudnik* who believes he's profound is even worse than just a plain *nudnik*.

nudnik—what Somerset Maugham called a crashing bore; a dull, tiresome person whom it is difficult to shake off. From Russian *nudniy*, tiresome.

Nice variation in some circles; *phudnik*, a *nudnik* with a Ph.D.

shiksa

Mary is a 22-year-old *shiksa* he sometimes jogs home with.

shiksa—a non-Jewish woman. The equivalent male is *sheigitz* (pronounced *shay-gitz*).

shlemiel, schlemiel, shlemihl, schlemihl

This is the rebellious *shlemiel*, the vulnerable social misfit and loser, preternaturally gauche and clumsy.

shlemiel—Yiddish has borrowed many words from German, but this is one word that German has borrowed from Yiddish, although it does not appear by itself in standard German dictionaries. *Schlemihl* is found in the expression *a Peter Schlemihl* taken from Adelbert von Chamisso's novel (1814) *Peter Schlemihls wundersame Geschichte* ("Peter Schlemihl's Wonderful Story"), in which the hero gives up his shadow for a never-failing purse, a cornucopia. Hence, to the Germans, *a Peter Schlemihl* is one who makes a foolish bargain without thinking of the consequences. By itself, as we use the word, *schlemihl/shlemiel* characterizes an unlucky, foolish bungler, a person who allows others to take advantage of him.

shlep, shleppiness, shlepdom

> The limousine is a 1972 Cadillac last used mayorally to transport—*shlep,* in English—Mr. and Mrs. Beame in a Bicentennial motorcade from the yacht of Elizabeth II, who rode in a Rolls-Royce.

shlep—as a verb, to drag along, carry with difficulty. From German *schleppen,* to carry. As a noun, *shlepp,* a feckless, awkward person. Not a *mensh.*

shlimazel, shlimazl

> The *American Heritage Dictionary* defines a *shlemihl* as a waiter who spills hot soup and a *shlimazel* as the one who gets it in his lap. *Shlimazel* is "bad luck," a combination of German *schlimm,* bad, and Hebrew-Yiddish *mazel,* luck.

shlock

> His friends at Penguin say he's been restive under the mass-market conditions that make it necessary "to publish a great deal of *shlock* in order to fill 30 rack pockets with paperback books each month."

shlock—trash; anything cheap, inferior, of little worth.

shlump, shlumpy

> Doing Shakespeare, she said, was like putting beautiful music on the hi-fi and having a *shlumpy* rotten day turn into a nice day.

shlump—slob. *Shlumpy,* dull; disheveled; not "together."

shmaltz—rendered fat; chicken fat. (See also **schmalts** among German words.)

shmatta

> If the airports, the auto industry, and the *shmatta* trade could be successfully "researched" for mass entertainment, why not the Holocaust?

shmatta—literally, "a rag," but used disparagingly for anything cheap, tawdry, even disreputable. Used tendentiously to describe any Jewish musical comedy as contrasted with a serious play (by I.B. Singer, for example). In New York City, "the *shmatta* trade" is a colloquialism, especially on Seventh Avenue (and among its Madison Avenue admen), for the garment industry.

shmooze

> On Seventh Avenue they call it the "*shmooze*," the lunchtime gabfest in Yiddish, Spanish, Italian, and even English that gives the lonely crowd in the *shmatta* trade, the cutters, pressers, sewing-machine operators and cart pushers, the courage to go on toiling in New York's feverish rag jungle day after weary day.

shmooze—conversation, chit-chat, gabfest, although most often used as a verb, *shmoosen,* to chat.

shnorrer

> Mr. Kollek (Mayor of Jerusalem) is known best as a fund-raiser and *shnorrer.*

shnorrer—in *shtetl* days, one whose trade was begging, who went from house to house to get the stipend he was entitled to by custom, sometimes a cube of lump sugar, sometimes a small coin. *Shnorr* is something like our word *cadge*.

shtetl

Despite valiant efforts by Rumanian Jews to preserve one of the last viable communities of Jewish life and religion in Eastern Europe, the *shtetl*, the village memorialized in countless writings and in the memories of hundreds of thousands, is disappearing.

shtetl—from the diminutive of the German word *Stadt*, city. It is Shalom Aleichem, for most readers and playgoers, who memorialized the life of the *shtetl*. The musical play *Fiddler on the Roof*, adapted from his story "Tevye and His Daughters," introduced the Jewish family drama of the Ukrainian *shtetl* of Anatevka—matchmaking and carousing, persecutions and rescues, joys and fears—to an incredibly large audience in many lands. Less roseate and less nostalgic accounts of the *shtetl* have been written by several contemporary historians.

shtik

Groucho Marx brought to dancing what George Burns brought to singing. All art has an element of *shtik* in it, but it was Groucho's walk that told all.

shtik—bit, routine, specialty, "thing," literally "piece" (of business).

tsuris, tsooris, tsores

And as though that weren't *tsuris* enough, two other troubled families are examined in this lachrymose made-for-television drama, which will be seen from 9 to 11 o'clock tonight on NBC. (Tom Buckley)

tsuris—troubles, woes, miseries. The singular *tsore* is rarely heard. *Tsuris* are the troubles that come (as Shakespeare says in *Macbeth*) "not in single spies but in battalions."

yenta

> He plays Woollcott not as a *yenta* but as a sprite, cuddlesome, even vulnerable, and deeply worried that he may be only a *nebbish*.

yenta—a talkative, gossipy, loud person; a vulgar and sentimental woman. Probably from the name *Yenta*.

7. Upper to Lower Case

And a single day's Assembly speeches produced three Swords of Damocles, two Pandora's boxes and one pig-in-a-poke. (It was not quite up to the standard set by a now-forgotten Assemblyman who once characterized the impact of a bill as "a Sword of Damocles hanging over Pandora's box.")

(The N.Y. Times)

Many of the entries in this chapter, not so familiar as those mentioned in the epigraph, were originally capitalized because they are names—names of heroes in mythology, legend, or history, names of characters in works of fiction, names of cities or countries. Through frequent use, most of them have lost their capitals and have become ordinary common nouns.

Aesopian, Aesopic

At other points, of course, he was using the oblique *Aesopian* style familiar to Russian radicals and conveying highly subversive ideas in an apparently servile manner.

Aesopian—Aesopian language is veiled in allegorical statement so as to conceal the real purpose or intention and elude
political censorship. Writers who employ it wear the mask of
allegory in the same way Aesop employed animals to teach
morals to human beings.

Alexandrine

Towards the end of the 12th century, the collabora-
tive verse-narrative known as *Roman d'Alexandre*
launched a new poetic line, having twelve syllables
with a caesura (a break or pause) after the sixth syllable, upon a proud centuries-long career. This line—
the *alexandrine*—is the meter of meters in France.

alexandrine—this form is an oddity in English poetry. Our
equivalent meter is the iambic pentameter of Elizabethan drama
and sonnets. Sir Philip Sidney, in the more than a hundred
sonnets addressed to Stella, used the alexandrine only in his
introductory sonnet and in a handful of others. The last two
lines of Sonnet 1 show how he used the alexandrine meter,
even respecting the caesura:

Biting my truant pen, beating myself for spite,
"Fool!" said my Muse, to me, "look in thy heart, and
write."

This is also an example of the more than occasional use of
a trochee (which see) in the first foot of an iambic line, and here
even in the foot following the caesura.

Apollonian and Dionysian

Mr. Solti has been characterized as *Dionysian* and Mr.
Karajan as *Apollonian,* and this general description
seems quite apt. . . . Mr. Solti is a bundle of nervous
energy, jabbing, angular, and intense, while Mr. Karajan stands stock still, with eyes closed, describing
serene, minutely calculated arcs of sound.

Apollonian—harmonious, measured, ordered, balanced. From
Apollo, god of sunlight, music, and poetry.

Dionysian—frenzied, ecstatic, having great creative and imaginative fire. From Dionysus, god of wine, who was also called Bacchus by both Greeks and Romans.

Armageddon

> Leaving *Armageddon* for later, the Canadian caper [the rescue and return of six Americans by the Canadian Embassy in Teheran] delighted Ottawa, where Prime Minister Joe Clark's re-election prospects brightened.

Armageddon—where the forces of good and evil are ultimately to meet in a last decisive battle. The term is symbolic of a battle or a war marked by overwhelming slaughter and destruction, making further combat impossible.

> And he gathered them together into a place called in the Hebrew tongue Armageddon . . .
> And there were voices, and thunders, and lightnings, and there was a great earthquake, such as was not since men were upon the earth, so mighty an earthquake, and so great.
>
> Revelation 16:16, 18

Augean

> It would be unfair to call New York racing an *Augean* stable at this point, but the aroma of corruption from the so-called Cinzano Caper is unmistakable.

Augean—One of the labors of Hercules was the cleaning of the stables of King Augeas of Elis, who had a herd of three thousand oxen. Their stalls had not been cleaned for thirty years. Hercules accomplished the task by diverting the course of two rivers and letting the streams run like a hose through the filthy stalls. "To clean the Augean stables" means to clean up a mess.

balkanization

> Because the potential *balkanization* of Canada (after the threat of secession by a group of zealots) has not yet become a crisis, the Carter State Department has not yet focused on it.

balkanization—the dividing of a region into mutually hostile political units, as was done by the European powers in the early twentieth century to form the Balkan states.

byzantine

> John le Carré has loosed imitators on the world, all of whom write spy stories marked by turgid *byzantine* maneuvering. In these stories it is impossible to distinguish good from evil.

byzantine—intricately involved, labyrinthine. From the ancient city of Byzantium. On its site in A.D. 330 the Emperor Constantine built Constantinople, now Istanbul.

Cadmean (See dragon's teeth, Pyrrhic)

Cannae

> They evolved a tortuous, complicated, unworkable plan for destroying the enemy's forces piecemeal and by a *Cannae-like* envelopment annihilating both the enemies' land and sea strength.

Cannae—pronounced *can-ee* (L. *can-eye*). In 216 B.C. at Cannae in Apulia, Italy, the Carthaginian general Hannibal achieved the classic dream of every military commander. He encircled and destroyed a Roman army. A defeat of this kind or a total defeat is known as a *Cannae*. Von Hindenburg achieved a Cannae at the expense of the Russians near Tannenberg in 1914, and the Russians retaliated in World War II at Stalingrad for one of the decisive battles of the war.

One of the two Roman generals at Cannae was named Paullus. The Nazi army near Stalingrad led by General von Paulus (!) was surrounded by the Russians and surrendered to them after losing a quarter of a million men. If history doesn't always repeat itself, names sometimes do.

Canossa

Mr. Nixon's trip to Peking not only was unnecessary but the spectacle of the American President going to *Canossa* to honor the anti-Pope of "Calvinist" Communism simply demeaned the United States.

Canossa—"To go to Canossa" means to humiliate oneself. The powerful Holy Roman Emperor Henry IV once defied Pope Gregory VII. The Pope excommunicated him, and the Emperor's supporters began to abandon him. Henry IV then made a pilgrimage in January 1077 to the village of Canossa, Italy, where the Pope was then staying. For three days the Emperor stood barefoot and bareheaded in the snow and did penance until the Pope received him. A Canossa is therefore a scene or place of humiliation or submission.

Charybdis (See Scylla)

chimera, chimerical

The nub of the matter is that the notion of exterminating pests by chemical means is quite *chimerical*; a remnant will always escape.

Chimera or *Chimaera*—a monster that breathed fire, had the head of a lion, the body of a goat, and the tail of a serpent. The name of such a fantastic and incongruous combination is used to denote a wild dream, an illusion; the adjective *chimerical* means unreal, visionary, extremely fanciful.

Robert Louis Stevenson ends his essay "El Dorado" on this note: "A strange picture we make on our way to our chimeras, ceaselessly marching, grudging ourselves the time for rest; indefatigable, adventurous pioneers."

cicerone

> This memoir is not intended as a guide to all the places this good-natured *cicerone* has been.

cicerone—because of the traditional talkativeness of all guides, they are sometimes referred to by an Italian word formed from the name of Rome's greatest orator, Marcus Tullius Cicero (106 B.C.–43 B.C.). The term *cicerone* (pronounced *sisseronee,* or It. *cheecheronay*) may also be a tribute to their eloquence and knowledge.

clerihew

A four-line short poem that humorously characterizes a person whose name must appear in the first line and be one of the rhymes. It was invented by Edmund Clerihew Bentley, better known as E. C. Bentley, author of one of the classics in detective fiction, *Trent's Last Case.*
    The following example of a *clerihew* is attributed to Anon. However, a note in the appendix tells us that it was "orally communicated" to the editor, Kingsley Amis. I have always suspected that Anon. didn't write his own stuff.

> SPINOZA
> Collected curiosa:
> Bawdy belles-lettres,
> Etc.
>
> Anon.*

cynic, cynical

> *Cynics* have suggested that commencement speakers tend to make daring appeals largely because they feel that nobody is listening.

cynic—a certain school of Greek philosophers taught the principles of self-control and independence. Some of their

---

*The anonymous clerihew "Spinoza" from *The New Oxford Book of Light Verse,* chosen by Kingsley Amis (1978), No. 185, is reprinted by permission of Oxford University Press.

disciples mistrusted humanity and assigned only selfish motives to people's actions. Diogenes, the man who with a lantern
in broad daylight went searching for an honest man or, more
cynically, for a *man*, is cited as the classic example. The
founder of the school of Cynics taught at Kynosarges. Playing
on the first part of this name, which is similar to the Greek word
for dog, and disliking the snarling manner some members of
the sect used, the Athenians referred to them as Cynics. One
day, Diogenes, seeing officials of a temple carrying away a thief
who had stolen a sacred bowl, commented: "The big thieves
have caught a little one."

    Cynicism indicates disbelief in man's sincerity and
questions human values. The adjective *cynical* has many interesting synonyms, some strong, some weak: *captious*; *carping*; *caviling*; *censorious*; *misanthropic*; *pessimistic*; *sarcastic*.

> "Life is too short to waste
> On critic peep or cynic bark,
> Quarrel or reprimand.
> 'Twill soon be dark;
> Up, mind thine own aim and
> God speed the mark."
>
> Emerson, "To J.W."

decibel

    Even in the more unthinking raucous dorms, the
baiting has been lowered by several *decibels*.

decibel—a *bel*, named in tribute to Alexander Graham Bell, is a
scientific unit for measuring the volume of sound. A *decibel*,
one-tenth of a *bel*, is just about the smallest degree of difference in loudness that the human ear can distinguish. There are
about 25 *decibels* (abbreviated to *db*) in the softest note of the
violin and about 100 in the *fortissimo* of a full orchestra. The
word *decibel* is often used figuratively, as in the excerpt above.

Dionysian (See Apollonian)

draconian

> Our society needs *Draconian* justice, swift and sure, to contain such offenders.

draconian—in about 621 B.C. Draco (or Dracon) compiled the first written code of laws in Athens. Death was the punishment he assigned to almost all crimes, even petty ones; the saying arose that his laws were written in blood, not in ink. Hence *draconian* means very rigorous and severe, extremely harsh or cruel.

dragon's teeth

> This is not the first revolution to soil itself by terror. The strange thing is that the Revolutionary Council and Ayatollah Khomeini should have felt their bloodshed was necessary.... Purges sow *dragon's teeth*.

dragon's teeth—Cadmus, a Phoenician prince, in one of his adventures sent some of his men to a well that was guarded by a dragon, who killed them. Being a hero, Cadmus killed the dragon and, on the advice of Athena, sowed the monster's teeth; out of these grew armed men, who killed each other, only five being spared. So evidently *to sow dragon's teeth* is to produce internecine warfare.

A *Cadmean victory* is so called because it is achieved at a ruinous cost to the victor, often a victory that loses more than it gains. Herodotus: "They joined battle and the Phocians won, yet it was but a Cadmean victory."

Gadarene

> Already it seems impossible to believe that someone so uncommonly like an *ersatz* Chaplin could come so near to treating the population of an entire continent like the *Gadarene* swine of the Bible.

Gadarene—at Gadara, near the sea of Galilee, Jesus drove out the devils that had entered two men. The demons then entered into the swine, which rushed headlong into the waters. Hence, *gadarene* means rushing into headlong or precipitate flight. Usually the word is met in the phrase *Gadarene swine* to characterize persons carried along and swept up by a mass movement, as in the above excerpt from a review by Alan Pryce-Jones of *The Men Who Tried to Kill Hitler* by Roger Manvell and Heinrich Fraenkel.

gasconading

> Above all, there was the General's *Gasconading*—the gold-encrusted cap, the carefully cocked corncob pipe, the blaring rows of military ribbons—a lifetime of melodramatics with its constant intimation that he yearned to be America's man on horseback.

gasconading—showing off, swaggering, praising oneself, boasting. From Gascony, a region and former province of S.W. France. The Gascons are traditionally garrulous and given to bragging. In Edmond Rostand's *Cyrano de Bergerac*, Cyrano is described by his good friend Ragueneau, the pastrycook-poet, as "Prouder than all the swaggering Tamburlaines/Hatched out of Gascony." Another famous braggart of Gascony is Alphonse Daudet's hero in his delightful stories *Tartarin of Tarascon.*

hector

> Even during the World Series in 1978, when Billy Martin was winning the championship of the baseball universe, and when another organization would have been promoting him for manager-of-the-year, he was being *hectored* and humiliated and threatened with instant dismissal.

hector—one would expect the name of Hector, the charismatic hero of the *Iliad,* to be used as the ultimate in praise of heroism and honor. Hector was certainly superior to Achilles as a human being and his equal as a fighter. Yet the gods played a

cruel trick on the Trojan so that he was overcome by Achilles.
Then history, the history of words, played still another trick on
his name.

Although at one time the name Hector was synony-
mous with *hero,* and in medieval lore it was listed among the
Nine Worthies (superior beings including King David, Alexander the Great, and Charlemagne), nevertheless, at about the
end of the sixteenth century the word *hector* came to mean a
bully or braggart, and the verb *to hector* meant to act the bully
or braggart, to badger, to intimidate.

Jacobin, Jacobite

In the section on George I, we learn about the abortive
Jacobite rebellion.

Jacobin, Jacobite—the best known of the radical republicans
during the French Revolution, called *Jacobins*, are Mirabeau,
Robespierre, Danton, and Marat. The term *Jacobin* has come
to denote someone with strong leftist feelings.

Jacobite, however, refers to James II of England and
his era. The Latin for James is Jacobus; in French, it is Jacques,
the name Dickens uses for revolutionaries in *A Tale of Two
Cities*. (Both words come from Jacobus, the Latin form for
James.)

Kafkaesque

"The Prisoner" is a *Kafkaesque* story of a British
citizen who finds himself the captive of unknown
captors, and who has no knowledge of why he is being
held or whether he will be released.

Kafkaesque—Franz Kafka, the Austrian-Czech novelist, whose
name probably appears somewhere in every issue of *The New
York Times Book Review,* is one of the seminal writers of the
twentieth century. In his short life (1883–1924) he created
short stories and novels which have had an incalculable impact

on the literature of the absurd. They reflect anxiety, guilt, loss of contact with reality, awareness of arbitrary powers ruling an irrational world. To the absurdist playwright Eugene Ionesco, the basic theme in Kafka's work is "man lost in a labyrinth, without a guiding thread." Perhaps the most famous *Kafkaesque* character is in *The Trial*, the character K, accused of a crime against a law he has never known. (In *The Castle*, there is the other K, a surveyor summoned to a castle he is unable to penetrate.) Today *Kafkaesque* is used to describe a nightmare situation of modern man.

laconic, laconism

> One of his most intimate friendships was with Frost, which the late Mr. Untermeyer explained as "largely a complement of temperaments." "He was a *laconic* New Englander," he said. "There was nothing at all laconic about me. I love to talk."

laconic—the Spartans, inhabitants of that part of Greece known as Laconia, were noted for saying the most in the fewest possible words. For example, when the Persian invader Xerxes demanded that the Spartan leader Leonidas surrender his weapons, the latter replied, "Come and take them!" One of Plutarch's anecdotes tells about King Archelaus, who when asked by a prating barber how he would be trimmed, answered, "In silence."

> Spartan women were also fond of short stinging replies. A society lady of Athens said to a Spartan woman: "I'm bringing my husband as dowry six houses, 200,000 drachmas, three farms, 500 slaves—and more. What are you offering to your husband that I haven't given?" The Spartan lady replied: "Chastity."

> Such economy of words is called a *laconism* after the name of the Spartans' homeland. The adjective is *laconic*.

limerick

> The term *limerick* is said by some to have been applied to verses popular with veterans of the Irish Brigade

who served King Louis IV after the surrender of
Limerick to William of Orange. These verses were
probably obscene. Over two centuries later the term
was officially admitted to the language with the *OED*'s
definition of it as "innocent nonsense verse." (*TLS*)

limerick—

"There's a notable clan yclept Stein
There's Gertrude, there's Ep and there's Ein
    Gert's poems are bunk
    Ep's statues are junk
And nobody understands Ein."

Arthur H. R. Buller
(1874–1944)

Usually this limerick or a variation of it retaining the essential
idea and characters is ascribed to Anon. In a poetry collection
edited by the writer tradition was continued. This is to set the
record straight. (See **clerihew**.)

W. S. Gilbert, probably fed up with the spate of lim-
ericks, got off this "send up" (which see):

"There was a young man of Tralee
Who was horribly stung by a wasp.
    When they said, 'Does it buzz?'
    He replied, 'Yes, it hurts,
It's a horrible brute of a hornet.' "

(There are various versions of this one, too.)

Lucullan

The picture of overstuffed American capitalists sitting
down to *Lucullan* feasts would be accepted readily by
many Soviet citizens.

Lucullan—Lucius Licinius Lucullus was a famous Roman
general of the first century B.C. On his return to Rome he
devoted himself to a carefree life of indolence and luxury in a

style of extraordinary magnificence. Plutarch tells us that "his daily entertainments were ostentatiously extravagant, not only with purple coverlets, and plates set with precious stones, and dancers, and dramatic recitations, but with the greatest diversity of dishes and the most elaborate cookery." Once when he ate alone the cook thought there was no need of display and served a simple one-course meal. Lucullus rebuked him with these famous words: "Dost thou not know, then, that today Lucullus dines with Lucullus?"

Synonyms: *sumptuous*; *lavish*; *luxurious*; *extravagant*.

macedoine

Macedoine is one of the most interesting names in French menu terminology. It means a mixture of numerous things, generally a combination of cubed fruits served as a dessert or a combination of diced vegetables.

macedoine—the name comes from Macedonia, the kingdom of Alexander the Great, which was formed by chopping up the nation into a number of smaller regions.

maenad

Now she is the prototypical dowdy faculty wife, now a blazing *maenad* unleashed on our libido.

maenad—a frenzied woman. *Maenades* was a name of the Bacchantes, from the Greek word *mainomai,* to be mad, because they became frenzied in the worship of Dionysus.

Manichean

He still sees the world in *Manichean* terms of conservative virtue assailed by liberal evil.

Manichean—a dualist doctrine dividing the world between light, or goodness, and darkness, identified with chaos or evil. Used figuratively, as in the excerpt, it means a conflict between two opposing views.

maudlin

> Although the play eventually vitiates its effectiveness by a sentimental, almost *maudlin,* scene of reconciliation, it nevertheless demonstrates an expenditure of talent in the writing, directing and performance.

maudlin—mawkish, tearfully sentimental, weakly emotional. This word comes from the name of Mary Magdalene, who watched the sepulcher of Christ.

> There were also women looking on afar off: among whom was Mary Magdalene . . .
>
> Mark 15:40

The British pronounce *Magdalen* of Magdalen College at Oxford, and *Magdalene* of Magdalene College at Cambridge, as if the names were written *maudlin.* The adjective has come to mean tearfully sentimental, because Italian paintings of Mary Magdalen usually show her weeping. John Ruskin speaks of "a smooth Magdalen of Carlo Dolci with a tear in each cheek."

Medusa

One of the Gorgons (*Gorgones*), three sisters whose heads were covered with hissing snakes instead of hair. Anyone looking at Medusa was turned to stone. Perseus, a Greek hero, killed her by looking at her reflection in his shield.

> "Gorgonized me from head to foot
> With a stony British stare."
>
> Tennyson, "Maud"

mithridate

In one of his Acrostic Puzzles in the *New York Times Magazine,* Thomas H. Middleton defined *mithridate* as an antidote against poisoning.

Mithridates the Great (132–63 B.C.), to protect himself against dying by poisoning, is believed to have immunized himself by taking gradually larger doses daily. So well did this immunity take hold that when he was captured by the Romans in 63 B.C., he finally had to call on a Greek mercenary to put him to death.

monadnocks

Such passages loom as *monadnocks* over an otherwise flat horizon.

monadnock—a rocky mass or mountain that looms above a *peneplane* (from L. *paena*, almost, as in *peninsula* and *penultimate*, almost or next to last). From Mt. Monadnock, New Hampshire, an isolated rocky hill rising above the eroded stretch of land below.

myrmidons

When and if the *myrmidons* of their coach learn to play as a complete unit, there will be very few teams who'll be able to stay on the same court with them.

myrmidons—soldiers who accompanied Achilles to Troy, hence loyal followers; subordinates who execute orders faithfully.

Oedipal

The past is always present in Greece, Mr. Cottrell says. Once a bus unexpectedly stopped and a Greek girl said, "Here you get out, because here there is something you must see."

"It was very quiet, save for the distant sound of the radio and the far-off bleating of sheep. We stood looking down the slope to where three lanes met beside a bridge. Then Zoë said, 'That is where *Oedipus* killed his father.' "

In a series of interpretive essays Bettelheim discusses such subjects as oral greed in "Hansel and Gretel," *oedipal* daring in "Jack and the Beanstalk," etc.

Oedipal—characterizing the tendency of a child to be attached to the parent of the opposite sex and hostile to the other parent.

Orphic

He defended the [book award] judges and said, "I suppose we can attribute the whole imbroglio to the lunacy that inevitably accompanies the National Book Awards spring fertility rite—publishing's own *Orphic* mystery, in which we tear each other to pieces as we struggle madly to resurrect our gods."

Orphic—mystic, occult, relating to the rites ascribed to Orpheus. Apparently the Orphic rites, as suggested in the excerpt, included the tearing and eating of animals. Still grieving over his second loss of Eurydice, Orpheus treated some Thracian women he met with contempt. A mistake! The women, enraged, tore him to pieces in the frenzy of their Bacchanalian orgies.

pasquinade

It strikes me that it may now be time to revive a rather rare English word—*pasquinade*—which seems accurately to describe the wall-poster phenomenon of the People's Republic of China.

pasquinade—in the Piazza Navona in Rome stood the mu-tilated remains of an ancient statue. During the sixteenth century there lived near it a tailor or a schoolmaster, a barber or a shoemaker—the occupation varies according to which tradition you believe. His name was Pasquino and he possessed a biting wit and an ability to compose epigrams, short pieces of verse with a whip in their tails. On the statue he is supposed to have placed his poems satirizing the events and personages of the day. For this reason the statue was given the nickname *Pasquino,* and the verses were called *pasquinatas*, from which we get *pasquinade*, meaning a lampoon or vicious satire.

The most famous of Pasquino's one-liners was directed against the Barberini family, one of whose members had torn down ancient monuments and landmarks to build palaces: *Quod non fecerunt barbari, fecerunt Barberini* ("What the barbarians have not done, the Barberini have done").

The practice of posting such satiric comments spread to other European countries. It is not a lost art. Recently, in the *Manchester Guardian Weekly* Anthony Burgess wrote: "Or you can do what I myself recently did in Rome—say what you have to say in four lines of verse and stick your holograph under the bust of Pasquino just off the Piazza Navona—hence *pasquinade*."

philippic

> In his speech, he delivered a *philippic* against the press, charging it with inaccuracy, guesswork, rumors, suppositions, hastiness, immaturity, superficiality, sen-sationalism, and misleading judgments—all without rectification.

philippic—in the fourth century B.C., in a series of celebrated speeches, Demosthenes of Athens, the greatest orator of ancient times, thundered against King Philip of Macedon, whose aim was to conquer all of Greece. The fiery invectives of Demosthenes were called *Philippics*; later, Cicero, the Roman counterpart of Demosthenes, gave the name *Philippics* to a set of speeches he delivered, or wrote, against a man named not

Philip, but Mark Antony. Hence, any speech of denunciation may be termed a *philippic,* no matter who is on the receiving end.

The word has some interesting synonyms: *tirade*, from a French word meaning to shoot; *invective*; *excoriation*; literally, "ripping the hide off"; and *vituperation*, act of finding fault.

Polynicean

> Three months after the terrible deaths in Guyana, nearly two-thirds of the bodies still lie unclaimed, unwanted, unburied, in some government depot under a *Polynicean* gloom of disapproval. (Diane Johnson in *NYRB*)

Polynicean—Polynices was the son of Oedipus and Jocasta. His brother was Eteocles; his sisters, Ismene and Antigone. In a battle against Thebes, ruled by his uncle Creon, Polynices fought against Eteocles, and the brothers killed each other. Because Polynices had fought against him, Creon *forbade his burial.* Antigone, mindful of the higher law of the gods and of her own conscience, performed one of the classic acts of civil disobedience. Under sentence of death, she defied the tyrant's edict and buried her brother.

Sophocles' great tragedy *Antigone*, which was first performed in Athens c. 442 B.C., remains a timeless tribute to the individual conscience in conflict with the state.

Potemkinize

> Foreign visitors [to the Olympics in Moscow] will then be shepherded around by well-briefed Intourist guides to view the *Potemkinized* cities. They'll shop in special foreign-currency stores and live in special hotels for foreigners, without the benefit of the average Russian's company.

Potemkinize—in 1790 Field Marshal Potemkin, a favorite of the reigning Catherine the Great, eager to make the queen proud of her country, had a grandiose stone village built—only for show. A *Potemkin village,* therefore, is all facade and no substance. Visitors to Hollywood studios in the old days became familiar with the *Potemkinized* sets for movies. Behind the facade of the main street of a western town, for example— the saloon front, the hitching posts, etc.—there was the open lot. Nowadays, of course, filmmakers go in for location shooting and the real thing.

Procrustean

> We impose a national system upon a multitude of individual and unique cases and insist that all sleep in the same *Procrustean* bed.

Procrustean—Procrustes, "the Stretcher," was an innkeeper-cum-highwayman who had an ingenious method of accommodating his guests. He insisted that each one must fit exactly the one iron bed in his inn. He stretched a guest who was too short and shortened the legs of one who was too tall. Hence, a system, especially a political or educational one, in which the individual must conform arbitrarily to a pattern without allowing for individual differences, is characterized as *procrustean*.

Promethean

> Yet while Ibsen gives Brand a *Promethean* grandeur, he also depicts him as ultimately hateful.

Promethean—daringly original, courageously innovative. Prometheus stole fire from heaven, carrying it in a hollow tube, gave it to mortals on earth, and taught them all the useful arts. How he was punished is told in Aeschylus' *Prometheus Bound* and Robert Lowell's "Prometheus." (Aeschylus' play is by way of being a protest play, a protest of the ancient world against divine oppression.)

Promethean appears in one of the loveliest and most moving passages in Shakespeare:

"Put out the light and then put out the light.
If I quench thee, thou flaming minister,
I can again thy former light restore,
Should I repent me; but once put out thy light,
Thou cunning'st pattern of excellent nature,
I know not where is that Promethean heat
That can thy light relume."

Othello

protean

The *protean* Mr. Papp tried everything—new plays,
revivals, star vehicles, classics.

protean—the sea god Proteus had one significant talent, the
gift of prophecy. But those who wanted a prophecy had to
catch him at midday when he assumed *every possible shape* to
avoid being forced to prophesy. Hence, the adjective *protean*
means varying, changing, and, in current use, *versatile.*

"So might I, standing on this pleasant lea,
Have glimpses that would make me less forlorn;
Have sight of Proteus rising from the sea;
Or hear old Triton blow his wreathed horn."
Wordsworth, "The World Is Too Much with Us"

Pyrrhic

To insist on a successful conclusion of SALT II as if this
result would be a feather in the battered cap of the
Administration is to seek an empty—a self-deceptive
and *Pyrrhic*—victory.

Pyrrhic—a Pyrrhic victory costs more than it gains. This kind of
hollow triumph is named after Pyrrhus, King of Epirus in
Greece, who invaded Italy in 280 B.C. and defeated the Romans
in a number of battles. However, he himself was wounded, and
he lost so many soldiers that he was unable to follow up his
victories. Pyrrhus won the battles but lost the war and had to

return home. According to Plutarch, Pyrrhus remarked, "Another such victory and we are undone."

quixotic

> The whole attempt at a frontal attack on the Soviet system of censorship—in the light of the exiling of the Nobel Peace Prize laureate Andrei Sakharov—seems particularly *quixotic*.

quixotic—describes someone idealistic to an impractical degree, symbolized by Don Quixote fighting windmills.

Rashomon

> Much of the questioning evoked the same *Rashomon* quality as has the whole Lance affair so far—different persons look at specific facts from different perspectives.

Rashomon—in 1951, Akira Kurosawa made the award-winning film *Rashomon* from the famous stories of Akutagawa. Set in the middle ages, *Rashomon* tells of the murder of a Samurai and the rape of his wife by a wandering bandit. At the trial, there are three different, contradictory versions of what happened: the bandit's, the wife's, and (through the lips of a sorceress) the Samurai's. Each version is true in its own fashion. The theme of this tale, that truth is elusive and reality is subjective, gives the word its current meaning; the "Rashomon quality" of an affair is its quicksilver, shifting view of the facts.

rodomontade

> Stoppard's script is filled with his usual felicitous turns of phrase, his deviously manipulative conceits, his lunatic lexicon of puns, literary allusions, and *rodomontade* wordplays.

rodomontade—Rodomonte, a Saracen king in Ariosto's sixteenth-century epic *Orlando Furioso,* is brave but a braggart of no mean proportions. So *rodomontade,* used as both adjective and noun, means boasting, blustering, braggadocio. (The latter is also from a literary source, Spenser's *The Faërie Queene*: but Braggadocchio is a great coward at heart—all rhetoric and no courage.)

satrap

> Not even the most cynical media *satrap* present could help but be touched by the drama of the beginning of communication between two strong spokesmen of nations that have spent a generation at war.

satrap—"protector of the kingdom"; a word known to readers of Greek history, where it appears as the title of a Persian viceroy, or governor of a province. The ancient Greeks used it as a special name for a rich man or for one who lived luxuriously. It is used today to designate either a person with final authority or else, in a pejorative sense, a henchman.

Synonyms: *nabob* (Hindi); *pasha* (Turkish); *tycoon* (Japanese); *mogul, bigwig.*

Scylla and Charybdis

> A well-tempered man, he learned to steer a course between the *Scylla* of estheticism and the *Charybdis* of art as propaganda.

Scylla and *Charybdis*—in Greek mythology, these are the names of two rocks between Italy and Sicily. In the one nearer to Italy dwelt Scylla, barking like a dog, with twelve feet and six long heads and necks, each head with three rows of teeth. On the other side, Charybdis swallowed the waters of the sea three times a day and three times threw them up again.

Wishing to avoid the overuse of these monsters of Greek myths, C. Lehmann-Haupt used "steer a careful course between the rock of scientific objectivity and the whirlpool of emotional mush." A current colloquial equivalent is to be "between a rock and a hard place."

Sisyphean, Sisyphian, Sisyphus

> The trainee is subjected to an incessant din of semi-intelligible commands, a torrent of invective that is usually as unimaginative as it is obscene, and a welter of meaningless *Sisyphean* tasks.

> Much as *Sisyphus* doggedly pushed his stone up the precipitous mountain, even though all past experience had shown him the stone would come tumbling down, so the delegates will meet, for it is the nature of man to continue to try.

Sisyphus—he was condemned by a cruel king of Corinth to roll a huge stone up a hill in Hades only to have it roll down again on nearing the top. *Sisyphean* toil may mean endless and ineffective effort—or, as in the second excerpt above, dogged and unremitting effort. Albert Camus's *The Myth of Sisyphus* (completed in 1941) is something of a classic in the literature of the absurd; yet Camus's originality lay in finding the absurdity of the world not a cause for despair. Senseless suffering, in his view, can invite one to live life more intensely. As an epigraph to *The Myth of Sisyphus,* Camus quoted Pindar: "O my soul, do not aspire to immortal life, but exhaust the limits of the possible."

solecism

> But she used the word "less" in a construction in which Fowler, the Grand Panjandrum of English usage, prefers "fewer." To judge from the spate of letters, that *solecism* gave a number of Americans a heady feeling of oneupmanship.

solecism—the inhabitants of Soloi in Asia Minor spoke a corrupt form of Attic, the Greek dialect of the Athenians. Hence, a *solecism* is an idiomatic mistake, incorrect grammatical usage. In its broader implications, a *solecism* is a deviation from the norm, something illogical, incongruous, absurd, or even an impropriety, a breach of etiquette.

Spoonerism

> The fashioning of *spoonerisms* still goes on. The late Kenneth Tynan, reviewing Rodgers' and Hammerstein's *The World of Susie Wong*, characterized it as "a world of woozy song."

spoonerism—the Reverend William A. Spooner (1844–1930) of New College, Oxford, was celebrated for his habit, accidental or cultivated, of transposing the first letters of words or phrases. It is reported that in conversation he referred to the well known two-wheeled vehicle as "a well-boiled icicle" and to a friend's new cottage as a "nosey little cook." They say he would startle listeners to his sermons by referring to "tearful chidings" or "this audience of beery wenches" or assuring them that something was as easy as for "a camel to go through the knee of an idol." It is also recorded (Bartlett's *Familiar Quotations*) that on dismissing a student, he said, "You have deliberately tasted two worms and you can leave Oxford on the town drain."

stentorian

> In such roles as Rodolfo his hefty voice has seemed fairly unwieldy. Canio, however, is better suited to his abilities—the *stentorian* ring is very much to the point, the lack of subtlety less important.

stentorian—the Greek herald in the Trojan War, Stentor, had a voice as loud as that of fifty men together, and it could be heard all over the Grecian camp.

Stygian

> In the next few minutes, the Cornell stands changed from wild elation to *Stygian* gloom.

Stygian—the Styx was the chief river by which the spirits of the dead, ferried by Charon, crossed to enter the Underworld. *Stygian* refers to this nether world; it implies gloom and darkness.

Milton's "L'Allegro" begins with the lines:

"Hence, loathed Melancholy,
  Of Cerberus, and blackest Midnight born,
In Stygian cave forlorn,
  'Mongst horrid shapes, and shrieks, and sights
  unholy."

Walter Savage Landor's lovely poem "Dirce" is different in mood:

"Stand close around, ye Stygian set,
  With Dirce in one boat conveyed!
Or Charon, seeing, may forget
  That he is old and she a shade."

sybarite, sybaritic

Other Polynesians were, and are, *sybarites*—singing, dancing, making love, finding their food in the trees, the fertile soil and the teeming lagoons, and doing no manual labor that was not essential.

sybarite—Sybaris, a celebrated Greek town in southern Italy, was notorious in the sixth century B.C. for its wealth and luxury. A *sybarite*, therefore, is a lover of luxury and pleasure, a voluptuary. It is a stronger word than *epicure* or *hedonist*.

thrasonical

The Romans had their idea of a Braggadocchio and Rodomonte, too. He was Thraso, a blustering soldier in Terence's play *The Eunuch*. In Shakespeare's *As You Like It*, Rosalind refers to "Caesar's *thrasonical* brag of 'I came, I saw, I overcame.'"

yahoo

There is a good deal of the *yahoo* in every gang of adolescents that goes berserk, whatever their color.

yahoo—in Dean Jonathan Swift's *Gulliver's Travels* (1726) the Yahoos are a tribe of brutes having human form and embodying all the vices of mankind. A *yahoo* is consequently a lout, a ruffian, a degraded specimen of the human race.

8. Words That May Fool You

In one of the most bitter campaigns in Florida history, during the 1950's, the opponent of Claude Pepper, speaking to a largely uneducated gathering in northern Florida, said:

"Are you aware that Claude Pepper is known all over Washington as a shameless extrovert? Not only that, but the man is reported to practice nepotism with his sister-in-law, and he had a sister who was once a thespian in wicked New York. Worst of all, it is an established fact that before his marriage Mr. Pepper practiced celibacy."

This shameless perversion of language, and disgraceful use of it to malign a good man, was successful in defeating Claude Pepper. (In 1962 he won a seat in the House, where he has since been very active.)

Nobody today except the most benighted would be fooled in this way, and so I am exercising a little bravado in trying to fill this chapter with words that may fool some enlightened people these days.

annular

> During the period of eclipse maximum, the sun is visible as a fiery ring around the moon—a so-called *annular* eclipse.

annular—related to or forming a ring (from L. *annulus*, ring). An *annular ligament* is a ligament that rings the ankle joint or wrist joint; in architecture, an *annulet* is a ringlike molding around the capital of a pillar.

bemused

> It is suggested that I have created a smoke screen in an attempt to *bemuse* the public by exaggerating the effect of the court order.

bemused—can mean anything from befuddled to hypnotized, from dazed to preoccupied. It is, therefore, seen around a great deal, most of the time in the sense of *befuddled, bewildered.* To Lorenz Hart's "bewitched, bothered, and bewildered" from *Pal Joey,* add "bemused."

bootless

> After an hour's *bootless* attempts to get through to the flooded area, he hung up.

bootless—fruitless, futile, useless, unprofitable.

> "When in disgrace with fortune and men's eyes
> I all alone beweep my outcast state,
> And trouble deaf heaven with my bootless cries. . . ."
>   Shakespeare, Sonnet 29

brackish

> My first reaction was astonishment; the Jordan River was skinny and *brackish.*

brackish—somewhat salty, briny, distasteful—not necessarily muddy.

cashiered

It is possible for soldiers to be *cashiered,* drummed out of service, given honorary and dishonorable discharges.

cashiered—dismissed in disgrace.

collegial

Justice Douglas, rated a genius by many a differing colleague, took less time to make up his mind because his absolutist views gave him less occasion to negotiate compromise in the time-consuming *collegial* manner.

collegial—has nothing to do with college except etymologically. It is the adjective for *colleague.*

comity

The white attitudes toward black Americans measured in this Times/CBS News Poll offered other, though less insistent evidence of recession's threat to *comity.*

comity—courteous behavior, politeness, civility—usually found in the expression *the comity of nations.* Gr. *komis,* polite.

concupiscence

Proud, indolent, predatory, and *concupiscent,* the Tuareg had become unaccustomed to work.

concupiscence—lust, one of the seven deadly sins. The word is related to Cupid, son of Venus, therefore god of love. Cupid's Greek twin was Eros, from whose name we get the words *erotic, eroticism, erotogenic, erogenous.*

consensual

The pact on wages and prices has set a conciliatory and *consensual* tone for politics that is absent in Portugal.

consensual—related to *consensus* and not to *sensual.*

contention, contentious

> That is a question not only about decision-making in the White House but about survival in a *contentious* world.

contention, contentious—both are related to the verb to *contend,* to struggle, to fight against; therefore *contentious* means full of struggle, pugnacious, argumentative.

> "Let the long contention cease!
> Geese are swans, and swans are geese."
> > Matthew Arnold, "The Last Word"

cupidity

> It is testimony to the growing venality of man as economic progress brings out his *cupidity.*

cupidity—avarice, greed (another one of the seven deadly sins). From L. *cupiditas,* eagerness, greed.

demiurge

> The heresy proposed that the world was created not by God, who is inaccessible, but by a vile *Demiurge,* who accidentally allowed some tiny divine spark to lodge in man.

demiurge—at first glance, and without a basic knowledge of etymology, one could easily come to the conclusion that *demi* is half and *urge* is urge, together forming a word that means "a halfhearted urge." Not so. This is the danger, mentioned in Chapter 1, in using one's intuition or imagination to unlock the meaning of a word through a mistaken derivation.
> *Demiurge* means any power or personality creating a world. From Gr. *demos,* the people + *-ourgous* (from *ergon,*

work), a worker for the people. The modern meaning originates in Plato's use of the word for the inferior god who created the material world; hence, a subordinate deity. *Demiurge* actually means a secondary deity, a blind force that created the world, one that lacks *nous* (a supreme intelligence; see **nous**).

Also: *dramaturgy*; *metallurgy*; *thaumaturgist* (*thauma*, miracle, wonder), a performer of wonders, a magician. (For other words with *-erg,* see **synergy**.)

doyen, doyenne

> Ngaio Marsh's *Last Ditch* is the latest and one of the best stories by the *doyenne* of mystery writers in the traditional British style.

doyen—the highest ranking or senior member (from L. *decanus*, originally a chief over ten [*dec-*] men); now a high officer in religious and academic circles; the senior member of a professional group. The French word *doyen*, from the same root, is often used instead of *dean*, especially in the sense of a person eminently qualified because of long experience. *Doyenne*, of course, is the feminine form.

effete

> He is forced to mask his fear of dissent with words like *effete*, when, in fact, he means that those who disagree with him are abnormal or homosexual or outside the circle of respectability.

effete—does not mean "effeminate," as it is mistakenly used in the passage above. From L. *ef* for *ex*, out + *fetus*, productive, meaning no longer able to bear young; hence, exhausted, worn out, enervated. The word for effeminate is *epicene* (which see).

empirical

> He not only had not hit a homer but also had driven in no runs and had batted only .146. So much for *empirical* evidence.

empirical—from a Greek word for experience, describes a practical method that relies on experience, observation, experimentation for drawing of conclusions—not on theory or logic alone. To arrive at something *empirically* is to do it through data or statistics. In the excerpt, the reader is being led to draw a conclusion from the facts given.

fitful

> It would destroy confidence and choke off whatever *fitful* starts there have been toward general economic recovery.

fitful—by fits and starts, intermittent, spasmodic.

> "Duncan is in his grave;
> After life's fitful fever he sleeps well."
> Shakespeare, Macbeth

footling

> There was not much in the way of entertainment—just introductions, self-congratulation, and *footling* recollections.

footling—silly, unimportant, trifling, trivial.

friable

> He rescued the paintings, in fragile colors on even more *friable* paper.

friable—easily crumbled. The word *friction* is related to it, as is *dentifrice*.

gloss

> The intelligent reader is advised to skip these pedantic *glosses* entirely.

gloss—a note of comment or explanation accompanying a text, generally limited to single words (from Gr. *glossa, glotta,* tongue). When a book like Anthony Burgess's *The Clockwork Orange* has many words that are unknown or unknowable without some explanation (Russian *chorosho* becomes "horror show"), a *glossary* is furnished at the back of the book.

Also: *glossolalia,* involuntary and often pathological repetition of words or phrases just spoken by others, as if echoing them; or utterance of unintelligible sounds sometimes viewed as manifestation of deep religious experience.

hapless

> The heart goes out to the *hapless* translator who misrendered some of Jimmy Carter's inconsequential rhetoric into Polish on the President's arrival in Warsaw on New Year's Eve. For Mr. Carter's reference to the Polish People's "desires for the future," he offered "lusts"; for Mr. Carter's "departing" from Washington, he used "abandoned."

hapless—luckless, unfortunate. Its rare use indicates that it means more than merely unlucky. A concatenation of miserable happenings, none of the translator's own making, made him *hapless*. He was kept shivering in freezing rain for three hours at the Warsaw airport before he was shown the President's arrival statement—a bare minute before the President delivered his speech.

hebetude

This word may fool you if you know your Greek mythology, for Hebe was the goddess of youth and cupbearer to the gods. *Hebetude,* however, comes from L. *hebetare,* to make dull or blunt; hence *hebetude* means dullness, lethargy. However, there is a rarely seen word *hebetic* (Gr. *hebe,* youth) which means youthful.

inveterate

> It pleases her that people as tough and practical-minded as the Marseillais should be *inveterate* flower-buyers.

inveterate—habitual, firmly established (from L. *in*, intensive +
veterare, to become old).
Also: *veteran.*

lubricious, lubricous, lubricity

Their excesses are dwelt on with the *lubricity* of a
gossip columnist.

lubricity—lewdness, prurience (from L. *lubricous*, slippery).
Also: *lubricate.*

mare's nest

This staunch advocate for tne authenticity of the
Vinland map has no fear of *mare's-nests* in geograph-
ical studies.

mare's nest—something supposed to be a wonderful discovery
but turning out to be a hoax; also a condition of confusion or
great disorder.

median

Men working full time earned a *median* income of
$13,859, compared with $8,312 for women.

median—if we take the sequence 1 2 4 8 9 9 9, the median is
8; the average or **mean** is 6 (42 ÷ 7); the **mode**, the item
appearing most frequently in this series, is 9.

mephitic

The friends of "raising the devil" generally are flocking
to their standards. The air is incarnadined and made
mephitic with their presence.

mephitic—the excerpt quoted is unfortunate, since it seems to
imply some relationship between the devil and *mephitic*.
Mephitic has nothing to do with *Mephistopheles*. It means
"bad smelling," sometimes to the point of being poisonous.

There is an interesting word in the second sentence: *incarnadined*, made red (from L. *carnis*, flesh, meat). Also: *carnal*; *carnation*; *carnage*; *incarnate*, in the flesh.

"Will all great Neptune's ocean wash this blood
Clean from my hand? No, this my hand will rather
The multitudinous seas incarnadine,
Making the green one red."
                                                          Shakespeare, *Macbeth*

miscreant

Just then the rock slide came and we could see the *miscreants* on the hillside who started the avalanche.

miscreant—has two derogatory meanings: one who holds false (*mis*) religious beliefs, a heretic; and more usually, one who behaves criminally or viciously, as in the passage above.

mishmash

The Senator is a charming, witty, hard-working *mishmash*, zestfully enjoying the legislative process, horse-trading, fulminating, and usually winning.

mishmash—what may fool you here—and it may come as something of a surprise—is that *mishmash* is a good old English word with a long history of use dating back to 1450! The first citation in the *Oxford English Dictionary* is dated c. 1450: "But, ser, I prey you this questyon to clarifye: Driff-draff, mysse-masche." In 1585, as if to "clarifye" this "questyon," this entry appears: "a confused or disordered heape of all things together: a mishmash" (the spelling is already modern). Then follows the use of this word in 1600, 1634, and so on through the centuries.

noisome

We proceed eastward to serene—and *noisome*—Venice. Although Europe offers plenty of contenders for odor pollution honors, the laurels must go to the Venetians.

noisome—has nothing to do with noise. A shortened form of *annoysome*, it describes an offensive odor. Synonyms: *smelly*; *stinking*; *fetid*; *disgusting*; *offensive*; *mephitic.*

odometer

> The 1977 Pontiac had nearly 25,000 miles on the *odometer.*

odometer—too many people ask, "What's the mileage registered on your speedometer?" The answer should be, "None." It's the *odometer* that registers mileage. From Gr. (*h*) *odus*, road.

Also: *exodus*, the road out; and such technical words as *electrode, cathode*, etc.

officious

> Momo finally helps Madame Rosa to escape the well-meaning but *officious* clutches of hospitals and social workers. (*TLS*)

officious—this word is sometimes equated by the unwary with domineering, "bossy" (a meaning not yet recorded in *Webster's Third*), but its specific meaning is meddlesome, intrusive, volunteering one's services where they are neither asked for nor needed, as when Robert Browning has the Duke of Ferrara complain that his last Duchess found pleasure in

> "The bough of cherries some officious fool
> Broke in the orchard for her. . . ."

olio

> "Tom Jones" is an *olio* of story, essay, personal philosophy and literary and social criticism.

olio—a medley of literary or musical items; a potpourri. Almost all the other synonyms are derogatory: *farrago*; *hodgepodge* or *hotchpotch*; *mess*. etc.

parlous

> Still others are wondering whether the country, in the *parlous* thicket of 1977 international diplomacy, can afford a patriarchal figure as its leader once again.

parlous—this is just the word *perilous* in transparent disguise. Other words showing the British influence in pronunciation: *sergeant*; *varmint* (*vermin*); *Barney* or *Barry* for *Bernard*. And in England: *derby, clerk*.

peculation

> It is a new problem of the well-informed spouse who seeks revenge and can reveal financial *peculation* . . . a problem that can threaten to break into the media on the eve of an election.

peculation—the stealing or misuse of public money entrusted to one's care (from L. *pecunia,* money). A cynic might say *speculation* is altogether different from *peculation*, since not much risk is involved in *peculation*.
>   Also: *pecuniary*; *impecunious* (*im* for *in,* without).

picaresque

> To many people, Brazil means Jorge Amado and his *picaresque,* combative, earthy, mixed race, and down-but-never-out characters.

picaresque—an episodic novel dealing with rogues and rascals (from Sp. *picaro,* rogue). As an adjective, involving or relating to rogues and adventurers.

presumptive

> It makes a sixth-grade education *presumptive* evidence of literacy.

presumptive—giving reasonable grounds for believing; founded on probability; assumed.
>   Another adjective having the same base is *presumptuous* (pronounced *chew*), not *presumptious*. It means impertinent, bold, forward, taking too much for granted. The word

presume, from which it comes, is a Janus-faced word having two meanings, *suppose* and *take liberties,* as this anecdote about Sir James M. Barrie illustrates. One day he opened the door on a reporter he didn't want to see.

"Mr. Barrie, I presume," said the reporter.

"Yes!" snapped back the usually calm Barrie and slammed the door closed.

proem (See prolegomenon)

prosody

Its perverse rhymes—"press" matches "highNESS"—constituted a comical defiance of English *prosody.*

prosody—it looks as if it had something to do with *prose*, a word of Latin origin, but it breaks down into Greek *pros*, near, and *ode*, song. *Prosody* is the study of versification, accents, meters, rhythms.

Pros appears in the words *proselyte* and *proselytize*, to convert or literally to "come near to." *Ody* sings its song in *melody, parody, rhapsody,* and *threnody*, a song of lamentation for someone dead.

restive

The *restive* Cuban refugees at Fort Chaffee, Arkansas, must learn that red tape in America takes a long time to cut.

restive—resisting control, balky, refractory. (From latin *re*, back, against + *stare*, stand.)

rusticate

Many *rusticated* Chinese want to go back to Peking.

rusticate—to go to or reside in the country; follow a rustic life (from L. *rus, ruris,* countryside). Not *rust* but close to it if used figuratively.

Also: *rural.*

scabrous

> Hell's Kitchen is that *scabrous* New York neighborhood where the leading characters try to hustle a living.

scabrous—squalid, scandalous, shocking, salacious.

scarify, scarification

> Matter from a pustule was introduced into the skin of the arm of a healthy individual by *scarification* with a needle or lance.

> You will find "Coma" a gripping, *scarifying* film.

scarify—used medically for the kind of scratches made in vaccination; used in literature, it means to leave an emotional scar, to lacerate the feelings. *Webster's Third* yielded to its use in the sense of *scare* and has a separate entry for it.
   Related to the word *scar* (from the Greek word meaning to scratch an outline), *scarify* is used both literally (to scarify the earth, scratch or cut into it) and figuratively, to make a cutting criticism, to flay, to excoriate.

subvention

> Can we be sure that all the right-wing terrorist gangs of Latin America, Italy, and Spain at the present time are entirely independent of outside *subvention*? (*TLS*)

subvention—subsidy, endowment. From L. *sub*, under + *venire*, to come; to come from under to one's assistance; come to the rescue; come up with something; to underwrite. In other words, *subsidy*.

temerity, temerarious

> Jimmy Byrnes had the *temerity* to think (which was probably right) and to say (which was undoubtedly wrong) that he was smarter than Truman. Unamused, Harry let him go.

> Winter seemed an unpropitious time for birds to nest, but then, whatever their faults, which are several, New York pigeons are a *temerarious* lot.

temerity—rashness, boldness, daring that results from underestimating the dangers or the probable consequences.

triage

> *Triage*—deciding which patients to give up on and let die—clearly violates our unconditional Hippocratic commitment to life.

triage—in wartime often used as a system of assigning priorities on the battlefield: those who could be saved; those who needed immediate attention to be saved; those who could not be saved. Because this use on the battlefield made the word familiar, many mistook it to mean to divide into three categories, especially if they thought *tri* meant three. The word comes from the French *trier,* to sort out, to sift, and has no etymological connection with *tri,* three. Another illustration of its use:

> She is officially the *triage* nurse in the emergency room during the busiest shift and as such she is the first to decide who is a medical emergency and who is not.

vetted

> A major point in the study was mere statistics that did not tell the whole story, because American publishers bring out what they wish, while Soviet works are *vetted* by Government agencies.

vetted—my first thought was that this was a typographical error and *vetoed* was intended. However, there it was in *Webster's New World Dictionary* and in *Merriam-Webster's Third*: "to inspect or examine with careful thoroughness." Chiefly British, the word has achieved a certain standing with readers of British detective stories, especially readers of Ngaio Marsh.

9. Upward Mobility; Colloquial and Slang Expressions

There are two kinds of slang. There are the expressions that shoot up like a rocket, brighten the scene for a while, and then fizzle out. Who today says *23 skidoo, so's your Aunt Tillie, your father's mustache, the cat's pajamas* (or *whiskers*), *dippy,* or *good night, nurse?* Not even mouth-to-mouth resuscitation can bring these back to life. They are museum pieces, tags for a bygone era.

Then there are the expressions that stay in orbit for a long time and, when they eventually come down, are given the status of colloquialisms. Some finally become words in good standing or, if you will, standard English. I think that of today's stock, *blow it, blow the whistle on, cop-out,* and *rip-off,* among others, have already made it; politicians and statesmen find it difficult not to introduce these into their remarks. Such words are sometimes found in good writing because they have roots in metaphor and a cutting edge and shadings that the conventional expressions do not provide.

In this chapter are some of the less familiar but frequently used slang or colloquial terms—I have left out *rap, hangup, uptight, goofed,* and the like because they are too well known. Some of these words may be found in your desk dictionaries, and not all of them are in Merriam-Webster's supplement *6,000 Words.*

Slang and colloquialisms that may once have been slang are here for the moment, perhaps for our age, until equally pointed or more vivid expressions take their place.

bash

Hollywood has its Oscars and now the Daytona Beach Playhouse has its Oscarettes. The local awards ceremony yesterday generated as much excitement as the Hollywood *bash.*

bash—celebration, party; perhaps related to Old English verb *bash,* to strike with a smashing blow. The word *smashing* is British slang for something or someone wonderful, unusually impressive, or striking.

blow it

To bring about communication with them on terms of respect and confidence is not an easy task. But if we *blow it,* posterity will not forgive us.

blow it—communicates more than *fail,* which on a scale of 100 may mean anything between zero and 55. When at the end of a film the two young men, with whom we have identified, look at each other and say, "We blew it!" it's also a cry of frustration: "How close we came to pulling it off."

blow the whistle on

He was reported last week trying to persuade President Carter to fire the one Federal official who has had the guts to *blow the whistle on* the Westway project.

blow the whistle on—today call a halt to is usually meant, although its other older meaning of to report or inform on may still be found.

bonkers

> Unscientifically, I'd bet about half of the editors in the United States agree with me and the other half think I'm *bonkers.*

bonkers—often used with "go"; crazy, mad; to go ape, to go bananas. There are so many variations for this idea that *bonkers* will probably soon be supplanted by another expression.

buzz words

> The situation is a very sensitive and delicate one, and it cannot be solved by the use of such *buzz words* as containment or détente.

buzz words—important sounding words that often have a fuzzy meaning and are used to impress (e.g., *mythic, resonant, linkage*).

camp, campy

> We are not going to ham up a romantic story of the 40's, not make it corny or *campy.*

camp, campy—something treated in a manner so outrageously affected, inappropriate, or so out of date as to be considered amusing.

candygram

> To use such language as "going abroad to live and work" and "seeking family reunions" for the refugee boat people is to smother crime and tragedy in the language of a *candygram.*

candygram—language that tries to sweeten what is bitter.

chockablock

> No chapter in this collection is longer than a dozen pages and most are considerably shorter; all are *chockablock* with quotations.

chockablock—jammed, crowded tightly together, "the sardine syndrome."

clunky

> The new set for the early morning news program, with its *clunky,* upholstered chairs, looks like the first-class cabin in a giant 747.

clunky—dull, unattractive; a dull metallic sound "goes *clunk*."

cockamamie

> I figure it has to be a lawyer to figure out this whole *cockamamie* scheme.

cockamamie—unbelievably absurd; almost worthless. *Cockamamie* is a shortening and alteration of *decalcomania.*

cop-out

> Objectivity is often a rationalization for non-involvement, the classic *cop-out* to avoid choosing sides.

cop-out—there are those who use the pretext that they don't know enough (or know too much) to tilt to one side or the other. They don't *want* to make a choice or commitment. That's a *cop-out*—a useful word, saying so much in so little.
      Words related in meaning: **fudge** and **waffle** (which see).

flab

> Two policemen, one lean and one gone to *flab,* were handcuffing junkies, preparatory to grilling them about the murder of a shopkeeper.

flab—a noun formed from the adjective *flabby.* There are many words that follow this trend. (See **hype**)

flack

> Everyone agrees she has been a splendid "director of communications" ("that means *flack*," she says good-naturedly).

flack—a press agent, a public relations person.

flak

> The move to insure that the programs would be tied in with private economic development has generated plenty of *flak*.

flak—originally, *flak* meant the burst of shells aimed at the enemy's aircraft. It is an acronym formed from a long German word: *Fliegerabwehrkanone,* breaking down to Flieger, flyer + Abwehr, defense + Kanone, cannon—"aircraft defense gun." Now it is used to refer to reactions or comments, generally unflattering and often abusive.

flakey, flaky, flake

> Republicans refer to him as the granola governor, appealing to *flakes* or nuts.

flaky, flake—*flaky* apparently means extremely eccentric ("off center"), crazy. The word was used several times by a Congressman about the Abscam "caper." A *flake* is an oddball, a screwball, a nut.

freak out

> If a young person *freaks out,* his friends are afraid to take him to a hospital because of the possible legal consequences.

freak out—both verb and noun; to withdraw from reality, chiefly by drugs.

fudge

> What makes Clarke such an effective popularizer of science is that, without bobbling a decimal point or *fudging* a complex concept, he gives voice to the scientific side of scientific inquiry.

fudge—to hedge, refuse to commit oneself.

> To *fudge* may also mean to be dishonest, to fake—as in the following:

Scientists, like priests, are presumed to be honest. So it is doubly dismaying when a scientist—devoted to the pursuit of objective truth—is found to have *fudged* data to make research results look more striking.

funky

Part of the reason why Mr. Baryshnikov is so funny in this *funky* take-off of jazz and classicism is that it is simply Mr. Baryshnikov the incorruptible stylist having a ball.

funky—odd or quaint in appearance or style.

gig

Years passed, and as her husband pecked away at his typewriter, she bounced from *gig* to *gig*, from Village cellar club to Broadway.

gig—a single theatrical engagement; any performance or routine.

glitch

Although today's news seems to promise a break-through in the liberation of the hostages, it may just be another *glitch*. ("Washington Week in Review," PBS-TV)

glitch—a false or spurious electronic signal; a hitch; a slip; a false signal (from German *glitschen,* to slip, slide; *glitschig,* slippery).

glitz, glitzy

You can find them this weekend doing what nearly all New York comics do while they wait for an audience to laugh them onto the Johnny Carson show and the *glitzy* stages of Las Vegas.

glitzy—not yet in any dictionary. My guess is that *glitz* and *glitzy* are a blend of glitter that is not gold plus a ritziness that comes close to being *schmaltz*. When a critic of the stature of Arlene Croce writes in *The New Yorker* that the climactic scene of *Der Rosenkavalier,* with "its mirrored walls and acres of streaming silk is just this side of *glitz,*" the word *glitz* has definitely acquired the momentum of upward mobility.

gridlock

> If either a natural or a man-made disaster occurs, the *"gridlock"* which we just weathered would be a picnic by comparison.

gridlock—here is a word right off the gridiron, coined during the 1980 subway strike to describe the situation at cross-sections in downtown New York City where cars almost inter-locked. A *grid* has an even intersection of horizontal and perpendicular lines. The word was picked up by a union leader who declared on radio: "The negotiations are in a *gridlock.*" Apparently a *gridlock* is worse than a deadlock or an impasse.

gussied up

> The American products tend to run in the proven groove of the top best sellers, heavy on sex and adventure, packaged glossily with name actors and *gussied up* with on-location shooting.

gussied up—decorated in a showy way; prettied; dressed up.

hairy

> The Afghanistan incursion sounds like another Gulf of Tonkin situation but much *hairier.*

hairy—scary, hazardous, frightening.

honcho

> Among those who recently defected from the administration was the lady known as the *honcha* on global affairs.

honcho—from Japanese "squad leader"; boss man, becoming boss woman in the passage by a change of *o* to *a*.

hunker down

> Mr. Muskie may be the principal spokesman of Washington's foreign policy, but the Russians are likely to find it is the same policy, and *hunker down* to see if anything better comes up in November.

hunker down—to squat or crouch; used here with the added figurative meaning of "waiting it out."

hype

> Not that "60 Minutes" is without flaws. It occasionally *hypes* a subject—a technique of exaggeration not by any means unknown in print journalism.

hype—publicize extravagantly. From Gr. *hypo*, under + *derm*, skin: "a shot in the arm." In this busy world there's a tendency to shorten words: *vibes, mod, pol, porn, perks, stats, out of sync(h), limo, condo,* and *vegan* (one who restricts his diet *totally* to vegetables).

jawbone, jawboning

> The steel price rollback does suggest that *jawboning*—tough talk, perhaps some threats—can make a difference.

jawbone—in his Acrostic Puzzle, Thomas H. Middleton defines *jawboning* engagingly as "super-echelon arm-twisting." This type of pressure through strong persuasion is especially used in urging voluntary compliance with government guidelines limiting prices and wages.

kneecap, kneecapping

> The newly invented slang verb, to *kneecap,* to shoot a man in the legs without killing him, is about the only interesting linguistic contribution of Italy's Red Brigades.

kneecap—explained in the excerpt above.

laid back

> In Never Never Land the people are mellow and *laid back* and the pulse of the city is defined by the arteries and veins of the highways.

laid back—completely relaxed, almost blissfully so.

luck into

> His brother, who dropped out of school when he was 14 and now has no time for education, may *luck into* something in the future, but his chances will diminish with age.

luck into—get hold of something good.

nerd

> When Gilda Radner made her Broadway debut last night she portrayed among other characters her famous "*nerd*," Lisa Loopner.

nerd—Walter Glange, deciding to add "nerd" to the paperback edition of the *Scribner-Bantam English Dictionary*, said: "*Nerd* has been around for about 15 years, but I notice it is being used with increasing frequency, especially among the 18- to 25-year-olds." The dictionary lists *nerd* as a noun meaning "a gauche, tacky or uncool personality."

rip-off

> Organized labor and the consumer lobbies tend to see many parts of the bill as a *rip-off* by the oil and gas interests.

rip-off—a tremendous swindle or robbery, but more picturesque and stronger than either. You can almost hear the physicality of it, the tearing sound.

scam

> Part of the *scam* the Government is putting forth is that making an A-bomb or an H-bomb is such a complicated matter that you couldn't make one yourself.

scam—a much used word, it means a fraudulent claim, swindle, obtaining of money fraudulently. In his novel *The Second Deadly Sin*, Lawrence Sanders used it twelve times, mostly as a noun; it can be both noun and verb. The Abscam "caper" gave it wider exposure.

send up

> She provides an amusing *send up* of Ingrid Bergman and all those noble, brave, passionate, beautiful, self-denying heroines Miss Bergman has ever played, and she does it in a way that I would hope even Miss Bergman would find funny.

> Perhaps the biggest loss in the revival of *The Man Who Came to Dinner* is its satirical thrust. Kaufman and Hart were *sending up* their Algonquin Round Table friends, all of whom were famous then, but not all of whom are well known now.

send up—a noun and a verb, it comes to us from England and has become almost a vogue word here. It means, as the passages imply, a satire, a spoof, a lampoon, a burlesque, a take-off, a travesty.

smarmy

> This book, fortunately, lacks the *smarmy* arrogance of some self-help books.

smarmy—you may have encountered *smarmy*—it appears often—and not bothered to look it up, knowing by its sound alone that it must have an unpleasant connotation. And so it does: gushy, slobbery, flattering in a Uriah Heepish way.

snit

> The news that a few local stations have refused to screen "Soap" has sent TV and advertising agency executives into a *snit*.

snit—a state of agitation, fit of anger, pique. Probably a merger of *snippy* + *fit*. A great favorite for crossword puzzles.

spook

> All institutions and bureaucracies like to keep their failures and outright disasters secret. But the C.I.A.'s approach to its *spooks*-turned-authors may be hastening the emergence of a new genre of nonfiction—the more-or-less true spy story.

spook—undercover agent, spy. Of course, *spook* also has its traditional meaning of ghost.

sting

> New Jersey law-enforcement officials said most of the indictments resulted from a "sting" operation called Operation Seashore in which six state police detectives opened a store on Atlantic Avenue, a major street, and posed as fences, or buyers of stolen property.

sting—usually followed by the word *operation*, designates a set-up for catching or entrapping criminals. The most famous was the operation called the "Abscam *sting*."

trendy

> He was a vegetarian long before it became *trendy* to be one.

trendy—following the trend, doing what's in fashion. (See **chic**)

waffle

The *waffling* of the American Olympic Games Committee has its curious echo in the statements of a Presidential candidate, whose desire to undercut Mr. Carter seems to take precedence even over his usually belligerent anti-Communism.

waffle—to swing from one side to another.

zap

"Disturbing and regrettable," the words used about the failure of our connection here, are diplomatese for "*zapped* again."

zap—to stun, defeat with sudden speed.

zinger

You might have mentioned The News's 1976 *zinger*: "Ford to City—Drop Dead." These five words may well have won New York State, and the election, for Jimmy Carter.

zinger—a pointed, witty remark; a brilliant punch line.

zonked out

They have ranged from conscientious objectors to connivers who have baffled their Selective Service boards by *zonking out* on speed.

zonked out—very high, a condition induced by strong drugs.

10. Rx—Use Only as Directed

Once I remember I used the words *sarcasm* and *irony* in an English essay. Mr. H. read them out and asked me what I meant by them and told the class he bet I didn't know. I replied that sarcasm was making fun of people, as he was making fun of me, but that irony was when the truth was funny, because it was quite different from what people pretended. It would be irony if he punished me.

David Garnett
The Golden Echo

Occasionally some confusion may exist where words are close in meaning (but not in use), close in sound, or close in appearance. Often one of the words is an interloper, the one whose use for the other is not approved. For example, *infer* is frequently found where *imply* should be, and *flaunt* is used for *flout,* but never the other way around; so *infer* and *flaunt* are not welcomed in such situations. Sometimes there is only a superficial resemblance between the paired words, but I thought it might be a good way to present words of some difficulty.

abjure, adjure

The governor insists on this billion-dollar project he once *abjured*, because he thinks it will get him elected next fall.

The President sternly *adjured* his appointees to heed his examples in bringing Sparta to Washington.

abjure—to swear off the use of, to renounce, to give up. L. *jurare*, to swear + *ab*, off.

adjure—entreat, appeal to earnestly.

acolyte, neophyte, anchorite, cenobite

Even Jawaharlal Nehru, his *acolyte* and India's first Prime Minister, was puzzled by Gandhi's oblique obsession with sex.

The acquisition of Winfield by the Yankees most likely would be a severe blow to the Mets. This would be a case of an experienced and shrewd operator, Steinbrenner, outfoxing a *neophyte*, Fred Wilpon, who has been president of the Mets for less than a year.

acolyte, neophyte, anchorite, cenobite—all four have their origin in religious life or ceremonies; the first three more often have secular meanings. *Acolyte:* follower; *neophyte:* new convert, beginner, novice, tyro (from Gr. *neo-*, new); *anchorite:* one who lives in seclusion for religious reasons, hermit; *cenobite:* a monk who (unlike an anchorite) lives in a monastery.

affect, effect

Which did the doctor order?
(a) A large glass of brandy at this time may *affect* his recovery.
(b) A large glass of brandy at this time may *effect* his recovery.

A placard on a blood pressure machine read:

> The Silent Killer: High Blood Pressure
>
> It Can Effect You at Any Age Without Symptoms

Whoever put up the sign, however, played it safe by using the word *affect* on the other side of the sign.

affect—usually a verb meaning to influence; move emotionally; to have an effect on.

effect—as a verb, means to bring about as a result, as in "to effect a cure." As a noun *effect* means the result or consequence.

ambiguous, equivocal

> In order to avoid *ambiguity* in the future, the bureaucracies have been asked to "laymanize" the language used in their releases.

Though generally used interchangeably to mean having two or more possible interpretations (*ambiguous,* "going off in two, *ambi,* directions"; *equivocal,* equal voice, double-talk), the nice distinction made is that while *ambiguity* is always unintentional, *equivocation* may be purposeful, intending to deceive. In other words, an *ambiguous* statement is made by someone who doesn't know how to make himself clear, while an equivocal statement is made by someone who doesn't want to make himself clear, who wants to use double-talk. Anybody can be *ambiguous*; you have to be clever to be *equivocal*—a diplomat, for instance, an official spokesman, a Delphic Oracle, or the witches in *Macbeth.*
    When Macbeth becomes disillusioned with the witches' equivocal prophecies, he says:

> "And be these juggling fiends no more believ'd,
>   That palter* with us in a double sense;

---

*act deceitfully

That keep the word of promise to our ears,
And break it to our hope."

Shakespeare, *Macbeth*

When the negative is to be expressed, the word *unequivocal* is used almost exclusively. It is a strong denial.

The adverb is not *unequivocably* (which I have spotted several times), but *unequivocally*. And *undoubtably* (sic) is *undoubtedly* wrong.

archetype, prototype

Moscow has called the neutron bomb an *archetypal* apitalist weapon, destroyer of people but not of property.

Frisbee's *prototype*—an ordinary, unshined, 10-inch metal pie tin from the Frisbie (sic) Pie Company of Bridgeport, Conn.—has been placed [in the Smithsonian Institution] next to a colorful collection of more modern Wham-o Company disks that bear the Frisbee trademark.

archetype, prototype—although they are used interchangeably to describe an early or first model (from Gr. *archae, arche-,* beginning, ancient, primitive; Gr. *proto-,* first), *The Merriam-Webster Book of Synonyms* makes this interesting distinction:

"*Archetype* is the pattern that serves as the model for all created things of the same type, whereas *prototype* is the original or first (*proto-*) instance of something which is imitated or reproduced."

atavistic, avatar

The *atavistic* tendencies of Hinduism have fostered a national regression, a yearning for the simplicities of village life and the old Indian ways. (*N.Y.R.B.*)

He is not merely a conservative, but the very archetype, the *avatar* of conservatism.

atavistic—reverting to primitive forms or behavior; ancestral. From a Latin word for an ancestor.

avatar—a word coming to us from India, where it refers to the reincarnation or embodiment of a god as a person on earth. Today it often means the embodiment of some idea or concept.

bring, take

> Which would Joe's mother prefer?
> (a) Joe *took* the dirty-looking dog home.
> (b) Joe *brought* the dirty-looking dog home.

bring—carry *toward* the speaker or to his home (analogous to *come here*).

take—carry *away from* the speaker (analogous to *go there*).

You *bring* someone home when you are going to your own home. You *take* someone home when you act as an escort.

But don't get uptight about these verbs, the way a friend of mine, a chemistry teacher, did a long time ago. He needed a thermos bottle for an experiment he was going to perform that week. To make sure he'd have it at school, he decided to write himself a postcard. "Dear Jess," he wrote. "Bring a thermos bottle to school on Thursday." He read over what he had written and frowned. "Let's see. *Bring* is right because I want it here at school. But tomorrow when I get this card I'll be at home, so it really should be *Take* a thermos bottle to school." He mumbled, *"Bring, take; take, bring."* Finally, he tore up the card and wrote another. All it said was, "Don't forget the thermos bottle."

cabal, cabala

> I never cease to be amazed at those few among us, who spot a controversy under every rock, a *cabal* under every corner.

> He studied the *cabala* and other mystical teachings, finding in them everything he had been pondering.

cabal—a small conspiratorial political group. In the reign of Charles II the word was popularized when by chance the initial letters of the notorious group of ministers, Clifford, Ashley, Buckingham, Arlington, and Lauderdale, formed the acronym *cabal*.

cabala—from Hebrew: an occult religious philosophy developed by a group of rabbis in the Middle Ages, based on mystical interpretation of the Bible.

captious, capricious

Still, when a "Boheme" has as gaily busy a Second Act and as gently touching a Third Act as this did, it is *captious* to complain about anything.

"Changing the name of the Alaskan mountain to Denali will rectify a long-standing injustice," said Senator Mike Gravel, who argues that the name had been *"capriciously"* changed to McKinley.

captious—petty fault-finding, carping, caviling. From L. *captus*, p.p. of *capere*, to seize or catch, hence eager to catch, pounce on the shortcomings and mistakes of others.

capricious—arbitrary, as the mood dictates, impulsive. An adjective from *caprice*, a whim.

chary, wary

The result is often of dubious value, for Soviet officials are *chary* of candor with the foreign press.

The average broker, like his client, has become very *chary* (sic) of a stock market that can lose billions as easy as a decimal point can be shifted.

chary, wary—obviously, the item about the stock market contains a misuse of the word *chary*. Though somewhat similar in meaning, *chary* and *wary* are not interchangeable. *Wary* stresses suspiciousness, fear of being taken in or taken advantage of (like *beware*), while *chary* stresses carefulness, discretion. If you are *chary* of praise, you give it sparingly; if you are *wary* of praise, you are on guard against it because you may suspect the motive behind it.

climatic, climactic

> In which sentence did the first nighters miss a thrilling speech about the weather?
> (a) On opening night a gun refused to fire and a premature curtain cut off a *climatic* speech.
> (b) On opening night a gun refused to fire and a premature curtain cut off a *climactic* speech.

> The Monday night telecasts were not the first instances in which diplomatic communications were conducted in the news media, and they were only the *climatic* (sic) developments in a series of public statements covered by the press the previous week that served as an exchange between the two leaders.

climatic, climactic—the second excerpt is not the first (or the last) instance of the incorrect use of *climatic* for *climactic*. *Climactic* is from *climax*; *climatic* is from *climate*.

complacent, complaisant

> She was married when they met, and remained so in name for many years, until her *complaisant* husband died.

complacent—very pleased (with oneself); self-satisfied; smug.

complaisant—willing to please others; therefore, obliging, agreeable, compliant, affable. A *complaisant* husband, as in the passage above, is presumably a cheerful party to his wife's infidelity, since he is willing to overlook it. (See **wittol**.)

Though they are very different in meaning, there is no difference in the pronunciation of these words. Both are derived from the same root, L. *plac,* to please. *Complacent* is closer to the latin; *complaisant* made a detour through French. In both words the prefix *com* is intensive, meaning *very.*

cosset, cozen

Cosseted by the two women, Wordsworth used them as scribes, for when he used a pen it brought on painful trials—perspiration, nervousness, pain in the chest.

The fact that the United States encouraged the revolt against Colombia that created Panama and then *cozened* that insecure infant into a one-sided treaty did not seem to concern Americans at the turn of the century.

cosset—pamper, coddle.

cozen—defraud by trickery, deceive, use chicanery (from Italian *cozzone,* horse trader).

credible (incredible), credulous (incredulous), creditable

Which performance made Iago seem real?
(a) His performance in the controversial role of Iago was *credible.*
(b) His performance in the controversial role of Iago was *creditable.*

Entered here only because at a Congressional hearing on the grounding of DC 10's, a Congressman said, "The basis for this action seems to me *incredulous.*" *Incredible!*

credible—believable.

credulous—disposed to believe, gullible.

creditable—deserving of some praise.
All from L. *credere,* to believe.
Also: *credo; credit; credence; credentials; accredited.*

deprecate, depreciate

> It is more than probable that the "Oresteia" cannot be rendered into a tongue other than Greek. There is no ground for *depreciating* Robert Lowell; he did what he set out to do and did it well. (Helen Vendler)

deprecate, depreciate—to deprecate an action is to disapprove ot it, to frown upon it; the idea of regret that the action has occurred is implied. To *depreciate* an action is to belittle it, to lessen it in value. However, today *depreciate* is used almost solely to mean a decrease of value in stocks, currency, real estate, etc., while *deprecate* and *deprecatory* have taken over the duties formerly assumed by *depreciate* and *depreciatory.*

There are two different Latin roots that have the same form in English—*prec.* One of them means price or value and is used in the words *precious* and *appreciate,* "to attach a price to (*ad*)," to value properly. As an antonym of *depreciate,* the word *appreciate* means to rise in value.

The other *prec* comes from the Latin *precari,* to pray. You "pray down" (*de*) or disapprove when you *deprecate.* An *imprecation,* "a praying against," is a curse. A *precarious* situation is a dangerous one in which prayer is of the essence.

The excerpt shows the fairly rare use of *depreciate* correctly. The adjective *deprecatory* is seen almost always to mean *depreciatory.* This is a lost cause except among the most discriminating users of English. One can see that under some conditions the meanings come close to each other. Fifty-two percent of the Usage Panel found *deprecatory* for *depreciatory* acceptable.*

discrete, discreet

> The book is lined with sharply isolated madnesses, like jars on a shelf, *discrete* little psychoses and neuroses, with the lids on.

---

*The Usage Panel referred to in this chapter appears in *The American Heritage Dictionary* with entries that are in dispute. A panel of more than 100 writers, well known in their fields, discussed and then voted on the acceptability of such words.

discrete—separate, distinct, unrelated.

discreet—careful, prudent.

    Discrete statements have no relation to one another; *discreet* statements are tactful and prudent.

disinterested, uninterested

    Which judge would most lawyers prefer?
    (a) The judge was completely *disinterested*.
    (b) The judge was completely *uninterested*.

    There are just two things wrong with this very fine first novel: a meaningless title and a mistaken impression on page 312 that *"disinterested"* means the same thing as *"uninterested."*

    She commits the elementary solecism of saying *"disinterest"* when she means "lack of interest." (*TLS*)

disinterested, uninterested—apparently there are critics who still care and who take authors to task if *they* don't. *Disinterested* means objective, impartial, having no personal interest or stake in, no axe to grind. The Usage Panel voted 93% against usage of *dis* for *un*

enormity, enormousness

    Only now are we beginning to realize the *enormity* and importance of the musical contribution and production of Poulenc.

enormity, enormousness—the sentence quoted should make you wince. What is meant, of course, is the wide range, the immensity, of Poulenc's musical contribution. Instead a word is used that means abnormality, outrageousness, even great wickedness! The *enormities* of the Third Reich. Yes. If *enormousness* is too much of a mouthful, *hugeness, vastness,* or *immensity* will do nicely. How beautiful it is to come across a phrase like "the hugeness of this project," referring to the Alaskan pipeline. The Usage Panel upheld the cause by 93%.

eschatological, scatological

> His three linked tales make up an *eschatological* fantasia, including death, judgment, heaven and hell, and ending with the end of everything.

> There were *scatological* suggestions for a new pronoun combining "she," "he" and "it."

eschatological—refers to a branch of theology or doctrine dealing with the ultimate destiny of mankind, what the apocalyptic vision is about. From a Greek word meaning last, farthest.

scatological—at the opposite end of this spectrum, since its meaning has to do with excrement and obscenity. From the Greek *skatos,* dung.

exigent, exiguous

> Isn't Spain for us a dream—remote indeed from "the *exigencies* of reality"?

> Information on the early periods of Russian history is *exiguous,* and he encapsulates it in about eleven pages.

exigent—urgent, requiring immediate attention, exacting. In an old TV commercial, the coffee taster, *El Exigente,* the exacting one, used to make villagers deliriously happy when a smile suffused his face at the first sip.

exiguous—meager, trifling, scanty.

fictive, fiction

> The most striking feature of the author's achievement is the bigness and richness of the Roman scene he paints, so thickly peopled with hustlers, bankers, socialists, prostitutes and artists, among them historical persons and *fictive* monstrosities.

fictive—a word gaining prominence, meaning any kind of imaginative treatment, not necessarily fictional.

flaunt, flout

> In which case was Joe trying to cash in on his father's prominence?
> (a) Joe *flouted* his father's authority.
> (b) Joe *flaunted* his father's authority.

> This new class *flaunts* its wealth in the nightclubs and casinos near the Pyramids, in the string of new boutiques for luxury imports and in shiny Mercedes cars on the shabby pockmarked streets of Cairo.

> The P.L.O. has been effectively banned from Jordan since September 1970, when King Hussein's army, goaded by the guerrillas' open *flouting* of Jordanian authority, suppressed them and later drove them from the kingdom.

flaunt—to make a show of or display ostentatiously.

flout—to disregard contemptuously, defy, pay no attention to. *Flout* comes from the Anglo-Saxon verb *flouten,* meaning to play the flute, an instrument which when used for obbligatos, seems to mock the coloratura singer's cadenzas; *mock* was one of the early meanings of *flout. Flout* generally has a much stronger meaning today, having become a synonym for *defy.*

Though W3 gives *flaunt* as a synonym for *flout,* the Usage Panel voted 91% against such usage.

fortuitous, fortunate

> The possibility that Oswald acted on his own, inspired by Castro's statement, cannot today be proved, but it has the elements of the *fortuitous* and the lunatic that sometimes govern history.

fortuitous, fortunate—fortuitous until recently meant only one thing—happening by chance, accidental. Now it is sometimes used to mean *fortunate* or lucky. In the following passage, it is obvious that "luckily" is meant, not "fortuitously":

> The deal shown today was defended by Ambrose Casner, a regular player in New York tournaments until his recent illness, who held the West hand and got off to a start that seemed unfortunate at the time, but more *fortuitously* (sic) proved to introduce the only effective defense.

It is not a question of whether *disinterested* is correct for *uninterested,* or *fortuitous* for *lucky*. The difficulty, it seems to me, is that two good words are being thrown away, for whenever *fortuitous* is used now it brings with it ambiguity. "Saved by the fortuitous arrival of a cargo from Peru"—what does it mean, accidental or lucky? Neither; it is just an ambiguity added to a language that doesn't need it. In the same way, to be perfectly clear we have to use *objective* or *impartial* for fear *disinterested* might be ambiguous.

The Usage Panel stood by *fortuitous* to mean "accidental" by an 85% vote.

hominid (hominoid), humanoid

> Anthropologists have not been sure, but recent studies by British scientists of fossil footprints of *hominids* made in Tanzania about 3.75 million years ago, indicate that ape-like creatures walked erect some three-quarters of a million years earlier than previously believed.

These two words can be dealt with quickly. They both mean a humanlike creature, but *hominid* comes to us from prehistoric anthropological research whereas *humanoid* comes to us from outer space via science fiction.

imbricate, embrocate

> His hair was arranged in scallops, scalp to tip, like *imbricated* roofing tile.

imbricate—overlap evenly, like the scales of a fish.

embrocate—moisten, rub the body with an oil or lotion.

imply, infer

> The motion picture code on sex says: "No film shall *infer* (sic) that casual or promiscuous sex relationships are the accepted or common thing."

imply—suggest indirectly, hint at, insinuate. Any sentence that begins somewhat angrily with: "Do you mean to —?" should fill in the blank with *imply*.

infer—to draw a conclusion, deduce.
 Obviously the word that should have been used in the passage is *imply*. It's the viewer of the film who can *infer*. The same distinction holds true for the respective nouns.
 Infer is so frequently used for *imply* that W3 gives it as a synonym. But *infer* is always the wrongdoer; at least so 92% of the Usage Panel *imply*. From which you can *infer* that you are not in good company if you use *infer* where *imply* is indicated.

inchoate, chaotic

> During a tour in Africa last year, Castro noted that building socialism is much easier in the *inchoate* nations of Africa than in Latin America, where the bourgeoisie is entrenched.

inchoate—just beginning, therefore still undeveloped or rudimentary.

chaotic—adjective of *chaos*; in a state of complete disorder, confusion.
 These words come close in meaning because things in their early stages *(inchoate)* may also be in a state of confusion *(chaos)*, but *inchoate* means disordered only in the sense of not yet being in order, not fully developed.

indict, indite

Many aspects of American life are baffling to the British, including the tendency to confuse *"indictment"* with "conviction."

These pieces are daily *indited* in haste, and the thought that underlies them seems rather conventional.

Though pronounced exactly alike and though identical in origin, these words have very different meanings.

indict—make a formal charge against someone. In legal procedure, a grand jury *indicts,* draws up the formal charge; the case is then tried before a petit (petty) jury, which may acquit or convict the person against whom the *indictment* has been brought. *Indict* does not mean convict—a mistake many people make.

indite—a literary term meaning to compose, write, express in words.

indigenous, indigent

In this country the only *indigenous* inhabitants are the Indians, who were so brutally treated by subsequent arrivals.

Indigent workers from the Third World and also from poorer European countries enter richer industrial lands in search of work. One of the fine foreign films of recent years that explored this situation is "Bread and Chocolate."

indigenous—native, born in the country where one's ancestors have lived from the beginning. (See **autochnous**)

indigent—poor, needy, destitute.

maunder, meander

Now the *maunderings* of subcommittee members and a tepid agreement to tinker with portions of the code are about all there is to show for 23 days of hearings.

The professor may construct a *meandering* "story line" to avoid the facts that don't exist, to bury what is pertinent.

maunder—to talk incoherently in an aimless, rambling way. Its meaning probably influenced by

meander—to go off course, to drift, to twist and turn (from *Maiandros,* the Greek name, and *Meander*, the Latin name, of the Menderes River in Asia Minor, which has been famous since ancient times for its winding, tortuous course.

mendacity, mendicancy

Lying is not peculiarly Nixonian. The fact is that *mendacity* is intrinsic to the government process.

On St. Francis, the author quotes briefly, inaccurately, and misleadingly ("*mendacity*" for "*mendicancy*"). (*TLS*)

mendacity, mendacious—lying (noun and adjective).

mendicant—begging for alms (from L. *mendicus*, a poor man or a beggar).The word gave its name to a group of *mendicant* friars or religious brothers who took the vow of poverty, practiced collective ownership of property, and lived by begging alms and charity. Among these religious groups were the Franciscans, Dominicans, Carmelites, and Augustinians.

meretricious, meritorious

"Doublespeak Awards" are intended to dishonor exceptionally *meretricious* service in duping, gulling, confusing, and hoodwinking.

meretricious, meritorious—though both come ultimately from the same Latin word (*meritum,* earned) these two words are not synonyms. Quite the contrary. *Meretricious* means tawdry, flashy, cheaply gaudy (from L. *meretrix*, harlot, literally "a woman who earns").

metastasis, metathesis

> Considering the *metastasis* rate for new agencies (taking the Department of Energy as a horrible example) and the trend toward deregulation of industries, another sprawling bureaucracy can hardly be considered a cure.

metastasis—originally a medical term used to describe the progress of certain diseases to other parts of the body, it is now frequently used as a weak synonym for *proliferate*. From Gr. *meta-*, beyond + *stasis*, a standing, thus a spreading beyond its original location to surrounding areas.

metathesis—in language, transposing of syllables or letters in a word. From Gr. *meta*, beyond + *thesis*, a placing. Examples are *modren* and *pattren*, and, of course, that monstrosity *nukeyoular* which has been metastasizing on TV and radio.
> An example of metathesis in the history of a word can be seen in *espadrilles* (shoes of soft twisted rope), which has been altered by metathesis from *espardilles*.

mettlesome, nettlesome

> So long was the reign of Elizabeth I and so full of incident, and so *mettlesome* was she in person that it is easy to think of her as the centerpiece of all sorts of dramatic offerings.

> The *nettlesome* problem of court jurisdiction over adoptions is being handled once again in a compromising manner by the State Legislature.

mettlesome—spirited, courageous, ardent; comes from the word *metal*.

nettlesome—irritating, stinging, causing vexation. From the word *nettle*, a plant one is advised not to handle, in spite of the poem that follows:

"Tender-handed stroke a nettle
  And it stings you for your pains;
Grasp it like a man of mettle,
  And it soft as silk remains."

Aaron Hill (1685–1750)

Shakespeare, too, has something to say on this subject:

"Out of this nettle, danger, we pluck this flower, safety."
Henry IV, Part I

militate, mitigate

The lumber industry contends that the adverse effects observed by conservationists are largely attributable to nature rather than to man, and that enlarging the park would not *mitigate* these effects.

It is sad to see the author using the barbarism *"mitigated against"* for *"militated against."* (*TLS*)

Anything that *militates* against nature is to be roundly deplored.

militate—to work against, fight against (related in origin to *militant* and *military,* from L. *miles,* a soldier).

mitigate—to make milder, softer, lessen the severity of.
  Militate is always followed by *against; mitigate,* never.

mundane, secular

Mr. Sadat's domestic headaches are a lesson for any politician who concentrates on glittering international issues to the detriment of more *mundane* bread-and-butter concerns at home.

Israeli law requires that all schools be publicly supported and that schools be designated either "religious," meaning Orthodox, or *"secular."* The secular schools outnumber religious institutions by about three to one.

mundane, secular—though these words are sometimes used interchangeably, *mundane* generally refers to the transitory occurrences of the workaday world (*Sic transit gloria mundi*). *Secular* is contrasted with religious (*secular* schools, *secular* buildings); it often stresses the materialistic as contrasted with the spiritual. *Secularism* is sometimes used as a synonym for materialism.

obfuscation, obscurantism

A director is supposed to clarify, not *obfuscate*; to enhance, not distort. He used the opera for another of his ego trips. This was not interpretation. It was vandalism.

Amendments to make the plain-language law plainer and more workable are of course welcome. But we trust that the legislators will hold fast against pressures to burrow back into *obscurantism*.

obfuscation, obscurantism—of these two, *obscurantism* (sometimes seen as *obscuranticism*) is the much stronger word.

To *obfuscate* means to darken where there is already some light and thus confuse and bewilder. *Obfuscation* is therefore the act of confusing others or the state of being confused oneself.

An *obscurantist* is one who wants to keep things dark (*obscure*), who strives to prevent enlightenment and is opposed to progress in knowledge and to new ideas and methods. (See **ambiguous**, **equivocal**)

precipitate, precipitous

We strongly believe that any *precipitate* withdrawal of American troops from the Korean peninsula would have a dangerous destabilizing effect on security relationships in East Asia.

In the harshest sense, dumping would be the sale of city notes or bonds that were previously held by the banks in the knowledge that they were about to drop *precipitously* in value, in part because of contemplated action by the banks themselves.

precipitate—hasty, rash, "headlong" (literally, L. *caput*, head + *pre*, in front).

precipitous—extremely steep.

prescribe, proscribe

Iranians today may no longer purchase, possess or consume liquor or pork. In August, the consumption of caviar, Iran's most famous product other than crude oil, joined the *proscribed* list. The sturgeon that lays the eggs is considered *majas*, filthy.

prescribe—to lay down the rules for, to order.

proscribe—to prohibit, forbid, outlaw, interdict.

Prescribe and *proscribe* are almost opposites. If a course of action is *prescribed,* the blueprint for it is furnished. If a course of action is *proscribed*, it is forbidden, outlawed, condemned.

Sulla, an early Roman dictator, issued a general order condemning to death all who had fought against him. Such terror resulted that a Senator asked Sulla to list those whom he meant. Sulla then had posted in a public place a list on which the names of 80 persons were inscribed. So began the *proscriptions*, lists on which the victorious leaders in Rome's many civil wars wrote (*script*) down before (*pro*) the public the names of those they wanted liquidated.

prone, supine, pronate

prone—flat on one's face (*pro* means forward, hence thrown forward). *Prone* also means having a tendency, inclination to.

supine—lying on one's back (associate with *spine*). *Supine* also means passive, indisposed to act, spineless.

pronate—a verb meaning to turn the palm of the hands downward.

Though often used interchangeably (incorrectly), *prone* and *supine,* as seen from a reclining position, are opposites. In a letter to the *Times Literary Supplement* on the subject of *prone* and *supine,* P.L. Warnett writes: "It seems curious that Joyce, a writer who pays a good deal of attention to detail, should make such an error. In the Nighttown sequence of *Ulysses,* he describes Stephen after he has been knocked down by Private Carr as follows: 'He lies prone, his face to the sky, his hat rolling toward the wall' (page 697, Bodley Head). This is more than simply a slip of the pen as he makes the same mistake a little further on: 'Stephen, prone, breathes to the stars' (page 700)."

ravage, ravish

The comments in Winners & Sinners were stippled with puns. Criticizing a headline that read, "Elm Beetle Infestation *Ravishing* Thousands of Trees in Greenwich," the late Theodore M. Bernstein titled his comment "Insex" and went on to say: "Keep your mind on your work, buster. The word you want is *'ravaging.'* "

ravage—to destroy, devastate.

ravish—to rape. However, the adjective *ravishing* can also mean very lovely, enchanting, unusually attractive.

in regard to, as regards

The price to us will certainly be a minor economic inconvenience *as regards to* (*sic*) oil, a sorting out of our real Allies and a temporary hardship for those firms dealing with Iran.

in regard to, as regards—you can send *regards* to Aunt Minnie, but if you refer to Aunt Minnie, it must be *in regard to* Aunt Minnie or *as regards* Aunt Minnie. You hear *in regards to, with regards to, as regards to* more often than you see it in print as here.

regrettably, regretfully

Have we learned anything about the suitability of Shakespeare to a medium (television) with which he was *regrettably* unfamiliar?

regrettably—unfortunately; "too bad it didn't happen." A situation or a happening can be *regrettable* (unfortunate).

regretfully—with regret ("Sorry, but . . ."), as in *"Regretfully,* I must decline, etc." A person can be *regretful.* Or put more beautifully:

"And love, grown faint and fretful,
With lips but half regretful
Sighs, and with eyes forgetful
Weeps that no loves endure."
Swinburne, "The Garden of Proserpine"

Now as an anticlimax read this short letter printed in the *Times* recently. Any confusion you ever had may, regrettably, return.

To the Editor:
Regretfully one must note that, regrettably, we've begun to say "regretfully" when we mean "regrettably."

specie, species

FEMALE OF THE SPECIE
Monday's official debut of the Susan B. Anthony dollar, the first coin to bear the likeness of an American woman, is going to be celebrated throughout the country.

And humans are not the only *species* with a sometimes-violent reaction to the antibiotic.

specie—of course, the usual expression is "female of the *species,*" but *specie* is correct above because *specie* refers to gold, silver, or copper coins.

species—the taxon lower than the genus is the species. (See **taxonomy**.)

tortuous, torturous

> Today's arrival in Teheran of the five-member United Nations panel of lawyers from Geneva followed *tortuous* negotiations between Iran and Secretary General Kurt Waldheim of the United Nations.

> That was in fact the most *torturous* part of the book for me. Usually, I don't struggle writing. I just write. But I really struggled over those five or ten pages.

tortuous—twisting, winding.

torturous—cruelly painful.

turbid, turgid

> Not even the fact that in some homes the new water was slightly *turbid* for the first few hours dampened their enthusiasm.

> Its *turgid* style and tangled syntax stand as additional proof that the misuse of language is indeed a problem in America today.

turbid—muddy, roiled, clouded (from L. *turbare,* to disturb, agitate, muddy, throw into confusion).
Also: *disturb; turbine; turbulent; imperturbable.*

turgid—swollen, inflated, pompous. As can be seen, *turgid* is used mainly for a style of writing that is bombastic, pompous.

venal, venial

> Throughout Watergate, as *venality* was compounded by stupidity, many of us wondered how men we were convinced were well-meaning could sow such wrong, or how smart politicians could make such horrendous mistakes.

venal, venial—a knowledge of their roots can help keep these words apart. *Venal* literally means "salable," hence capable of being bought, open to corruption, mercenary. It comes from the root *ven*, part of the Latin verb *vendere*, to sell.

Also: *vend*, to sell; *vendor*, one who sells.

Venial, from L. *venia* (forgiveness, pardon), means pardonable, excusable, slight, trivial. In the Roman Catholic Church a *venial sin* is minor in nature and warranting only temporal punishment, as distinct from a *mortal sin*. Associate *venial* with *trivial*: two synonyms ending in *-ial*.

Index